Studies in the Philosophy of G. E. Moore

STUDIES IN THE PHILOSOPHY OF G. E. MOORE

Edited with an
Introduction by
E. D. KLEMKE

QUADRANGLE BOOKS
Chicago 1969

Manufactured in the United States of America. Published simultaneously in Canada by Burns and MacEachern Ltd., Toronto.

Library of Congress Catalog Card Number: 74-78311

To

Arthur and Joan Jacobson

PREFACE

IT IS GENERALLY recognized that G. E. Moore was one of the foremost philosophers of the twentieth century. (His first published articles actually appeared in 1897.) He has been described as "the spearhead of the attack" on Idealism and "one of the major leaders of the modern movement known as philosophical realism. . . . His work occupies a place of unique significance and lasting value in contemporary philosophy."[1] His published works cover a span of sixty years, ending in 1957, and two volumes of his writings have appeared posthumously. "Over a long period," writes G. A. Paul, "he was the life of many of the gatherings of philosophers in Britain. When Moore was to read a paper or take part in discussion, one could be sure that things would *go*."[2]

Moore was born in Upper Norwood, a suburb of London, in 1873. He began his undergraduate work at Trinity College, Cambridge, in

1. P. A. Schilpp (ed.), *The Philosophy of G. E. Moore* (2d ed.; New York: Tudor, 1952), p. xiii.
2. G. A. Paul, "G. E. Moore: Analysis, Common Usage, and Common Sense," in A. J. Ayer *et al.*, *The Revolution in Philosophy* (New York: St. Martin's Press, 1957), p. 69.

1892. Here he met Bertrand Russell and attended lectures by Sidgwick, Stout, Ward, McTaggart, and others. He spent six years, 1898-1904, as a Fellow of Trinity. From 1904 to 1911 he was away from Cambridge, but he returned to accept a university lectureship in Moral Science in 1911 and later was granted a professorship. Altogether, he spent 28 years teaching at Cambridge, and thereafter continued as a Fellow and still lectured. He held visiting professorships at various American universities during 1940-41. He died on October 24, 1958, at the age of 85.

Almost three decades ago, a volume was devoted to Moore in the "Library of Living Philosophers Series" that contained, among other things, several critical essays on Moore.[3] Since that time, a large number of other papers, chapters, etc., on Moore have been published. Many of these essays are not so accessible as one might desire them to be. Hence it seemed appropriate to reprint a number of them, along with several new essays written for this volume. I have divided the papers into three main categories: (1) Moore's ethics; (2) his ontology; and (3) his methodology and epistemology. In some cases, of course, a paper may cover more than one of these areas.

I would like to express my gratitude to all of the authors, editors, and publishers who so kindly granted their permisison to include various essays in this volume. I would also like to express my appreciation to all those who have helped in or encouraged the preparation of this book. I am greatly indebted to Professors Gustav Bergmann, William A. Earle, Moltke S. Gram, Herbert Hochberg, and Henry Veatch. I am especially grateful to Professors Gram and Hochberg for having contributed new essays written expressly for this volume. Special thanks are due to Mr. Truman Metzel; to Mr. G. Moor, who aided in the compiling of the bibliography and in many other ways; to Robert Birnbaum, who compiled the index; to Mrs. Mary Facko, who worked diligently at the task of typing the manuscript; and to President Rolf Weil, Dean Otto Wirth, and Dean George Watson of Roosevelt University for granting me a reduced teaching load in order to complete this work.

E. D. KLEMKE

Chicago, Illinois
March, 1969

3. Schilpp, *op. cit.*

viii

CONTENTS

Studies in the Philosophy of G. E. Moore

Introduction

DID G. E. MOORE
REFUTE IDEALISM?

E. D. Klemke

In "MY MENTAL DEVELOPMENT,"[1] Bertrand Russell vividly describes the period in which he and G. E. Moore became dissatisfied with Hegelian philosophy, which both had for a time accepted. Speaking of Moore, Russell writes:

> He took the lead in the rebellion, and I followed with a sense of emancipation. Bradley had argued that everything that common sense believes in is mere appearance; we reverted to the opposite extreme, and thought that *everything* is real that common sense, uninfluenced by philosophy or theology, supposes real. With a sense of escaping from prison, we allowed ourselves to think that grass is green, that the sun and stars would exist if no one was aware of them, and also that there is a pluralistic timeless world of Platonic ideas. The world which had been thin and logical, suddenly became rich and varied and solid.

Russell here pays tribute to Moore for what was undoubtedly one of Moore's most distinctive philosophical achievements or, at least, goals: his attack on and refutation of idealism and the concomitant support for realism. As is well known, Moore attempted a refutation in his famous

3

paper of 1903, "The Refutation of Idealism." And he continued to oppose idealism in many other works.

But, of course, Moore is an important and widely renowned philosopher for various other things too. Among these are: his emphasis upon common sense and the role of common sense in philosophical pursuits; his stress on analysis as an important activity in philosophy, and his insistence that very often the philosophical task is not to dispute the truth of certain propositions but to seek for their correct analysis; his ethical doctrines that good is unanalyzable and a nonnatural property; his claim that metaphysics is one of the most important branches of philosophy. Since most of these points are covered in the various parts of this volume, I shall here concentrate on the first that I mentioned—Moore's attack on idealism. The chief question which I shall explore is: Can it be said that, in any sense, Moore succeeded in refuting idealism, and if so, in what sense? I shall begin with an analysis of Moore's paper, "The Refutation of Idealism," but I shall later move to a consideration of other works as well.

I

Did G. E. Moore refute idealism? I want to give a qualified "Yes" in answer to the question. I say a qualified "Yes" because: (1) There may be doubts in some minds as to whether anyone could *refute* idealism, or for that matter, any philosophical "ism." I want to argue that, in the sense in which Moore specifies what he means by a refutation of idealism (and that is a limited sense, to be sure), he came close to refuting it. And this leads me to the next qualification. (2) Not every part or aspect of Moore's refutation is completely explicit in his essay "the Refutation of Idealism" (or anywhere else in his writings). Hence, a large part of my task will be to make the arguments fully explicit, without, if possible, reading anything into Moore's work that is not already there. (3) In many ways, Moore's famous paper is confused and disorganized—a fact which led him to doubt whether it should have been reprinted in his book, *Philosophical Studies*. I hope to bring out the structure of the overall argument in a more coherent way. I hope to show that much of the essay is better than Moore later thought it was, even though it contains various flaws. (4) At least one of Moore's arguments is unsound. But I shall attempt to show that certain views of Moore's which occur in later essays may provide a way of making the argument sound. With these qualifications, then, I maintain that Moore achieved or nearly achieved a refutation of idealism.[2]

We must begin, then, with the question: What did Moore *mean* by a refutation of idealism? He takes pains to point out that he does *not* mean by this a criticism of the main *thesis* of idealism, namely, the thesis 'Reality is spiritual.' ("I devoutly hope it is," he says, perhaps in jest.) He emphasizes that he has a more limited objective. There is, he believes, a certain *premise* which is essential to all idealistic *arguments* which attempt to prove the central idealistic conclusion that reality is spiritual. And he hopes to show that *this* proposition, which functions as a premise in *all* idealistic arguments, *is false*—"in all the senses ever given to it." Let us call this premise P and the idealistic conclusion (that reality is spiritual) C. If Moore can show that the premise P is false, then although the conclusion C *may* be true, nevertheless C cannot be *proved* to be true (since P is essential to every proof of C). Thus Moore hopes to refute idealism, not by showing that C is false, but by showing that all arguments for C include a false proposition P as a premise; and hence C cannot be inferred to be true from P (along with whatever other premises may be used).

And what is this essential premise P? It is, of course:

(P) Esse is percipi (To be is to be perceived) (p. 5).[3]

Strictly speaking, Moore says, the idealist's argument is a little more complicated than just 'P (plus other premises), therefore C.' To prove C the idealist needs as a premise and thus first needs to prove:

(Q) Esse is percipere (To be is to perceive) (p. 6).

Hence his argument is 'P (and other premises—call them R), therefore Q; and Q (and other premises), therefore C.' However, Moore points out that we need not worry about Q. For if P is false, then Q cannot be inferred to be true, and therefore C cannot be inferred to be true. Thus we can concentrate on P. If it is false, then we can never infer that C is true.

Moore then turns to the crucial premise P ('Esse is percipi'). In order to show that P is false, we must be clear as to what it means, since the terms are ambiguous. For one thing, 'percipi' has both a narrow and a broader meaning. Moore proposes to follow the Idealists and use it in the wider sense. In this sense, 'percipi' means 'to be experienced.' Therefore P is equivalent to:

(P₁) To be is to be experienced (Whatever is, is experienced) (pp. 6, 7).

But the copula, 'is,' is also ambiguous, and this allows for several possible interpretations of P₁ (and hence of P). (*a*) Under one interpretation, P might be meant as a synonymous definition, like "'Sleuth' = df. 'detective.'" But under this interpretation, P would be merely a trivially true tautology, reducible to the form 'A is A.' (*b*) P might be meant to be an analytically true statement, such as 'Uncles are males.' Under this interpretation, P would also be trivially true, and reducible to the form 'AB is A.' Thus, in order for P to be significant, it must be more than either a synonymous definition or an analytically true statement, both of which are trivially true. Thus P must be a *synthetic* proposition. It cannot merely say 'Whatever has percipi has percipi' or 'Whatever has percipi plus other qualities has percipi.' Rather, it must say (*c*) that two *distinct* "terms" are related, and that whatever has the one (esse) has the other (percipi). (I omit all the *X* business, which is not essential to the argument.)

Furthermore, Moore apparently holds that P (as P₁ [c]) cannot merely be a contingent proposition either. He gives no reason for this, but I assume that he would say that, if it were contingent, then it would be justifiable in terms of empirical evidence, etc. Thus P must mean:

(P₂) Esse is necessarily connected with percipi (p. 10).

That is, two distinct things are *necessarily* connected—'Whatever is, *must* be experienced' (p. 11). Now P is a significant proposition, in fact, a necessary synthetic proposition asserting a necessary connection between esse and percipi. As Moore sees it, in order for P to be both true *and* important, it must mean P₂, otherwise, even if it were true, it would be analytic (or contingent).

Thus, we must understand P as P₂: 'Esse and percipi are necessarily connected.' Very well; so understood, is P true? Moore states that if an idealist were to say that it is self-evident, then all that he could say in return is: "It doesn't appear so to me." And if P is understood in that way, Moore says that he cannot refute it. But Moore holds that probably no idealist has really ever taken P to be self-evident. Instead, the idealist interprets P in another sense; and in this sense, P turns out to be an important *falsehood,* because it is self-contradictory. To see this requires a number of steps. First, the idealist identifies P with:

(P$_3$) The object of experience is inconceivable apart from the subject. (p. 12).

(Or subject and object are necessarily connected.) Why does the idealist hold P$_3$? Because, according to Moore, he fails to see that the subject and the object of experience are *distinct,* that they are two and not one. Thus the idealist takes P$_3$ (and therefore P) to mean:

(P$_4$) The object of experience is not distinct from the experience of it (p. 13).

(What is experienced is not distinct from the experience of it.) For example, yellow is not distinct from the sensation of yellow. And P$_4$, of course, is equivalent to:

(P$_5$) The object of experience is *identical* with the experience of it.

For example, yellow and the sensation of yellow must then be identical. But if the two are identical, says Moore, then there cannot be any-thing in the sensation of yellow which is not in yellow. But then to deny that yellow could *be* apart from the sensation of yellow is to deny merely that yellow can ever be other than it is. But this means that P$_5$ (and hence P) is a purely analytic proposition once again. Thus if one said that 'Yellow is necessarily an object of experience,' he would be merely saying that 'Yellow is necessarily yellow.'

Therefore the idealist must mean something else than P$_5$ by P$_3$ (and by P), and some idealists will insist upon meaning something else (says Moore). First, many idealists interpret P$_3$ to mean:

(P$_6$) What is experienced is inseparable from the experience of it (p. 14).

That is, the two are distinct but form an inseparable unity; e.g., yellow and the sensation of yellow are distinct but inseparable. The two form an organic unity (p. 15). In other words, each of the two would not be what it is apart from its relation to the other. And (although Moore does not make this explicit until later in the essay), the idealist takes P_6 to mean:

(P_7) The object of experience cannot exist *independently* of the experience of it.

For example, yellow cannot exist independently of the experience of it. Now P_7 is not an analytic proposition, but idealists hold it to be an important truth. Hence, since it claims to be a significant truth, it must be a synthetic proposition. But, Moore says, now we have caught the idealist holding a contradiction, and this is what refutes his argument.

Let us first look at the idealists' argument.

IDEALIST ARGUMENT:

1. P_7
2. P_5
3. $P_7 \equiv P_3$
4. $P_5 \equiv P_3$
5. $P_3 \equiv P$
6. P
7. (Q, R)
8. $\therefore C$

At this point, Moore has the material for his first argument. He has some trouble making it explicit (pp. 15-17). Let us attempt to do so.

ARGUMENT I

1. By P_3, the idealist means *both* P_5, an analytic proposition, and P_7, a synthetic proposition.
2. But no proposition can be both analytic and synthetic.
3. Hence P_3 is self-contradictory, and therefore false.
4. Since $P_3 \equiv P$, P is false.
5. Therefore C cannot be inferred to be true from P (and any other premises, Q, R, etc.).

A second form of the argument, somewhat more explicit, is as follows:

1. By P_3 the idealist means both P_5 and P_7.

2. P_5 says that the object of experience is identical with the experience of it.
3. P_7 says that the object of experience is not identical with (but merely independent of) the experience of it.
4. Since P_3 means P_5 *and* P_7, it is self-contradictory.
5. Since $P_3 \equiv P$, P is self-contradictory.
6. Therefore C cannot be inferred to be true from P.

II

Before continuing, let us consider a possible objection to one of the premises of Moore's argument. This, of course, is the assertion that, by P_3 and hence P, the idealist means *both* P_5 and P_7—yielding a self-contradiction. Perhaps some would maintain that no idealist in fact ever held P in the form in which it meant both P_5 and P_7. Moore is quite explicit in maintaining that idealists probably did take P to mean both P_5 and P_7, holding it to mean P_5 in one context, and P_7 in another. He states that "it is fair to suppose" that idealists have maintained that certain propositions are analytic (provable by the law of contradiction alone) and also that they are not analytic (but synthetic). He says, "It is very easy to hold two mutually contradictory opinions" (p. 13). However, even if it were established that no idealist ever did hold P in such a way that it meant both P_5 *and* P_7 and hence was self-contradictory, Moore has further arguments in store. So let us proceed.

I have thus far dealt with only the first half of Moore's essay (pp. 1-17). At this point, Moore says that he proposes "to make a complete break" in his argument. So far he claims to have proved: (1) If, by P, the idealist means some things, then his proposition is merely a tautology, and hence even if C followed, it too would be merely a tautology. (2) If, by P, the idealist means something else, then he ends up with a self-contradiction, and therefore C cannot be inferred to be true. Moore says that he now proposes to show that "certain propositions" which idealists hold, to prove P are false (p. 17). Significantly, these turn out to be P_5 and P_7. Hence this is a most important task which Moore undertakes. For if anyone were to raise the objection mentioned above— that no idealist in fact ever held P in the form in which it means *both* P_5 and P_7, but merely one or the other—then Moore's reply would be:

Well, nevertheless P_5 and P_7 *are both false.* And this will provide Moore with a new argument (actually taken as two by Moore): P_5 and P_7 are both false. Since they are equivalent to P, P is false. Therefore C cannot be inferred to be true from P (along with any other premises).

In order to arrive at the falsity of P_5 and P_7, we must get at the correct analysis of a sensation. (Actually, any type of experiencing would do.) And this process, it turns out, provides Moore with still another argument against idealism (in addition to the two pertaining to P_5 and P_7). Let us turn then to the correct analysis of a sensation. Moore holds that in every sensation there are two distinct "elements": (1) *consciousness,* that by which all sensations are alike; and (2) the *object* of consciousness, that by virtue of which they differ. This must be the correct analysis in order (a) to distinguish a sensation of blue from one of green, and (b) to show what they have in common. Thus, of the three answers which are theoretically possible to the question 'When a sensation of blue exists, what exists?'—namely, (i) blue alone, (ii) consciousness alone, or (iii) both—only the last can be correct (p. 17).

Now we must be clear, says Moore, that all three of these alternatives are different. Therefore, if anyone says that 'Blue exists' means the same thing as 'The sensation of blue exists,' he makes a self-contradictory statement, for he then says that 'Blue exists' means the same thing as 'Both blue and consciousness exist.' But these two facts—(a) that all three alternatives are different, and (b) that only the last is true (both blue and consciousness exist)—imply that P_5 must be false. The object of experience cannot be identical with the experience of it. For to say that the object of experience is identical with the experience of it is to say that the object (e.g., blue) is identical with that object plus consciousness. And that is a self-contradiction. Hence, P_5 must be false. This now gives us a second argument against all idealists who interpret P to mean P_5. Here, schematically, is Moore's argument.

ARGUMENT II

1. Since the object of experience (e.g., blue) is not identical with the experience of it, P_5 is false.
2. Since $P_5 \equiv P$, P is false.
3. Therefore C can never be inferred to be true from P.

But perhaps the above argument would not be effective against most idealists. For, as Moore sees it, in answer to the question 'When a sensation of blue exists, what exists—blue alone, or consciousness alone, or both?' everyone, including idealists, has replied: both (p. 20). However, although idealists have held that both exist, they have given a different *analysis* as to *what* the two things are and how they are related. *They* distinguish (*a*) the *existence* of a sensation and (*b*) its *content*, and they hold that these two are inseparable aspects of one whole. And hence they use this analysis to substantiate P_7.

Moore then argues that this analysis is incorrect. *First*, in a sensation of blue, blue is *not* the content of the sensation. We may see this if we ask 'What is *meant* by saying that one thing is the content of another?' (A) We may say that blue is *part* of the content of a blue flower. The relation between blue and a blue flower is that of a thing to its qualities. Now if blue is part of the content of a sensation, then it must have the same relation to consciousness that it has to the other parts of a blue flower. It is doubtful that blue is part of the content of a sensation. For if it were, then when we say that a sensation of blue exists we would have to say that there exists a blue awareness, and that seems odd. (B) However that may be, the idealist's view is that blue is *the* content, not *part* of the content, of the sensation of blue. Now the term 'content' may be used in two senses, and as Moore sees it, in both senses, the idealist's view is false. (1) 'Content' may mean what Bradley called the "what"—i.e., the whole of what exists when a thing exists. In this sense of 'content,' blue is *not the* content of a sensation of blue, for it is not the whole of what exists; *part* of the content is the other element, consciousness. (2) 'Content' may be taken to mean the *form* of what exists as opposed to its substance or matter. In this view, since consciousness is common to all sensations, it would be the substance, and the content would be that by virtue of which one sensation differs from another, i.e., blue, green, etc. But, says Moore, this sort of analysis of a sensation into the two aspects content and existence is inadequate, for under 'existence' we would be limited to including *what* exists *other than* blue, since blue comes under 'content' and not under 'existence.' But surely blue exists just as much as consciousness. We may conclude this first point, then, by saying that there seems to be no good reason for thinking that blue is *the content* of a sensation (pp. 21-24).

However, *second,* even if blue were the content, this analysis would still be defective, for it leaves out the most important element in the analysis of a sensation. A sensation, says Moore, is a case of "knowing," or "being aware of," or "experiencing," something. Take a case of a sensation of blue. What exists here is an awareness *of* blue. Hence what exists must be: (1) blue; (2) an awareness; and (3) also a *unique relation* between the two, expressed by 'of'—the relation of *knowing* which is an utterly distinct relation, one which is not reducible either to the relation of a substance to its content or to the relation of one part of a content to another part of that content (the two relations stressed by idealists) (pp. 24-26). This presents Moore with another argument against idealism—again not directly against the idealist's conclusion C and not directly against P, but rather against the idealist analysis of a *sensation,* an analysis which is essential to statements such as P (which are then used to prove C). Moore's argument is:

ARGUMENT III

1. The most important component in the analysis of a sensation is the relation between the object of an awareness and the awareness, the relation designated by 'of.'
2. The idealist analysis of a sensation omits this.
3. Therefore any statement such as P which in any way rests on the idealist analysis must be false or inadequate.
4. Hence, C can never be inferred to be true from P.

Finally, let us turn to Moore's last argument—the argument to show that P_7 is false and that therefore C can never be inferred to be true from P. P_7 once again is: 'The object of experience cannot exist independently of the experience of it.' (The two are inseparable but not identical.) In holding P_7, says Moore, idealists do not deny that there are some things which exist independently of *their* experience. Thus by P_7, the idealists mean: The object of experience cannot exist independently of *some* experience of it. (What exists must be an inseparable aspect of *some* experience.) Why do idealists hold this? Because they think that some things *are* inseparable aspects of *their* experiences and thus cannot exist independently of *their* experience—e.g., the content of a sensation, say, blue. But according to Moore this is false. Blue can exist independently of the experience of it, and the same holds for *all* other objects of experience. Therefore P_7 is false. For *any* object of experience whatever, that object can exist independently of (apart from) the experience of it (p. 18).

But what is Moore's argument to show that P_7 is false? (A) First he points out that P_7 is based on the faulty idealistic analysis of a sensation and thereby leads to some objectionable consequences. (1) If the object of experience were an inseparable aspect of the experience of it, then no idealist (among others) could ever be aware of himself or anything else. For on his theory, he and all other persons are "mere *contents* of an awareness, which is aware *of* nothing whatever" (p. 28). Furthermore, the idealist could never be aware of the fact that reality is spiritual, even if it actually were! For by his theory, "his existence and the spirituality of reality are *contents* of an awareness which is an awareness of nothing—certainly not, then, of its own content" (p. 28). (2) If the idealist were to hold that *he* exists because things are contents of *his* experience, then nevertheless he would have no good reason for holding that anything else *besides* himself exists. Nothing *else* could be known to exist except as "an inseparable aspect of his awareness, that is, as part of himself" (p. 29).

(B) So far, Moore has not directly attacked P_7. However, he also has an argument to attempt to show that P_7 is false. The argument may be stated in this way. Sometimes I have a sensation of blue. *What* I am here aware of is *blue*. We may diagram this as follows:

(Fig. 1)   awareness₁ ——→ | blue |

At other times I am not merely aware of *blue*, but I am aware of: being aware of blue (as when I reflect and know that a sensation of blue exists). The object of this awareness is not *blue*, but *awareness of blue*. We may diagram this as:

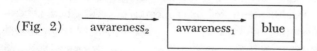

(Fig. 2)   awareness₂ ——→ | awareness₁ ——→ | blue | |

Now the awareness₁ of blue can exist independently of awareness₂. There are times when I have had the awareness₁ of blue without having an awareness₂ of that awareness₁ of blue. But if it is possible (and at times actual) for the awareness₁ of blue to exist independently of the awareness₂, then it is equally plausible to hold that blue can exist independently of awareness$_1$, for both are awarenesses. The same holds for *every* object of awareness, including material things: any object can exist independently of the awareness of it. Moore writes:

> If . . . we clearly recognize the nature of that peculiar relation which I have called "awareness of anything"; if we see that *this* is involved equally in the analysis of *every* experience . . . if further, we recognize that this awareness is . . . of such a nature that its object, when we are aware of it, is precisely what it would be, if we were not aware, then it becomes plain that the existence of a table in space is related to my experience of *it* in precisely the same way as the existence of my own experience is related to the experience of *that*. Of both we are merely aware: if we are aware that the one exists, we are aware in precisely the same sense that the other exists; and if it is true that my experience can exist, even when I do not happen to be aware of its existence, we have exactly the same reason for supposing that the table can do so also [pp. 29-30].

Here, then, we have a fourth argument against the idealist thesis.

ARGUMENT IV

    1. Since the object of an awareness$_2$ can exist independently of the awareness$_2$, the object of an awareness$_1$ can exist independently of the awareness$_1$.
    2. P_7 is therefore false.
    3. Hence, since $P_7 \equiv P$, P is false.
    4. Therefore, C cannot be inferred to be true from P (and any other premises).

And so Moore holds that, in the sense which he specified, idealism has been refuted. His *main* argument, composed of the four component arguments, is: In every significant (non-tautological) sense, P is either self-contradictory (and hence, false) or (noncontradictorily) false. Therefore, since P is essential to all proofs of the idealistic conclusion C, that conclusion can never be inferred to be true.

III

What are we to think of Moore's arguments?

It seems to me that Argument I is a good one. There are two forms of this argument. In the first, Moore rejects P on the grounds that it is held to be both analytic and synthetic, and is therefore self-contradictory. I believe that Moore is right in maintaining that no statement can be both analytic (in the sense of provable by the law of noncontradiction) and synthetic (in the sense of not provable by the law of noncontradiction) without being self-contradictory. Hence any argument which includes such a statement as a premise is an argument whose conclusion can never be inferred *to be true,* however valid the form of the argument may be. In the second form of this first argument, P is held to mean both that the object of experience is identical with the experience of it and that it is not identical but inseparable from the experience of it. Again, P is self-contradictory. Hence neither C nor anything else may be inferred to be true as long as P is a premise.

Argument II seems to me to be conclusive. The object of experience cannot be *identical* with the experience of it. For one thing, if, say, blue were not different from the sensation of blue, then I would not be able to distinguish an awareness of blue from an awareness of the awareness of blue. But I *can* distinguish the two, for the object of the former awareness is merely *blue,* whereas the object of the second is not merely blue but *awareness of blue,* i.e., blue *and* the awareness of it.

A proper appraisal of Argument III would be an enormous undertaking and require at least a whole chapter or book in itself. This is the argument in which Moore criticizes the idealist analysis of a sensation and maintains that any experiencing or awareness includes, besides consciousness and the object, a unique relation expressed by 'of,' a relation which is not reducible to any other relation, such as that of a substance to its content or one part of a content to another part. I am inclined to think that Moore is right. If this is so, then any statement such as P which in any way reflects or relies upon an analysis of a sensation which overlooks this relation must be false. And, therefore, any argument which includes P as a premise is one whose conclusion can never be inferred to be true.

What about Moore's Argument IV—the one to show that P_7 is false and that therefore C can never be inferred to be true when P is understood as P_7? This argument has problems, but perhaps it can be salvaged. The main difficulty lies in Moore's claim that there are absolutely no cases in which P_7 is true.

In a criticism of Moore's "The Refutation of Idealism," C. J. Ducasse maintained that "There is a certain class of cases concerning which it is true that *esse* is *percipi*" (in the sense of P_7: the object of experience cannot exist independently of the experience of it) and "another class of cases concerning which it is false that *esse* is *percipi*" (again, in the sense of P₇).⁴ Although Moore appears, in his "Reply," not to have been convinced by Ducasse's *arguments*, nevertheless he says: "I now agree with Mr. Ducasse. . . . As an argument for my present view I should give the assertions that a toothache certainly cannot exist without being felt, but that, on the other hand, the moon certainly can exist without being perceived."⁵

Thus in his "Reply," published almost forty years after his "Refutation," Moore held that there is one class of cases for which P (understood as P₇) is true and another class of cases for which it is false. But exactly what are the two classes, and how do we distinguish the members of the one from the members of the other? In his "Reply," the closest that Moore comes to providing an answer is as follows. He says that words such as 'blue,' 'bitter,' etc., can be used in two different senses. To say that a ball or a tie is blue is different from saying that an after-image (seen with closed eyes) is blue. He holds that when we say that a tie is blue we are attributing a *property* to the tie, whereas if we say that a sense-datum or after-image is blue, we are attributing a *quality* to it. In the former case we are speaking of a property which is something that can belong to *physical objects* and which therefore may exist even when it is not being perceived. But if we say that an after-image or sense-datum is blue, we are speaking of a *sensible quality* (and not a property). Finally, Moore says that in his "Refutation," he was maintaining (in his last argument) that the *sensible quality* blue *could* exist independently of its being perceived, and he now holds that on *that* point he was wrong. For it is as impossible for any sense-datum to exist unperceived as it is for a headache to exist unfelt. However, oddly enough, several pages later he says that, although he now is inclined to think that no sense-data can exist except while they are being perceived, he nevertheless sees no contradiction in holding the opposite! And he concludes his discussion by saying that, although neither Ducasse nor he has given a good reason for holding that the *esse* of sensible qualities is *percipi*, he still believes that there must be some reason.⁶

Thus, although Moore was groping, in his "Reply," for a criterion by which to distinguish the cases for which P₇ (and hence P) is true and those for which it is false, he did not provide one. Yet it is important to do so, for, if a criterion can be provided, then Moore's last argument, when amended, may be a good argument. Let us see why this is so. First, consider those cases where the object of an awareness is itself an awareness$_1$ of X (where 'X' designates the object of an awareness$_1$). Moore did *not have* to maintain that *every* awareness$_1$ of X exists independently of the awareness$_2$, or even that every one of them *can* (although this appears to be what Moore actually held), but only that there are *some* awarenesses$_1$ of X which either can or do exist independently of the awarenesses$_2$. It is easy to cite cases where this has actually occurred. For example, last week, while I was reading a paper by J. L. Austin, I was aware$_1$ of certain black marks on a page and also, because of utter boredom, aware$_2$ of being aware$_1$ of those marks. But when I turned to some magnificent papers by M. S. Gram, an awareness$_1$ of marks existed *without* my having an awareness$_2$ of my awareness$_1$ of marks. Second, the same holds for the objects of awareness$_1$. In order to falsify P_7, Moore need not hold that *every* object of awareness$_1$ of X is such that it does or can exist independently of the awareness$_1$, but only that there are some which either can or do. Thus, if it is possible also to hold that even *one* object of awareness$_1$ exists or can exist independently of the awareness$_1$ then this falsifies P_7, and hence Moore's last argument (when so modified) holds up. Thus the main problem is: Is there any criterion by which we can decide with respect to any X whether or not X can or does exist independently of the awareness$_1$ of X?

Someone might ask: "But if only one negative case is enough to falsify P_7, then must we go any further? After all, Moore has already come up with one falsifying case in showing that the awareness$_1$ of blue often exists independently of the awareness$_2$ of it. So this falsifies P_7, and hence Moore's argument stands as it is." Unfortunately, this will not do. For, even if one grants that there are falsifying cases of this type, this only shows that the objects of *awareness$_2$* can exist independently of awareness$_2$. But Moore holds that the same is true with regard to objects of *awareness$_1$*, that they too can or do exist independently of the awareness$_1$. The fact that there are cases where the objects of awareness$_2$ exist independently of the awareness$_2$ does not entail that the objects of awareness$_1$ exist independently of the awareness$_1$. Therefore, to falsify completely P_7, we must also show that at least one object of awareness$_1$ can or does exist independently of the awareness$_1$.

Let us then turn to the problem of providing a criterion by which to distinguish those cases in which P as P_7 is true and those in which it is false, a criterion which holds for *both* types of cases. In his paper, "Proof of an External World" (published long after the "Refutation" but before the "Reply"), Moore suggests a criterion, or at least makes a distinction which may be the basis for one.[7] In a passage in this paper, Moore seeks a criterion for distinguishing those things which are "in my mind" from those which are "external to my mind." The criterion which he puts forth is this: An object is in *my* mind if, from a proposition asserting that it exists at a specific time, there logically follows a further proposition that *I* was having an experience at that time. And an object is external to *my* mind if, from a proposition that it exists at a specific time, there does *not* follow a further proposition that *I* was having an experience at that time. I was having an experience at a given time if and only if either "(1) I was conscious at the time or (2) I was dreaming at the time or (3) something was true of me at the time which resembled what is true of me when I am conscious and when I am dreaming."[8]

Let us see if this criterion, rough as it is, will be helpful. First let us formulate it in terms of our problem:

(A$_1$) For any object X and any person Y, X exists independently of Y's experience of X if a proposition asserting that X exists at time t1 does *not* entail the proposition that Y was having an experience at t1.

(A$_2$) For any object X and any person Y, X does *not* exist independently of Y's experience of X if a proposition asserting that X exists at t1 *entails* the proposition that Y was having an experience at t1.

In case (1), the esse of X is *not* percipi; in case (2), the esse of X *is* percipi.

Now, of course, the criterion does not, as formulated, consider the possibility that someone other than Y is having the experiences at t1. But one might argue that it may be formulated as:

(B$_1$) For any object X, X exists independently of the experience of X if a proposition asserting that X exists at t1 does *not* entail the proposition that there is some Z such that Z was having an experience at t1.

(B$_2$) For any object X, X does *not* exist independently of the experience of X if a proposition asserting that X exists at t1 *entails* the proposition that there is some Z such that Z was having an experience at t1.

Furthermore, (B_1) and (B_2), as well as (A_1) and (A_2), are undoubtedly meant to state both necessary and sufficient conditions, in which case the 'if' in each should be changed to 'if and only if.'

But suppose that someone refuses to admit any cases of (A_1) or (B_1)? Would we have to resort to merely saying, "It's just obvious that there are"? Perhaps all that one could do if anyone refused to admit cases of (A_1) and (B_1) would be to take examples of various objects and attempt to show that there are differences. Let us now do just that and consider various candidates for X in the criterion. By the criterion, the esse of the planet Mars is *not* percipi, for the proposition that Mars exists at t1 does not entail that I or anyone was having an experience at t1. On the other hand, the esse of an after-image is percipi for it entails that someone was having an experience at the time. What about Moore's case of *blue*? If we can distinguish (as Moore does) between sensible qualities and physical properties, then if 'blue' refers to a sense-datum, its esse is percipi; whereas if it is possible that blue can be a property of physical objects, then its esse is not percipi. Now, suppose that the object X is, not blue, but the *awareness of blue*. Then it may seem that, contrary to Moore's last argument (in the "Refutation"), its esse *is* percipi, for the assertion that, say, my awareness$_1$ of blue exists at t1 entails that I was having an experience at t1. But to say that the awareness$_1$ of blue is percipi goes against Moore's main point (in his last argument) and against common experience, in that we sometimes do have an awareness$_1$ of X without having an awareness$_2$ of the awareness$_1$ of X, which seems to indicate that the awareness$_1$ of X exists independently of the experience of it. But if the awareness$_1$ of X can exist independently of the awareness$_2$ of *it*, then it would be something whose esse is *not* percipi, and from the proposition that I was having an awareness$_1$ of blue at t1 it would *not* follow that I was having an experience at t1. We seem to have a paradox here. Is there any way to resolve it?

One might argue that we must distinguish two senses of the expression 'exist independently.' In the first sense of the expression, to say that X exists independently of the experience of X is to say simply that the former can occur without the latter's occurring. In this sense, my awareness$_1$ of blue *can* exist independently of my awareness$_2$ of my awareness$_1$ of blue, as a result of my not having focused my consciousness on my awareness$_1$ of blue. But my awareness$_1$ of blue *cannot* exist independently in a second sense, that is, as an "object" such that, from the proposition that it exists at t1, it does *not* follow that *someone* was having an experience at t1. Following this line of argument, one might hold the real issue is not whether the awareness$_1$ of blue (or, in general, the awareness$_1$ of X) can exist independently of the *awareness$_2$* of it (i.e., without my having a second-level awareness of it)—for I may, through inattention, a state of rapture, drugs, or engrossment in the works of Henry Veatch, not happen to bring the awareness$_1$ into my field of consciousness at the given time. The issue *is* whether X can exist without there being *any* consciousness of *anything* occurring at that time. The awareness$_1$ of blue can exist without my having an awareness$_2$ of it. But it cannot exist without my being aware of *anything at all,* for the proposition asserting that I was aware$_1$ of blue at t1 entails that I was having an experience at t1. Therefore the esse of an awareness$_1$ of blue *is* percipi. It cannot exist independently (in the second sense) of the experience of it.

However, this line of argument does not come to grips with the main points of Moore's "Refutation." Furthermore, it might be argued that the apparent paradox and its solution result from appealing to either of the above criteria. But the criterion which Moore at times seems to hold in his 1903 essay is neither A nor B, but rather:

(C_1) For any object X and any person Y, X exists independently of Y's experience of X if a proposition asserting that X exists at t1 does *not* entail the proposition that Y was having an experience *of* X at t1.

(C_2) For any object X and any person Y, X does *not* exist independently of Y's experience of X if a proposition asserting that X exists at t1 entails the proposition that Y was having an experience *of* X at t1.

This criterion is never explicitly stated by Moore, although it seems to underlie much of his reasoning. In order for this criterion to be successful, it must avoid the defects of Moore's last argument. That argument, you may recall, is: The awareness$_1$ of blue often exists independently of the awareness$_2$ of the awareness$_1$ of blue. But if it is possible for the object of an awareness$_2$ to exist independently of the awareness$_2$, then blue can exist independently of the awareness$_1$ of blue, for both are awarenesses. And hence P_7 is false, and C can never be inferred to be true. However, it does not follow that, since the object of an awareness$_2$ exists (or can exist) independently of the awareness$_2$, therefore the object of an awareness$_1$ exists (or can exist) independently of the awareness$_1$. Hence to falsify P$_7$, we need to find at least one instance in which the object of an awareness$_2$ exists independently of the awareness$_2$, and also at least one instance where the object of an awareness$_1$ can or does exist independently of the awareness$_1$. In terms of this last criterion, let 'X' refer to an awareness$_1$ of blue. A proposition asserting that the awareness$_1$ of blue exists at t1 does *not* entail that I was having an experience of the awareness$_1$ of blue at t1; therefore it is an object that exists independently of my experience of it. Next, let 'X' again refer to the planet Mars. A proposition asserting that Mars exists at t1 does *not* entail that I was having an experience of Mars at t1; therefore it, too, is an object which exists independently of my experience of it. (It might be noted that there is no longer a paradox.)

However, we still have not gone far enough to falsify P$_7$ conclusively. For up to now we have been interpreting P$_7$ as:

(P$_7$a) For any person Y, the object of his experience cannot exist independently of Y's experience of it.

But you may recall that Moore himself stated that most idealists would not deny that there are some things which exist independently of *their* experience. Thus what they take P$_7$ to mean is:

(P$_7$b) For any Y, the object of experience cannot exist independently of any experience of it. (Its existence is dependent upon *some* experience of it.)

Hence we need a new criterion by which P$_7$b (and not merely P$_7$a) can be falsified. Once again, although Moore does not specifically state one, he often seems to rely upon and doubtless would have agreed to the following:

(D$_1$) For any object X, X exists independently of the experience of X if a proposition asserting that X exists at t1 does *not* entail the proposition that there is some Z such that Z was having an experience *of* X at t1.

(D$_2$) For any object X, X does *not* exist independently of the experience of X if a proposition asserting that X exists at t1 entails the proposition that there is some Z such that Z was having an experience *of* X at t1.

But by using this criterion we end up with the same results, and again for both types of cases. First let 'X' again refer to an awareness$_1$ of blue. A proposition asserting that an awareness$_1$ of blue exists at t1 does *not* entail that there is some Z such that Z was having an experience of that awareness$_1$ of blue at t1. And once more, let 'X' refer to the planet Mars. A proposition asserting that the planet Mars exists at t1 does *not* entail that there is some Z such that Z was having an experience of Mars at t1. Hence both the awareness$_1$ of blue and the planet Mars are objects such that each exists independently of *any* experience of it.

Thus we have provided a criterion by which to establish that there are both objects of awareness$_2$ and objects of awareness$_1$ which exist independently of the experience of them. The existence of such objects does not entail that either we ourselves or anyone else is having any experience of them. And since P$_7$, in either sense a or sense b, is meant to be a universal proposition ('For *all* X, X cannot exist independently of the experience of X'), and since we have found some cases (of both types) where the object of experience can or does exist independently of the experience of it, *P$_7$ is still false.* Thus Moore's main point remains, although, admittedly, it is poorly argued in his 1903 paper (because of, among other things, his failure to distinguish the types of cases in which the object of experience can exist independently of the experience of it from those in which it cannot). And if we consider Moore's refutation to include not only his explicit statements in "The Refutation of Idealism," but also certain views in "Proof of an External World" (which often seem to be implicit, here and there, in the earlier paper), then I think that we may admit that Moore has shown—or nearly shown —that, in all the senses ever given to it, *P is false; hence C can never be inferred to be true.* And as long as P is false, the idealistic conclusion C remains (as Moore said) but a "pleasant supposition."

IV

However, suppose that a Berkeleian Idealist were to argue: "P has not been falsified. The reason is this. I don't say that, for all X's that are sensible things, the being of X consists in its being perceived by *me,* but only that the being of X consists in its being perceived by *some* mind. Now since no finite mind perceives all, it follows that (A) there must exist an infinite *Mind* that perceives all. And since it perceives everything, it follows that (B) Esse is percipi."

In answer to this we may say: First, the argument assumes what it intends to prove. For one cannot logically infer A unless one has an additional premise, namely: 'The being of X consists in its being perceived.' Upon adding this premise we would then have the following argument:

1. For all X (sensible things), the being of X consists in its being perceived.
2. No finite mind perceives everything.
3. ∴ There exists an infinite Mind that preceives everything.

Now even if this be a valid argument, nevertheless, Moore would reply that, since (1) (which is a case of P_5) is false, (3) cannot be inferred to be true. Second, one could, of course infer 'Esse is percipi' from the above argument because the first premise *is* the statement 'Esse is percipi.' Hence we would have a (merely formally) valid argument of the form p, q / ∴. p. But nevertheless, if p (i.e., 'Esse is percipi') is false as a premise, then it is equally false as a conclusion. And we have already shown P_5 to be false. The being of X does *not* consist in its being perceived.

And of course we would end up with the same result if we took P_7 as the first premise.

1′ X cannot exist independently of its being perceived.
2′ No finite mind perceives all.
3′ ∴ There exists an infinite Mind which perceives all.

Again since (1′) (a case of P_7) is false, (3′) cannot be inferred to be true, however *formally* valid the argument may be.

Notes

1. In Paul A. Schilpp (ed.), *The Philosophy of Bertrand Russell* (3d ed., New York: Harper, 1963), p. 12.
2. After writing this paper, I read the treatment by D. Lewis of Moore's refutation in his monograph, "Moore's Realism," in Addis and Lewis, *Moore and Ryle: Two Ontologists* (Iowa City: University of Iowa, and The Hague:

Martinus Nijhoff, 1965). I agree with much of Lewis' chapter, but I believe that he did not succeed in structuring the actual arguments and the overall design of Moore's refutation. Also he has not given sufficient attention to an appraisal and hence tends too readily to concede that "Moore has refuted Idealism" (p. 118).

3. All page numbers in parentheses refer to Moore's "The Refutation of Idealism," in *Philosophical Studies* (London: Routledge & Kegan Paul, 1922), pp. 1-30.

4. C. J. Ducasse, "Moore's 'The Refutation of Idealism,'" in Paul A. Schilpp (ed.), *The Philosophy of G. E. Moore* (2d ed., New York: Tudor, 1952), pp. 225, 226.

5. G. E. Moore, "A Reply to My Critics," *ibid.*, p. 653.

6. *Ibid.*, pp. 655-60.

7. In *Philosophical Papers* (London: Allen & Unwin, 1959), pp. 127-50.

8. *Ibid.*, p. 142.

PART ONE
MOORE'S ETHICS

Introduction

IT HARDLY SEEMS necessary to say much here regarding Moore's main ethical doctrines, since they have been given wide consideration and have been the subject of much dispute. Among those which are most important are his notion of the indefinability of good (or, as he sometimes says, of 'good') and his thesis of the naturalistic fallacy, both of which are elaborated in *Principia Ethica*.[1] As most readers are doubtless aware, Moore holds that the question "how 'good' is to be defined, is the most fundamental question in all Ethics."[2] Unless this question is "fully understood, and its true answer clearly recognized, the rest of Ethics is as good as useless from the point of view of systematic knowledge."[3] Moore then turns to the question: How is good to be defined? And his answer is that it cannot be defined. "Good is good, and that is the end of the matter."[4] That is to say, good (or sometimes 'good') is a simple notion, in some ways, analogous to yellow. Both are simple notions, out of which definitions may be composed, but they themselves are indefinable, since, being simple, they are not "composed of any parts."

Now many have attempted to define notions such as yellow or good.

27

Some have tried to define yellow by stating the sort of light vibrations which stimulate the eye, etc. But no such definition can be adequate, for light vibrations, etc., are not what we *mean* by yellow: we do not perceive light vibrations. Many philosophers have, as Moore sees it, made a similar mistake with regard to 'good.' They purported to give "definitions" of good by enumerating the other properties which belong to all things which are good, and then thought that they were defining good. The view which holds that other properties are identical with goodness is called by Moore the "naturalistic fallacy." Thus anyone who, say, holds that good is identical with pleasure or that 'good' means 'desirable' commits the naturalistic fallacy. (Moore also holds that any one who confuses two natural "objects" with one another and defines one via the other would be committing the same fallacy, although, in that case, there would be no reason to call the fallacy "naturalistic.")

In "The Naturalistic Fallacy" (Essay 1 in this volume), W. K. Frankena maintains: (*a*) that the naturalistic fallacy is often taken as if it were a logical fallacy and hence used as a weapon; but (*b*) that there are passages in *Principia Ethica* which indicate that it should not be used as a weapon and must be proved to be a fallacy. According to Frankena, these passages imply that the fallaciousness of the naturalistic fallacy is the very point at issue in arguments between intuitionists and their opponents. And he argues that the charge of committing the fallacy "can be made, if at all, only as a conclusion from the discussion and not as an instrument for deciding it."[5] To attempt to do otherwise is to beg the question.

R. M. Hare has maintained that, although Moore's refutation of naturalism was badly stated, nevertheless, there is "something about the way in which, and the purposes for which, we use the word 'good' which makes it impossible to hold the sort of position which Moore was attacking although Moore did not see clearly what this something was."[6] In "The Refutation of Naturalism in Moore and Hare" (Essay 2 in this volume), Roger Hancock criticizes both Moore's and Hare's refutations of naturalism and questions the possibility of ever conclusively refuting any naturalistic ethical theories.

In "On Moore's Analysis of Goodness" (Essay 3 in this volume), R. F. Tredwell discusses Moore's view that goodness is a nonnatural, indefinable property and argues that: "goodness is not *a* property; it is not a *property*; it is not nonnatural; and it is not indefinable."[7]

In "On the Naturalistic Fallacy" (Essay 4 in this volume), George

Nakhnikian points out six distinguishable errors to which Moore calls attention. Nakhnikian maintains that Moore was right in calling them mistakes but that he was wrong in thinking that this implied the indefinability of 'good.'

Notes

1. Cambridge: Cambridge University Press, 1903; reprinted several times.
2. *Ibid.*, p. 5.
3. *Ibid.*
4. *Ibid.*, p. 6.
5. Below, p. 32.
6. R. M. Hare, *The Language of Morals* (Oxford: Clarendon Press, 1952), pp. 83-84.
7. Below, pp. 53-54.

One

THE NATURALISTIC FALLACY

W. K. Frankena

THE FUTURE HISTORIAN of "thought and expression" in the twentieth century will no doubt record with some amusement the ingenious trick, which some of the philosophical controversialists of the first quarter of our century had, of labelling their opponents' views "fallacies." He may even list some of these alleged fallacies for a certain sonority which their inventors embodied in their titles: the fallacy of initial predication, the fallacy of simple location, the fallacy of misplaced concreteness, the naturalistic fallacy.

Of these fallacies, real or supposed, perhaps the most famous is the naturalistic fallacy. For the practitioners of a certain kind of ethical theory, which is dominant in England and capably represented in America, and which is variously called objectivism, non-naturalism, or intuitionism, have frequently charged their opponents with committing the naturalistic fallacy. Some of these opponents have strongly repudiated the charge of fallacy, others have at least commented on it in passing, and altogether the notion of a naturalistic fallacy has had a considerable

Reprinted by permission of the author and the editor from *Mind*, XLVIII (1939).

currency in ethical literature. Yet, in spite of its repute, the naturalistic fallacy has never been discussed at any length, and, for this reason, I have elected to make a study of it in this paper. I hope incidentally to clarify certain confusions which have been made in connexion with the naturalistic fallacy, but my main interest is to free the controversy between the intuitionists and their opponents of the notion of a logical or quasi-logical fallacy, and to indicate where the issue really lies.

The prominence of the concept of a naturalistic fallacy in recent moral philosophy is another testimony to the great influence of the Cambridge philosopher, Mr. G. E. Moore, and his book, *Principia Ethica*. Thus Mr. Taylor speaks of the "vulgar mistake" which Mr. Moore has taught us to call "the naturalistic fallacy,"[1] and Mr. G. S. Jury, as if to illustrate how well we have learned this lesson, says, with reference to naturalistic definitions of value, "All such definitions stand charged with Dr. Moore's 'naturalistic fallacy.' "[2] Now, Mr. Moore coined the notion of the naturalistic fallacy in his polemic against naturalistic and metaphysical systems of ethics. "The naturalistic fallacy is a fallacy," he writes, and it "must not be committed." All naturalistic and metaphysical theories of ethics, however, "are *based* on the naturalistic fallacy, in the sense that the commission of this fallacy has been the main cause of their wide acceptance."[3] The best way to dispose of them, then, is to expose this fallacy. Yet it is not entirely clear just what is the status of the naturalistic fallacy in the polemics of the intuitionists against other theories. Sometimes it is used as a weapon, as when Miss Clarke says that if we call a thing good simply because it is liked we are guilty of the naturalistic fallacy.[4] Indeed, it presents this aspect to the reader in many parts of *Principia Ethica* itself. Now, in taking it as a weapon, the intuitionists use the naturalistic fallacy as if it were a logical fallacy on all fours with the fallacy of composition, the revelation of which disposes of naturalistic and metaphysical ethics and leaves intuitionism standing triumphant. That is, it is taken as a fallacy in advance, for use in controversy. But there are signs in *Principia Ethica* which indicate that the naturalistic fallacy has a rather different place in the intuitionist scheme, and should not be used as a weapon at all. In this aspect, the naturalistic fallacy must be proved to be a fallacy. It cannot be used to settle the controversy, but can only be asserted to be a fallacy when the smoke of battle has cleared. Consider the following passages: (*a*) "the naturalistic fallacy consists in the contention that good *means* nothing but some simple or complex notion, that can be defined in terms of natural qualities"; (*b*) "the point that good is indefinable and that to deny this involves a fallacy, is a point capable of strict proof."⁵ These passages seem to imply that the fallaciousness of the naturalistic fallacy is just what is at issue in the controversy between the intuitionists and their opponents, and cannot be wielded as a weapon in that controversy. One of the points I wish to make in this paper is that the charge of committing the naturalistic fallacy can be made, if at all, only as a conclusion from the discussion and not as an instrument of deciding it.

The notion of a naturalistic fallacy has been connected with the notion of a bifurcation between the 'ought' and the 'is,' between value and fact, between the normative and the descriptive. Thus Mr. D. C. Williams says that some moralists have thought it appropriate to chastise as the naturalistic fallacy the attempt to derive the Ought from the Is.⁶ We may begin, then, by considering this bifurcation, emphasis on which, by Sidgwick, Sorley, and others, came largely as a reaction to the procedures of Mill and Spencer. Hume affirms the bifurcation in his *Treatise*: "I cannot forbear adding to these reasonings an observation, which may, perhaps, be found of some importance. In every system of morality which I have hitherto met with, I have always remarked, that the author proceeds for some time in the ordinary way of reasoning, and establishes the being of a God, or makes observations concerning human affairs; when of a sudden I am surprised to find, that instead of the usual copulations of propositions, *is*, and *is not*, I meet with no proposition that is not connected with an *ought*, or an *ought not*. This change is imperceptible; but is, however, of the last consequence. For as this *ought*, or *ought not*, expresses some new relation or affirmation, it is necessary that it should be observed and explained; and at the same time that a reason should be given, for what seems altogether inconceivable, how this new relation can be a deduction from others, which are entirely different from it. But as authors do not commonly use this precaution, I shall presume to recommend it to the readers; and am persuaded, that this small attention would subvert all the vulgar systems of morality, and let us see that the distinction of vice and virtue is not founded merely on the relations of objects, nor is perceived by reason."⁷

Needless to say, the intuitionists *have* found this observation of some importance.⁸ They agree with Hume that it subverts all the vulgar systems of morality, though, of course, they deny that it lets us see that the distinction of virtue and vice is not founded on the relations of

objects, nor is perceived by reason. In fact, they hold that a small attention to it subverts Hume's own system also, since this gives naturalistic
definitions of virtue and vice and of good and evil.[9]

Hume's point is that ethical conclusions cannot be drawn validly from
premises which are non-ethical. But when the intuitionists affirm the
bifurcation of the 'ought' and the 'is,' they mean more than that ethical
propositions cannot be deduced from non-ethical ones. For this difficulty
in the vulgar systems of morality could be remedied, as we shall see,
by the introduction of definitions of ethical notions in non-ethical terms.
They mean, further, that such definitions of ethical notions in non-ethical
terms are impossible. "The essential point," says Mr. Laird, "is the
irreducibility of values to non-values."[10] But they mean still more. Yellow
and pleasantness are, according to Mr. Moore, indefinable in non-ethical
terms, but they are natural qualities and belong on the 'is' side of the
fence. Ethical properties, however, are not, for him, mere indefinable
natural qualities, descriptive or expository. They are properties of a
different *kind*—non-descriptive or non-natural.[11] The intuitionist bifurcation consists of three statements:

(1) Ethical propositions are not deducible from non-ethical ones.[12]
(2) Ethical characteristics are not definable in terms of non-ethical ones.
(3) Ethical characteristics are different in kind from non-ethical ones.

Really it consists of but one statement, namely, (3) since (3) entails
(2) and (2) entails (1). It does not involve saying that any ethical
characteristics are absolutely indefinable. That is another question, although this is not always noticed.

What, now, has the naturalistic fallacy to do with the bifurcation of
the 'ought' and the 'is'? To begin with, the connexion is this: many
naturalistic and metaphysical moralists proceed as if ethical conclusions
can be deduced from premises all of which are non-ethical, the classical
examples being Mill and Spencer. That is, they violate (1). This procedure has lately been referred to as the "factualist fallacy" by Mr.
Wheelwright and as the "valuational fallacy" by Mr. Wood.[13] Mr. Moore
sometimes seems to identify it with the naturalistic fallacy, but in the
main he holds only that it involves, implies, or rests upon this fallacy.[14]
We may now consider the charge that the procedure in question is or
involves a fallacy.

It may be noted at once that, even if the deduction of ethical conclusions from non-ethical premises is in no way a fallacy, Mill certainly

did commit a fallacy in drawing an analogy between visibility and
desirability in his argument for hedonism; and perhaps his committing
this fallacy, which, as Mr. Broad has said, we all learn about at our
mothers' knees, is chiefly responsible for the notion of a naturalistic
fallacy. But is it a fallacy to deduce ethical conclusions from non-ethical
premises? Consider the Epicurean argument for hedonism which Mill
so unwisely sought to embellish: pleasure is good, since it is sought by
all men. Here an ethical conclusion is being derived from a non-ethical
premise. And, indeed, the argument, taken strictly as it stands, *is* fallacious. But it is not fallacious because an *ethical* term occurs in the
conclusion which does not occur in the premise. It is fallacious because
any argument of the form "A is B, therefore A is C" is invalid, if taken
strictly as it stands. For example, it is invalid to argue that Croesus is
rich because he is wealthy. Such arguments are, however, not intended
to be taken strictly as they stand. They are enthymemes and contain
a suppressed premise. And, when this suppressed premise is made explicit, they are valid and involve no logical fallacy.[15] Thus the Epicurean
inference from psychological to ethical hedonism is valid when the
suppressed premise is added to the effect that what is sought by all
men is good. Then the only question left is whether the premises are
true.

It is clear, then, that the naturalistic fallacy is not a logical fallacy,
since it may be involved even when the argument is valid. How does
the naturalistic fallacy enter such "mixed ethical arguments"[16] as that
of the Epicureans? Whether it does or not depends on the nature of
the suppressed premise. This may be either an induction, an intuition,
a deduction from a "pure ethical argument," a definition, or a proposition which is true by definition. If it is one of the first three, then the
naturalistic fallacy does not enter at all. In fact, the argument does not
then involve violating (1), since one of its premises will be ethical. But
if the premise to be supplied is a definition or a proposition which is
true by definition, as it probably was for the Epicureans, then the argument, while still valid, involves the naturalistic fallacy, and will run as
follows:

(*a*) Pleasure is sought by all men.
(*b*) What is sought by all men is good (definition).
(*c*) Therefore, pleasure is good.

Now I am not greatly interested in deciding whether the argument as here set up violates (1). If it does not, then no "mixed ethical argument" actually commits any factualist or valuational fallacy, except when it is unfairly taken as complete in its enthymematic form. If it does, then a valid argument may involve the deduction of an ethical conclusion from non-ethical premises and the factualist or valuational fallacy is not really a fallacy. The question depends on whether or not (b) and (c) are to be regarded as ethical propositions. Mr. Moore refuses so to regard them, contending that, by hypothesis, (b) is analytic or tautologous, and that (c) is psychological, since it really says only that pleasure is sought by all men.[17] But to say that (b) is analytic and not ethical and that (c) is not ethical but psychological is to prejudge the question whether 'good' can be defined; for the Epicureans would contend precisely that if their definition is correct then (b) is ethical but analytic and (c) ethical though psychological. Thus, unless the question of the definability of goodness is to be begged, (b) and (c) must be regarded as ethical, in which case our argument does not violate (1). However, suppose, if it be not nonsense, that (b) is non-ethical and (c) ethical, then the argument will violate (1), but it will still obey all of the canons of logic, and it is only confusing to talk of a 'valuational logic' whose basic rule is that an evaluative conclusion cannot be deduced from non-evaluative premises.[18]

For the only way in which either the intuitionists or postulationists like Mr. Wood can cast doubt upon the conclusion of the argument of the Epicureans (or upon the conclusion of any parallel argument) is to attack the premises, in particular (b). Now, according to Mr. Moore, it is due to the presence of (b) that the argument involves the naturalistic fallacy. (b) involves the identification of goodness with 'being sought by all men,' and to make this or any other such identification is to commit the naturalistic fallacy. The naturalistic fallacy is not the procedure of violating (1). It is the procedure, implied in many mixed ethical arguments and explicitly carried out apart from such arguments by many moralists, of defining such characteristics as goodness or of substituting some other characteristic for them. To quote some passages from *Principia Ethica*:

(a) " . . . far too many philosophers have thought that when they named those other properties [belonging to all things which are good] they were actually defining good; that these properties, in fact, were simply not 'other,' but absolutely and entirely the same with goodness. This view I propose to call the 'naturalistic fallacy.' . . ."[19]

(b) "I have thus appropriated the name Naturalism to a particular method of approaching Ethics. . . . This method consists in substituting for 'good' some one property of a natural object or of a collection of natural objects. . . ."[20]

(c) ". . . the naturalistic fallacy [is] the fallacy which consists in identifying the simple notion which we mean by 'good' with some other notion."[21]

Thus, to identify 'better' and 'more evolved,' 'good' and 'desired,' etc., is to commit the naturalistic fallacy.[22] But just why is such a procedure fallacious or erroneous? And is it a fallacy only when applied to good? We must now study Section 12 of *Principia Ethica*. Here Mr. Moore makes some interesting statements:

". . . if anybody tried to define pleasure for us as being any other natural object; if anybody were to say, for instance, that pleasure *means* the sensation of red. . . . Well, that would be the same fallacy which I have called the naturalistic fallacy. . . . I should not indeed call that a naturalistic fallacy, although it is the same fallacy as I have called naturalistic with reference to Ethics. . . . When a man confuses two natural objects with one another, defining the one by the other . . . then there is no reason to call the fallacy naturalistic. But if he confuses 'good,' which is not . . . a natural object, with any natural object whatever, then there is a reason for calling that a naturalistic fallacy. . . ."[23]

Here Mr. Moore should have added that, when one confuses 'good,' which is not a metaphysical object or quality, with any metaphysical object or quality, as metaphysical moralists do, according to him, then the fallacy should be called the metaphysical fallacy. Instead he calls it a naturalistic fallacy in this case too, though he recognizes that the case is different since metaphysical properties are non-natural[24]—a procedure which has misled many readers of *Principia Ethica*. For example, it has led Mr. Broad to speak of "theological naturalism."[25]

To resume: "Even if [goodness] were a natural object, that would not alter the nature of the fallacy nor diminish its importance one whit."[26]

From these passages it is clear that the fallaciousness of the procedure which Mr. Moore calls the naturalistic fallacy is not due to the fact that it is applied to good or to an ethical or non-natural characteristic. When Mr. R. B. Perry defines 'good' as 'being an object of interest' the trouble is not merely that he is defining *good*. Nor is the trouble that he is defining an *ethical* characteristic in terms of *non-ethical* ones.

Nor is the trouble that he is regarding a *non-natural* characteristic as a *natural* one. The trouble is more generic than that. For clarity's sake I shall speak of the definist fallacy as the generic fallacy which underlies the naturalistic fallacy. The naturalistic fallacy will then, by the above passages, be a species or form of the definist fallacy, as would the metaphysical fallacy if Mr. Moore had given that a separate name.[27] That is, the naturalistic fallacy as illustrated by Mr. Perry's procedure, is a fallacy, not because it is naturalistic or confuses a non-natural quality with a natural one, but solely because it involves the definist fallacy. We may, then, confine our attention entirely to an understanding and evaluation of the definist fallacy.

To judge by the passages I have just quoted, the definist fallacy is the process of confusing or identifying two properties, of defining one property by another, or of substituting one property for another. Furthermore, the fallacy is always simply that two properties are being treated as one, and it is irrelevant, if it be the case, that one of them is natural or non-ethical and the other non-natural or ethical. One may commit the definist fallacy without infringing on the bifurcation of the ethical and the non-ethical, as when one identifies pleasantness and redness or rightness and goodness. But even when one infringes on that bifurcation in committing the definist fallacy, as when one identifies goodness and pleasantness or goodness and satisfaction, then the *mistake* is still not that the bifurcation is being infringed on, but only that two properties are being treated as one. Hence, on the present interpretation, the definist *fallacy* does not, in any of its forms, consist of violating (3), and has no essential connexion with the bifurcation of the 'ought' and the 'is.'

This formulation of the definist fallacy explains or reflects the motto of *Principia Ethica*, borrowed from Bishop Butler: "Everything is what it is, and not another thing." It follows from this motto that goodness is what it is and not another thing. It follows that views which try to identify it with something else are making a mistake of an elementary sort. For it *is* a mistake to confuse or identify two properties. If the properties really are two, then they simply are not identical. But do those who define ethical notions in non-ethical terms make this mistake? They will reply to Mr. Moore that they are not identifying two properties; what they are saying is that two words or sets of words stand for or mean one and the same property. Mr. Moore was being, in part, misled by the material mode of speech, as Mr. Carnap calls it, in such

sentences as "Goodness is pleasantness," "Knowledge is true belief," etc.
When one says instead, "The word 'good' and the word 'pleasant' mean
the same thing," etc., it is clear that one is not identifying two things.
But Mr. Moore kept himself from seeing this by his disclaimer that he
was interested in any statement about the use of words.[28]

The definist fallacy, then, as we have stated it, does not rule out
any naturalistic or metaphysical definitions of ethical terms. Goodness
is not identifiable with any 'other' characteristic (if it is a characteristic
at all). But the question is: *which* characteristics are other than goodness, which names stand for characteristics other than goodness? And
it is begging the question of the definability of goodness to say out of
hand that Mr. Perry, for instance, is identifying goodness with something else. The point is that goodness is what it is, even if it is definable.
That is why Mr. Perry can take as the motto of his naturalistic *Moral
Economy* another sentence from Bishop Butler: "Things and actions are
what they are, and the consequences of them will be what they will be;
why then should we desire to be deceived?" The motto of *Principia
Ethica* is a tautology, and should be expanded as follows: Everything
is what it is, and not another thing, unless it is another thing, and even
then it is what it is.

On the other hand, if Mr. Moore's motto (or the definist fallacy)
rules out any definitions, for example of 'good,' then it rules out all
definitions of any term whatever. To be effective at all, it must be
understood to mean, "Every term means what it means, and not what
is meant by any other term." Mr. Moore seems implicitly to understand
his motto in this way in Section 13, for he proceeds as if 'good' has
no meaning, if it has no unique meaning. If the motto be taken in this
way, it will follow that 'good' is an indefinable term, since no synonyms
can be found. But it will also follow that no term is definable. And
then the method of analysis is as useless as an English butcher in a
world without sheep.

Perhaps we have misinterpreted the definist fallacy. And, indeed,
some of the passages which I quoted earlier in this paper seem to imply
that the definist fallacy is just the error of defining an indefinable characteristic. On this interpretation, again, the definist fallacy has, in all
of its forms, no essential connexion with the bifurcation of the ethical
and the non-ethical. Again, one may commit the definist fallacy without
violating that bifurcation, as when one defines pleasantness in terms
of redness or goodness in terms of rightness (granted Mr. Moore's belief

that pleasantness and goodness are indefinable). But even when one infringes on that bifurcation and defines goodness in terms of desire, the *mistake* is not that one is infringing on the bifurcation by violating (3), but only that one is defining an indefinable characteristic. This is possible because the proposition that goodness is indefinable is logically independent of the proposition that goodness is non-natural: as is shown by the fact that a characteristic may be indefinable and yet natural, as yellowness is; or non-natural and yet definable, as rightness is (granted Mr. Moore's views about yellowness and rightness).

Consider the definist fallacy as we have just stated it. It is, of course, an error to define an indefinable quality. But the question, again, is: which qualities are indefinable? It is begging the question in favour of intuitionism to say in advance that the quality goodness is indefinable and that, therefore, all naturalists commit the definist fallacy. One must know that goodness is indefinable before one can argue that the definist fallacy *is* a fallacy. Then however, the definist fallacy can enter only at the end of the controversy between intuitionism and definism, and cannot be used as a weapon in the controversy.

The definist fallacy may be stated in such a way as to involve the bifurcation between the 'ought' and the 'is.'[29] It would then be committed by anyone who offered a definition of any ethical characteristic in terms of non-ethical ones. The trouble with such a definition, on this interpretation, would be that an *ethical* characteristic is being reduced to a *non-ethical* one, a *non-natural* one to a *natural* one. That is, the definition would be ruled out by the fact that the characteristic being defined is ethical or non-natural and therefore cannot be defined in non-ethical or natural terms. But on this interpretation, too, there is danger of a *petitio* in the intuitionist argumentation. To assume that the ethical characteristic is exclusively ethical is to beg precisely the question which is at issue when the definition is offered. Thus, again, one must know that the characteristic is non-natural and indefinable in natural terms before one can say that the definists are making a mistake.

Mr. Moore, McTaggart, and others formulate the naturalistic fallacy sometimes in a way somewhat different from any of those yet discussed. They say that the definists are confusing a universal synthetic proposition about *the good* with a definition of *goodness*.[30] Mr. Abraham calls this the "fallacy of misconstrued proposition."[31] Here again the difficulty is that, while it is true that it is an error to construe a universal synthetic

proposition as a definition, it is a *petitio* for the intuitionists to say that
what the definist is taking for a definition is really a universal synthetic
proposition.[32]

At last, however, the issue between the intuitionists and the definists
(naturalistic or metaphysical) is becoming clearer. The definists are all
holding that certain propositions involving ethical terms are analytic,
tautologous, or true by definition, e.g., Mr. Perry so regards the statement, "All objects of desire are good." The intuitionists hold that such
statements are synthetic. What underlies this difference of opinion is
that the intuitionists claim to have at least a dim awareness of a simple
unique quality or relation of goodness or rightness which appears in
the region which our ethical terms roughly indicate, whereas the definists
claim to have no awareness of any such quality or relation in that region,
which is different from all other qualities and relations which belong to
the same context but are designated by words other than 'good' and
'right' and their obvious synonyms.[33] The definists are in all honesty
claiming to find but one characteristic where the intuitionists claim to
find two, as Mr. Perry claims to find only the property of being desired
where Mr. Moore claims to find both it and the property of being good.
The issue, then, is one of inspection or intuition, and concerns the
awareness or discernment of qualities and relations.[34] That is why it
cannot be decided by the use of the notion of a fallacy.

If the definists may be taken at their word, then they are not actually
confusing two characteristics with each other, nor defining an indefinable characteristic, nor confusing definitions and universal synthetic propositions—in short they are not committing the naturalistic or definist
fallacy in any of the interpretations given above. Then the only fallacy
which they commit—the real naturalistic or definist fallacy—is the failure
to descry the qualities and relations which are central to morality. But
this is neither a logical fallacy nor a logical confusion. It is not even,
properly speaking, an error. It is rather a kind of blindness, analogous
to colour-blindness. Even this moral blindness can be ascribed to the
definists only if they are correct in their claim to have no awareness
of any unique ethical characteristics and if the intuitionists are correct
in affirming the existence of such characteristics, but certainly to call it
a 'fallacy,' even in a loose sense, is both unamiable and profitless.

On the other hand, of course, if there are no such characteristics in
the objects to which we attach ethical predicates, then the intuitionists,
if we may take them at their word, are suffering from a corresponding

moral hallucination. Definists might then call this the intuitionistic or moralistic fallacy, except that it is no more a 'fallacy' than is the blindness just described. Anyway, they do not believe the claim of the intuitionists to be aware of unique ethical characteristics, and consequently do not attribute to them this hallucination. Instead, they simply deny that the intuitionists really do find such unique qualities or relations, and then they try to find some plausible way of accounting for the fact that very respectable and trustworthy people think they find them.[35] Thus they charge the intuitionists with verbalism, hypostatisation, and the like. But this half of the story does not concern us now.

What concerns us more is the fact that the intuitionists do not credit the claim of the definists either. They would be much disturbed, if they really thought that their opponents were morally blind, for they do not hold that we must be regenerated by grace before we can have moral insight, and they share the common feeling that morality is something democratic even though not all men are good. Thus they hold that "we are all aware" of certain unique characteristics when we use the terms 'good,' 'right,' etc., only due to a lack of analytic clearness of mind, abetted perhaps by a philosophical prejudice, we may not be aware at all that they are different from other characteristics of which we are also aware.[36] Now, I have been arguing that the intuitionists cannot charge the definists with committing any fallacy unless and until they have shown that we are all, the definists included, aware of the disputed unique characteristics. If, however, they were to show this, then, at least at the end of the controversy, they could accuse the definists of the error of confusing two characteristics, or of the error of defining an indefinable one, and these errors might, since the term is somewhat loose in its habits, be called 'fallacies,' though they are not logical fallacies in the sense in which an invalid argument is. The fallacy of misconstrued proposition depends on the error of confusing two characteristics, and hence could also on our present supposition, be ascribed to the definists, but it is not really a *logical* confusion,[37] since it does not actually involve being confused about the difference between a proposition and a definition.

Only it is difficult to see how the intuitionists can prove that the definists are at least vaguely aware of the requisite unique characteristics.[38] The question must surely be left to the inspection or intuition of the definists themselves, aided by whatever suggestions the intuitionists may have to make. If so, we must credit the verdict of their inspection, especially of those among them who have read the writings of the intuitionists reflectively, and, then, as we have seen, the most they can be charged with is moral blindness.

Besides trying to discover just what is meant by the naturalistic fallacy, I have tried to show that the notion that a logical or quasi-logical fallacy is committed by the definists only confuses the issue between the intuitionists and the definists (and the issue between the latter and the emotists or postulationists), and misrepresents the way in which the issue is to be settled. No logical fallacy need appear anywhere in the procedure of the definists. Even fallacies in any less accurate sense cannot be implemented to decide the case against the definists; at best they can be ascribed to the definists only after the issue has been decided against them on independent grounds. But the only defect which can be attributed to the definists, *if* the intuitionists are right in affirming the existence of unique indefinable ethical characteristics, is a peculiar moral blindness, which is not a fallacy even in the looser sense. The issue in question must be decided by whatever method we may find satisfactory for determining whether or not a word stands for a characteristic at all, and, if it does, whether or not it stands for a unique characteristic. What method is to be employed is, perhaps, in one form or another, the basic problem of contemporary philosophy, but no generally satisfactory solution of the problem has yet been reached. I shall venture to say only this: it does seem to me that the issue is not to be decided against the intuitionists by the application *ab extra* to ethical judgments of any empirical or ontological meaning dictum.[39]

Notes

1. A. E. Taylor, *The Faith of a Moralist* (London: Macmillan, 1930), I, 104 n.
2. *Value and Ethical Objectivity*, p. 58.
3. *Principia Ethica*, pp. 38, 64.
4. M. E. Clarke, "Cognition and Affection in the Experience of Value," *Journal of Philosophy*, 1938.
5. *Principia Ethica*, pp. 73, 77. See also p. xix.

6. "Ethics as Pure Postulate," *Philosophical Review*, 1933. See also T. Whittaker, *The Theory of Abstract Ethics* (Cambridge: Cambridge University Press, 1916), pp. 19 f.

7. Book III, part ii, section i.

8. See J. Laird, *A Study in Moral Theory* (London: Allen & Unwin, 1926), pp. 16 f.; Whittaker, *op. cit.*, p. 19.

9. See C. D. Broad, *Five Types of Ethical Theory* (New York: Harcourt Brace, 1930), Chap. IV.

10. Laird, *op. cit.*, p. 94 n.

11. See his *Philosophical Studies* (London: Routledge & Kegan Paul, 1922), pp. 259, 273 f.

12. See Laird, *op. cit.*, p. 318. Also pp. 12 ff.

13. P. E. Wheelwright, *A Critical Introduction to Ethics* (Garden City: Doubleday, 1935), pp. 40-51, 91 f.; L. Wood, "Cognition and Moral Value," *Journal of Philosophy*, 1937, p. 237.

14. See *Principia Ethica*, pp. 114, 57, 43, 49. Whittaker identifies it with the naturalistic fallacy and regards it as a "logical" fallacy, *op. cit.*, pp. 19 f.

15. See *Principia Ethica*, pp. 50, 139; Wheelwright, *loc. cit.*

16. See C. D. Broad, *The Mind and Its Place in Nature* (New York: Harcourt Brace, 1929), pp. 488 f.; Laird, *loc. cit.*

17. See *Principia Ethica*, pp. 11 f., 19, 38, 73, 139.

18. See L. Wood, *loc. cit.*

19. *Principia Ethica*, p. 10.

20. *Ibid.*, p. 40.

21. *Ibid.*, p. 58; cf. pp. xiii, 73.

22. Cf. *ibid.*, pp. 49, 53, 108, 139.

23. *Ibid.*, p. 13.

24. See *ibid.*, pp. 38-40, 110-112.

25. *Five Types of Ethical Theory*, p. 259.

26. *Principia Ethica*, p. 14.

27. As Whittaker has, *loc. cit.*

28. *Principia Ethica*, pp. 6, 8, 12.

29. See J. Wisdom, *Mind*, 1931, p. 213, note 1.

30. See *Principia Ethica*, pp. 10, 16, 38; J. E. McTaggart, *The Nature of Existence* (Cambridge: Cambridge University Press, 1927), II, 398.

31. Leo Abraham, "The Logic of Intuitionism," *International Journal of Ethics*, 1933.

32. As Mr. Abraham points out, *loc. cit.*

33. See R. B. Perry, *General Theory of Value* (New York: Longmans Green, 1926), p. 30; cf. *Journal of Philosophy*, 1931, p. 520.

34. See H. Osborne, *Foundations of the Philosophy of Value* (Cambridge: Cambridge University Press, 1933), pp. 15, 19, 70.

35. Cf. R. B. Perry, *Journal of Philosophy*, 1931, pp. 520 ff.

36. *Principia Ethica*, pp. 17, 38, 59, 61.

37. But see Osborne, *op. cit.*, pp. 18 f.

38. For a brief discussion of their arguments, see *ibid.*, p. 67; L. Abraham, *op. cit.* I think they are all inconclusive, but cannot show this here.

39. See *Principia Ethica*, pp. 124 f., 140.

Two

THE REFUTATION OF NATURALISM IN MOORE AND HARE

Roger Hancock

HARE HAS expressed the view that although Moore's refutation of naturalism was badly stated and has been widely criticized, it nevertheless rests on secure foundations: "there is indeed something about the way in which, and the purposes for which, we use the word 'good' which makes it impossible to hold the sort of position which Moore was attacking, although Moore did not see clearly what this something was."[1] In the following discussion I would like, first, to restate and criticize one of Moore's arguments against naturalism, and second, similarly to restate and criticize Hare's refutation of naturalism. Third, I would like to question the possibility of any conclusive refutation of naturalism.

I

Hare remarks that the word 'naturalism' has been used loosely, and suggests that it be restricted to "those theories against which Moore's

Reprinted by permission of the author and the editor from *The Journal of Philosophy*, LVII (1960), 326-34.

refutation (or a recognizable version of it) is valid."[2] But this suggestion can hardly be understood as a definition of naturalism; so understood it would be trivially true that naturalistic theories are false, and no further argument would be required. And Moore himself could not have used this suggestion as a definition in setting out to refute naturalism.

'Naturalism' as used by Moore and Hare might be defined as the view that ethical words such as 'good' or 'right' are synonymous with expressions designating natural properties. But what is a natural property? It might be suggested that a natural property is one that can be observed. Yet Moore himself holds that 'good' designates a property which in some sense can be observed. And some properties which are not observable, e.g., the property of being conducive to life in self or others, are natural properties according to Moore. A better way to define 'naturalism' as used by Moore and Hare might be, simply, that naturalism is the view that ethical words are synonymous with non-ethical words. This is not entirely satisfactory, since there seems to be no way of picking out ethical from non-ethical words. Until a criterion is given, the decision to call a given theory 'naturalistic' is somewhat arbitrary; in practice Moore and Hare seem agreed that such expressions as 'pleasant' or 'conducive to life in self or others' or 'forbidden by the ruler of our State' are non-ethical.

The general outlines of Moore's open-question argument are clear, and the argument can be paraphrased as follows:

1. If naturalism is true, then some sentences of the form 'Whatever is F is good' is analytic, where 'F' is replaceable by a non-ethical expression.
2. If ethical sentences of the form 'Whatever is F is good' are analytic, then we cannot significantly ask 'Are F's good?'
3. But we can always significantly ask 'Are F's good?'
4. Therefore no sentence of the form 'Whatever is F is good' is analytic, and hence naturalism is false.

Formally the argument is valid, and superficially at least, it is clear. But there are difficulties in the notion of 'significance.' What does it mean to say that a statement can or cannot be significantly questioned, and why is it impossible to significantly question an analytic statement? One ordinary sense of 'significance' can probably be ruled out. This is the sense in which a question 'Is S P?' is significant if it is important; the sense in which events and actions as well as statements are significant. In this sense a question 'Is S P?' can be insignificant although 'S is P' is not analytic; e.g., the question 'Is the number of words in *Principia Ethica* greater than 100,000?' On the other hand the question 'Is a rhombus a parallelogram?' might very well be significant, although 'A rhombus is a parallelogram' is analytic. Moore probably would have wanted to say that questions like 'Are all pleasures good?' are significant in the sense of important. But that cannot be the sense in which he holds that such sentences can be significantly questioned, in the course of his refutation of naturalism.

Moore suggests two clues as to what might be meant by saying that a statement can or cannot be significantly questioned. The first is contained in the following passage:

> Moreover anyone can easily convince himself by inspection that the predicate of this proposition [whatever we desire to desire is good]—'good'—is positively different from the notion of 'desiring to desire' which enters into its subject: 'That we should desire to desire A is good' is *not* merely equivalent to 'That A should be good is good.' It may indeed be true that what we desire to desire is always also good; perhaps, even the converse may be true; but it is very doubtful whether this is the case, and the mere fact that we understand very well what is meant by doubting it, shows clearly that we have two different notions before our minds.[3]

Moore is arguing that no non-ethical expression is synonymous with the ethical predicate 'good.' His argument is that if this were so, then (for some non-ethical expression 'F') the sentence 'Whatever is F is good' would be equivalent to the tautology 'Whatever is F is F' which, Moore holds, it is not. And such sentences are never equivalent because while the former can always be doubted, the latter cannot be doubted. By saying that sentences of the form 'Whatever is F is F' cannot be doubted, Moore presumably means simply that their denials are self-contradictory. This suggests the possibility that when Moore says we can always significantly ask 'Are F's good?' he means that 'F's are not good' is never self-contradictory. Moore's argument, then, might be restated in the following way:

1. If naturalism is true, then (for some non-ethical expression 'F') the sentence 'F's are not good' is self-contradictory.
2. But sentences of the form 'F's are not good' are never self-contradictory.
3. Hence naturalism is false.

How does Moore know that it is never self-contradictory to deny sentences of the form 'Whatever is F is good'? To say this is, after all, only another way of saying that 'F's are good' is not analytic. And this is precisely what the naturalist affirms. The hedonist, for example, will surely have no trouble with Moore's argument; having defined 'good' as 'pleasant' and holding that 'Whatever is pleasant is good' is analytic, he will simply reply that in point of fact it is self-contradictory to say that something is pleasant and yet not good. Moore would have no answer; at the very most his argument only pushes the dispute back a step, without doing anything to settle it. I conclude that the above interpretation is not a satisfactory explanation of what Moore means by 'significant question'; if it is, then Moore's open-question argument is unconvincing.

A second clue to what Moore might have meant by 'significant question' is contained in the following passage:

> But whoever will attentively consider with himself what is actually before his mind when he asks the question 'Is pleasure (or whatever it may be) after all good?' can easily satisfy himself that he is not merely wondering whether pleasure is pleasant. And if he will try this experiment with each suggested definition in succession he may become expert enough to recognize that in every case he has before his mind a unique object, with regard to the connection of which with any other object, a distinct question may be asked.[4]

Again Moore is attacking the view that ethical words are synonymous with non-ethical expressions. And his argument is that when we ask 'Are F's good?' we can recognize on reflection that there are two distinct things before our minds, with regard to whose connection we are asking. The question 'Is S P?' is significant, then, if S and P designate two distinct things; it is not significant if they designate only one thing. Moore's argument, interpreted in this way, can be paraphrased as follows:

1. If naturalism is true, there are sentences of the form 'Whatever is F is good' in which 'F' and 'good' designate the same properties.
2. But whenever we ask 'Are F's good?' we can see, on reflection, that 'F' and 'good' designate two distinct properties.
3. Hence naturalism is false.

Understood in this way the dispute between Moore and naturalism reduces to the question of what is "before our minds" when we ask questions such as 'Are all pleasures good?' Frankena has pointed out that such questions reduce to "inspection or intuition"; the error of the naturalist would be a certain kind of "blindness" which prevents him from noting what in fact is before his mind.[5] But we can ask what the consequences are if the dispute is viewed in this way. First, the dispute between Moore and the naturalists might be an empirical question, a question of what in fact is observed to be before our minds when we make certain statements, or ask certain questions. If this is an empirical question then Moore has certainly given no evidence for saying that when we ask, for instance, 'Are all pleasures good?' we always have two distinct things before our minds. It might well be that some do and others, like Moore, do not; it might then be that naturalism is true for some and false for others. Or, it might be that sometimes we do and sometimes we do not have two distinct things before our minds, with the absurd result that naturalism is sometimes true and sometimes false. Further, what sort of evidence would be required to show that we have distinct things before our minds? In fact it is doubtful if this is an empirical question, in any simple sense. Many naturalists would question the very notion of properties, in the sense of mental entities which are designated by the words we use.

I conclude that Moore's argument, interpreted in either of the two ways discussed above, is not a convincing refutation of naturalism. In the following section I would like to consider some objections to Hare's refutation of naturalism.

II

Hare, like Moore, uses an argument of this general form in refuting naturalism: naturalism, if true, implies that certain ethical sentences are analytic; but ethical sentences are never analytic; hence naturalism is false. Hare sometimes argues as if it were evident, and needed no further argument, that ethical sentences are not analytic. Thus, he asserts:

> Suppose that someone were to maintain that 'It is not right to do A' is entailed by 'A has been forbidden by the ruler of our State', we should only need to point out that in that case 'It is not right to do what has been forbidden by the ruler of our State' would be entailed by the analytic sentence 'What has been forbidden by the ruler of our State has been forbidden by the ruler of our State', and would therefore be itself analytic, which in ordinary usage it is not.[6]

Generally, Hare's argument in this passage is that no ethical sentence, in ordinary usage, is analytic. But if this were Hare's argument, his refutation of naturalism would hardly be an improvement over Moore; Moore, too, held that ethical sentences are never analytic. Further, what sort of evidence would go to show that in ordinary usage ethical sentences are never analytic? It is certainly true that naturalists have used sentences such as 'Whatever is pleasant is good' in order to make analytic statements, and there seems to be no good reason for excluding such usages from what is called "ordinary usage."

The clearest statement of Hare's refutation of naturalism is contained in the following passage:

> Now our attack upon naturalistic definitions of 'good' was based on the fact that if it were true that 'a good A' meant the same as 'an A which is C', then it would be impossible to use the sentence 'An A which is C is good' in order to commend A's which are C; for this sentence would be analytic and equivalent to 'An A which is C is C.'[7]

By saying that we use sentences of the form 'An A which is C is good' to commend A's which are C, Hare presumably means more than saying that we apply an ethical word to A's which are C. If this were all that commending means, it would be trivially true that by commending A's that are C's we are not saying that A's that are C are C (when C is replaceable by a non-ethical expression). In order to evaluate Hare's argument we have to know what Hare means by commending.

Hare describes commending as follows: "When we commend or condemn anything, it is always in order, at least indirectly, to guide choices, our own or other people's, now or in the future."[8] Hare's refutation of naturalism might, then, be restated as follows:

1. If naturalism is true, then some ethical sentences of the form 'Whatever is F is good' are equivalent to 'Whatever is F is F.'
2. Sentences of the form 'Whatever is F is F' are never used to guide choices.
3. But ethical sentences of the form 'Whatever is F is good' are used to guide choices.
4. Hence sentences of the form 'Whatever is F is good' are never equivalent to 'Whatever is F is F' and, hence, naturalism is false.

Formally the argument is valid. But what evidence does Hare have for saying that sentences of the form 'Whatever is F is good' are used to guide choices? A naturalist could say (for some non-ethical expression F) such sentences are analytic, and hence do not guide choices. In reply to this, Hare might simply argue that in fact such sentences do guide choices. How is such a dispute to be settled; how is one to go about deciding whether a given sentence does or does not guide choices? Hare gives no way of deciding such a question.

A further objection to Hare's argument can be made. Hare holds that sentences of the form 'Whatever is F is F' cannot be used to guide choices, whereas sentences of the form 'Whatever is F is good' are used to guide choices. But is it impossible for a sentence of the form 'Whatever is F is F' to be used in order to commend F's? It would probably be granted by anyone, naturalist or intuitionist, that such sentences are not used in order to guide choices. But it is not so clear that sentences of the form 'All F's are good' are never used to guide choices when 'F' and 'good' are synonymous. A hedonist, for example, might want to say that since 'pleasant' and 'good' are synonymous, the sentence 'All and only pleasures are good' is equivalent to 'All and only pleasures are pleasant.' But he might also want to say that while the latter sentence does nothing to guide choices, the former sentence does guide choices, because the word 'good' guides choices in a way in which no synonym of 'good' does or can do. In general, a naturalist might argue, two expressions can be synonymous even if sentences containing one expression are not equivalent to sentences containing the other expression. For example, it might be argued that the sentence 'She is an elderly unmarried woman,' and the sentence 'She is a spinster' are not equivalent, in the sense that the latter conveys overtones and suggestions, and hence guides choices, in a way in which the former sentence does not, in spite of the fact that 'elderly unmarried woman' and 'spinster' are synonymous. Similarly, the naturalist could argue that the expressions 'pleasant' and 'good' can well be synonymous, even though replacement of 'pleasant' by 'good' might result in a sentence which guides actions in a way in which the former sentence does not.

In reply to the above objections, Hare might, of course, reply that if one sentence, S_1, guides choices, while another, S_2, does not guide choices, and the two sentences only differ because S_1 contains an expression E which does not occur in S_2, then the expression cannot be synonymous with the expression E_1 which replaces E in S_2. In other words,

Hare might want to make the choice-guiding usage of expressions a criterion of synonymity, so that it can never be the case that one of a pair of synonyms guides choices while the other does not. This criterion, plus the empirical fact (if it is a fact) that ethical words such as 'good' or 'right' guide choices whereas non-ethical expressions such as 'pleasant' do not, would be sufficient to refute naturalism.

In reply to Hare's argument, as sketched above, a naturalist could reply (1) that he does not accept choice-guiding usage as a criterion of synonymity, and (2) that it is not in fact true that ethical words guide choices whereas non-ethical expressions never do. As regards (1), there seem to be good reasons for rejecting choice-guidance as a criterion of synonymity. Consider, for instance, the expressions 'x told a lie' and 'x knowingly uttered a falsehood'; dictionaries tell us these are interchangeable and synonymous, but it is at least plausible to hold that the first has an effect on choices which the second does not have. In general, there are many expressions which are interchangeable without change of truth-value, and in that sense synonymous, which affect listeners in different ways and guide their choices in different ways: one might say that advertising is made possible by this fact. Of course Hare can still contend that interchangeability without changing truth-value is not a sufficient criterion of synonymity. But Hare's argument would then rest on an unusual and arbitrary proposal about synonymity. As regards (2), a naturalist might well argue that non-ethical expressions do in fact guide choices. (It is assumed that guiding choices is not a criterion of being an ethical word; if it were then it would of course be trivially true that no non-ethical expressions guide choices.) When someone says, for example, 'There is a law against x,' he usually intends to, and often does, guide our decision to do or not to do x. Hare might reply that this is so only because we understand the speaker to have implied an additional premise to the effect that whatever is illegal is wrong, the inference then being that x is wrong. But what reason is there to suppose that such an inference takes place in all cases? The assertion that it must take place seems to amount to nothing more than saying, in a complicated and misleading way, that the sentence 'There is a law against x' does in fact guide choices. I conclude that the naturalist has good reasons for rejecting Hare's argument; it does not seem to be generally true that, since ethical words guide choices and non-ethical expressions never do, the two sorts of expressions are never synonymous. Hence I conclude that Hare has not been successful in showing that sentences of the form 'Whatever is F is good' are never analytic.

In conclusion I would like to say something about the possibility of ever conclusively refuting naturalistic ethical theories. Underlying every naturalistic theory is an assertion that an ethical expression is synonymous with a non-ethical expression. Thus Hobbes, for example, asserts that 'just' and 'he that in his actions observeth the laws of his country' are "equivalent" and in fact "make but one name."[9] In general, an assertion that expressions are synonymous can be understood as an empirical assertion about ordinary language, or as a proposal which is one of the rules of an artificial language. In neither case, however, is the truth of naturalism a simple empirical question. The assertion that, e.g., 'good' and 'pleasant' are synonymous in ordinary language cannot be decided without deciding on a criterion of synonymity, and in the previous discussion I have tried to show that disputes about synonymity are an important part of disputes about naturalism. If, on the other hand, naturalism is viewed as based on a rule in an artificial language, acceptance of naturalism depends on adopting an artificial language. In neither case is the acceptance or rejection of naturalism a straightforward empirical issue; the refutation of naturalism, then, cannot be an argument that naturalistic theories are contradicted by the facts.

Notes

1. R. M. Hare, *The Language of Morals* (Oxford: The Clarendon Press, 1952), pp. 83-84.
2. *Ibid.*, p. 82.
3. G. E. Moore, *Principia Ethica* (Cambridge: Cambridge University Press, 1929), p. 16.
4. *Ibid.*
5. W. K. Frankena, "The Naturalistic Fallacy," p. 40 above.
6. Hare, *op. cit.*, p. 155.
7. *Ibid.*, pp. 90-91.
8. *Ibid.*, p. 127.
9. Hobbes, *Leviathan,* Pt. I, Chap. IV.

Three

ON MOORE'S ANALYSIS
OF GOODNESS

R. F. Tredwell

IF G. E. MOORE is correct and goodness is an indefinable, nonnatural property known by direct intuition, then my task in writing a good paper opposing him becomes both easier and more difficult. It is easier, because I will not have to worry about the cogency of my arguments or the accuracy of my quotations, so long as I am careful to add goodness to the paper. But on the other hand my task will be more difficult, because I confess quite frankly that, while I have only a little trouble in recognizing a valid argument when I see one, I have no ability to perceive this added property of goodness. Perhaps I ought to concentrate on cogency, then, in the hope that, if I am successful in attaining it, I will be able to argue that so far as philosophic papers are concerned, goodness *is* cogency.

In attacking Moore's thesis, I plan to be about as contrary as possible. Moore holds that goodness is a nonnatural, indefinable property; I shall take precisely the opposite position: goodness is not *a* property; it is not a *property;* it is not nonnatural; and it is not indefinable. On the

Reprinted by permission of the author and the editor from *The Journal of Philosophy,* LIX (1962), 793-802.

positive side, I shall maintain that goodness is a number of relations sharing several formal features; that these formal features can be specified without much trouble; and that, in addition, if we first answer the question, "A good *what?*" we can generally specify the properties (all of them natural) which lead us to say that a thing is good.

Because Moore is such an admirably clear writer, it is possible to say precisely where one thinks he goes wrong. Let me begin my examination of his position, then, by looking at some points Moore puts forward. Discussing goodness in the essay on "The Conception of Intrinsic Value," Moore writes,

> To say that a kind of value is "intrinsic" means merely that the question whether a thing possesses it, and in what degree it possesses it, depends solely on the intrinsic nature of the thing in question. . . . When I say . . . that the question whether and in what degree anything possesses it depends solely on the intrinsic nature of the thing in question, I mean to say two different things at the same time. I mean to say (1) that it is impossible for what is strictly one and the same thing to possess that kind of value at one time and in one set of circumstances and not to possess it at another; and equally impossible for it to possess it in one degree at one time, or in one set of circumstances, and to possess it in a different degree at another, or in a different set. . . . (2) The second part of what is meant is that if a given thing possesses any kind of intrinsic value in a certain degree, then not only must that thing possess it, under all circumstances, in the same degree, but also anything exactly like it, must, under all circumstances, possess it in exactly the same degree.[1]

These two assertions together, I shall call the "dependence criterion."

The third proposition comes from *Principia Ethica*. There, after saying that natural *objects* are those which exist somewhere and at some time, Moore turns to natural and nonnatural *properties*:

> There is, indeed, no difficulty about the 'objects' themselves, in the sense in which I have just used the term. It is easy to say which of them are natural, and which (if any) are not natural. But when we begin to consider the properties of objects, then I fear the problem is more difficult. Which among the properties of natural objects are natural properties and which are not? For I do not deny that good is a property of certain natural objects: certain of them, I think, *are* good; and yet I have said that 'good' itself is not a natural property. Well, my test for these too also concerns their existence in time. Can we imagine 'good' as existing *by itself* in time, and not merely as a property of some natural object? For

myself, I cannot so imagine it, whereas with the greater number of objects—those which I call the natural properties—their existence does seem to me to be independent of the existence of those objects. They are, in fact, rather parts of which the object is made up than mere predicates which attach to it. If they were all taken away, no object would be left, not even a bare substance: for they are in themselves substantial and give to the object all the substance that it has. But this is not so with good.[2]

A very similar statement, which will perhaps express Moore's point more concisely, appears in the "Intrinsic Value" essay:

> I can only vaguely express the kind of difference I feel there to be [between intrinsic properties and intrinsic values] by saying that intrinsic properties seem to describe the intrinsic nature of what possesses them in a sense in which predicates of value never do. If you could enumerate *all* the intrinsic properties a given thing possessed, you would have given a *complete* description of it, and would not need to mention any predicates of value it possessed; whereas no description of a given thing could be *complete* which omitted any intrinsic property [PS 274].

These two statements about goodness I shall call the "nondescriptive criterion."

Finally, then, to complete this survey of points that Moore makes about goodness, there is the statement in the essay on intrinsic value in which he says that he feels that only beauty, goodness, and perhaps a few other properties, are of this kind (PS 273).

Let me summarize briefly those assertions which I shall be concerned with: first, the *dependence criterion*, which says that the value of an object depends on its intrinsic nature in such a way that two objects cannot differ solely in their value; second, the *nondescriptive criterion*, which says that a complete description of the object would have to mention all its natural properties, but need not mention its value; and third, Moore's *hypothesis* that there are only a very limited number of properties that have these features.

Moore's hypothesis is clearly false: there are an infinite number of "properties" that meet the dependence and nondescriptive criteria; moreover, by examining these "properties" we can get a better idea what 'good' is.

The group of so-called properties which meet these two criteria are classification properties—such properties as 'human,' 'cow,' 'college professor,' 'large,' 'cousin,' and so on. Clearly classifications meet the dependence criterion: it is, strictly speaking, impossible for a single thing to belong to one class in one set of circumstances and to another nonoverlapping class in another set of circumstances; moreover, if one thing belongs to a certain class, then anything exactly like it will belong to that class as well.[3]

Classification properties meet the nondescriptive criterion as well. If you are describing a cow, the complete description would not include any mention of the fact that it is a cow you are talking about; if you were to give a complete description of a college professor—he is absent-minded, has chalk on his coat, patches on his elbows, a harassed look on his face, and so on—it might eventually become quite obvious what *kind* of object you were talking about, but the class itself would not be part of the description. Moreover, it is interesting to note that Moore's way of putting the nondescriptive criterion—in terms of substance and existence in time—closely parallels descriptions in idealistic logic of classification terms.

Now while these arguments do not prove that goodness is a classification term, they seem to suggest it; let us adopt this hypothesis and see whether it will hold up in relation to the other things Moore says about goodness.

Moore would certainly object that goodness is not a typical classification property any more than it is a typical natural property; for while goodness admits of degrees, properties like 'cow' do not.

But *does* goodness admit of degrees? Even in ordinary language we do not speak of one thing's having more or less goodness than another; instead, we speak of the thing's standing in the relation of better and worse, and when we use the adjective 'good' we usually mean "better than most" or "better than a certain arbitrary standard." For example, a "good apple" is one which has firm flesh, even color, and a tangy flavor; a good student is one who is better than most students; and so on. And here the thing that admits of degrees is not goodness, but firmness, evenness of color, and tang in the case of the apple, and intelligence, industry, and scholastic attainment in the case of the student. These features give rise to a ranking of apples and students, and the relative goodness of an apple or student depends on its position in this ranking.

Goodness, I should think, is a derived feature dependent on our willingness to compare a number of objects and say some are better than others. In this respect, it is not a property like yellow—Moore's favorite analogy—but a feature like 'large.' And like 'large,' goodness is dependent on a prior classification in terms of which it is measured. Let me illustrate this similarity between largeness and goodness and how they differ from colors by means of a few examples of the fallacies that arise from following Moore's analogy between yellow and good. Consider the argument: "Jupiter is a red planet; all planets are heavenly bodies; therefore, Jupiter is a red heavenly body." This is pretty clearly valid. But we would have been involved in a fallacy if we had argued in the following way: "Jupiter is a large planet; all planets are heavenly bodies; therefore, Jupiter is a large heavenly body." Now let us parallel these with arguments involving goodness. "My bicycle is a blue bicycle; all bicycles are modes of transportation; therefore, my bicycle is a blue mode of transportation." And the fallacious argument, "My bicycle is a good bicycle; all bicycles are modes of transportation; therefore, my bicycle is a good mode of transportation."

In each pair of arguments, the fallacy involved in the second one is the same: 'large planet' means "larger than the run of planets"; 'good bicycle' means "better than most bicycles." But it does not follow that what is large or good in relation to one class is large or good in relation to another.

From this argument, I think we can infer at least that goodness is not a property, for all properties will give valid inferences in this form of argument, and goodness does not; therefore, one part of my argument is complete, and we are ready for the next.

Goodness, it seems to me, is a feature that an object has by virtue of three things:

1. Its membership in a class.
2. The class's being ranked in terms of better and worse.[4]
3. The object's relatively high place in the ranking.

Now not all of these premises I wish to take have been thoroughly examined, and we ought to fix our attention on number 1: a thing's goodness depends on its membership in a class.

When Moore discusses goodness, he says that it is *a* property of a certain kind—in other words, that there is one property which is goodness. Now what difference does it make whether goodness is one property or many? It makes at least this much difference: if goodness is a single property, then if we take any two objects in the universe, x and y, we ought to be able to make one of three remarks about them: either 'x is

better than y,' or 'y is better than x,' or 'x and y are of equal value';
whereas, if goodness is *not* a single property, we need not be able to
make any of these remarks about x and y chosen at random.

It seems to me that, though we do not always make explicit the classification behind a comparison of value, still, a classification is always
implicit in such a comparison, and we ignore it at our peril. Consider
the following dispute: A says, "Pushpin is better than poetry, because
pushpin gives more pleasure than poetry," to which B replies, "On the
contrary, poetry is better than pushpin, because it sharpens our perceptions and instructs us." Are the remarks incompatible? No, because A
is implicitly classifying pushpin and poetry as harmless diversions, and
it is sufficient for a diversion's being good that it be pleasurable. B, on
the other hand, is classifying poetry and pushpin as cultivating in-
fluences, where pleasure is not only insufficient for goodness but is even
irrelevant.

To help make clear what I mean, let us consider a very small world
consisting of just two items: Kant's *Critique of Pure Reason* and
Santayana's *Reason in Science*. One thing we should like to be true in
every possible world, I suppose, is this: if x is better than y, then y is
not better than x. Now if, in this little world, we rank the books as
works of philosophy, the *Critique of Pure Reason* is better than *Reason
in Science*. But if we rank them as works of literature, Santayana's book
is better than Kant's. Here, then, we have just what we do not want:
each is better than the other.

We must, then, give up the idea that goodness is a single property,
and assert that the goodness of a thing depends on how it is classified.
For in every case where two things can be classified in two different
ways, it is possible that the first classification will show x to be better
than y and that the second will show y to be better than x. A second
reason for holding that goodness is not a single property is that not every
pair of things can be compared in value. (I will not develop this argument, for I think I could not produce a pair of things that everyone
would agree were incomparable; but I suspect that everyone could
himself produce an example that would satisfy him.)

Since we have now rejected two of Moore's major contentions—that
goodness is a property and that it is a single property—we might pause
long enough to agree with him in his rejection of classical naturalism.
If goodness is not a single property, it follows *a fortiori* that it is not a
single natural property. Here I think Moore's intuition in rejecting the

positions of Mill, Spencer, Clifford, *et al.* is absolutely sound, but his reasons are bad. The trouble is not that they confused one property with another, but that, like Moore himself, they supposed they were dealing with a single property. Moore's careful statement of the formal features of goodness—the nondescriptive and dependence criteria—is sufficient to bring out the mistake that both he and the naturalists make.

To return now to the main line of my argument: that goodness is not a nonnatural property follows in a straightforward way. We must distinguish between Moore's statement of the *definition* of nonnatural properties in terms of the dependence and nondescriptive criteria, on the one hand, and his *informal interpretation* of the results of his investigation, on the other. I accept fully the definition and reject the interpretation in which Moore likens goodness to colors and the knowledge of goodness to the intuition of color. Goodness is not like yellowness but like largeness, and it is known in a way analogous to the way largeness is known.

Goodness is nonnatural in one sense, therefore, and perfectly natural in another. If it were a property like yellowness, it would be a very odd one. But it is not; rather, it is a disguised relation, and as a relation it behaves quite normally. Goodness *does* accord with Moore's definition of "nonnatural properties"; but the definition does not define a group of properties.

We come now to the question whether good is indefinable. First, we ought to note that, in the extraordinarily narrow sense in which Moore defines "definition," goodness is indeed indefinable. But then, very few things of any importance *are* definable in Moore's sense. Moreover, the reasons Moore gives for good's being indefinable are not good reasons: he says it is like yellow, and yellow is indefinable, so good is indefinable. But we have decided that good is not like yellow.

Now as a matter of fact, it seems to me that goodness *is* definable, within certain limits, and I would do it this way: 'x is a good A' means

(1) x is an A, and
(2) all the things that are A's are ranked in terms of better and worse, and
(3) x is better than most of them.[5]

I have urged that, most of the time when we use the phrase 'x is good', we are speaking elliptically, and intend to say that x is a good A. Occasionally, however, we mean that, classify x any way you like, it is better than most other members of the class. And sometimes—when, for example, we say that everyone is good, really, when you come right down to it—we mean that there is *some* classification or other in which *x* ranks high in the class.

Now in stating this definition of 'good,' I have simply eliminated it in favor of 'better'; and the question must arise whether 'better' is definable. And the answer is yes and no.

It is definable in the sense that I can give formal axioms for its use—it is transitive, asymmetrical, and so on. But this is not a very interesting sort of definition. In another sense, it is not definable, just because the conditions under which we say one thing is better than another differ from class to class. That is to say, it is not possible to give a general statement of truth conditions for the sentence '*x* is better than *y*.'

For example, in his book on Columbus, Samuel Eliot Morison reports that the Great Discoverer wrote back to Spain that the natives ate a long, yellow fruit that tasted like rotten pears. He was speaking of the banana. It is clear, then, that the more a pear tastes like a good banana, the worse pear it is. Taste is a criterion of goodness in both cases, but in the one case, a certain taste shows that the thing is good, and in the other, that it is bad. Or to take an even more obvious example, a man would be a good poisoner if 95% of those whom he worked on died; but if 95% of the people a doctor worked on died, he would be a very bad doctor indeed.

The fact that there is no single criterion that holds in *all* classes, however, does not imply that there are no criteria at all. In fact, I would be inclined to assert just the opposite, namely, that there is some criterion for ordering just about any class you like. Moreover, in every class I can think of, the criterion is some natural property or group of natural properties.

Consider cars, for example. One car is better than another if it has better pickup, or lower gasoline consumption, or is more comfortable, or more stylish, or goes faster, or carries more load, or is easier to handle and park, and so forth. One piece of music is better than another if it is more pleasing, or stricter in form, or more clever, or more surprising in its development, or richer in its orchestration, or more ingenious in achieving its effect with more economical means, and so on.

We often have trouble in deciding what class a given object belongs to; but, once we are clear on that question, it is usually not too hard to decide whether the object is a good one of its kind. For instance, if one is teaching an introductory philosophy course, it may be hard to decide whether it is to be thought of as a terminal course for nonmajors—in which case it is better to try to give the students a broad acquaintance with philosophic ideas—or whether it is to be the first course for future philosophy majors—in which case logic and philosophic method are more in order. Similarly, when one is buying a car, it is often hard to decide whether it is to be a means of running around town, or a means of taking long trips, or merely a status symbol. But when this decision is made, it is usually not too difficult to decide what features to look for in order to ensure that the new car be a good one.

When we do run into trouble, it is usually that there are a number of different features that a thing of the given kind should have to be good, and we find that one object exceeds in one and another in another. Is Wagner better than Mozart? The one is more colorful, the other more ingenious and economical. Well, then, which is more important, color or ingenuity, and what weight should we give to each? Here, I confess, I am simply not sure. One *could* simply divide the class of composers and say that Wagner is the greatest of the nineteenth-century operatic composers and Mozart the best of the eighteenth, and that the criteria of excellence are different for the two periods. But this is the coward's way out.

To summarize, then, on the question of the indefinability of good, I maintain that 'good' *is* definable, and that, once the question "A good *what?*" has been answered, it is ordinarily possible to specify the truth conditions for the sentence 'x is better than y' in terms of natural properties.

One final point remains to be made about the specification of truth conditions for this narrower statement, 'x is a better A than y.' It would seem that there would be no way to test a suggestion as to how one might rank objects of a given kind except by reference to the formal properties of the better-worse relation. That is to say, suppose someone suggested that we rank apples in the following way: we will record the Greenwich mean time at which every apple is picked or falls off the tree; if an apple leaves the tree earlier than another, it is better and if they leave the tree at the same time, they are equally good. This will rank apples in accord with the *formal* properties we would like to have hold within a ranking of better and worse, but clearly this is not the "right" way to rank them. Does not the rejection of this suggestion show that we have an intuition of how apples *ought* to be ranked which is prior to the specification of truth criteria for the sentence 'x is a better apple than y'?

No, it does not. What it does show is that there are ways of cross-checking our ranking criteria against other orderings of the set of apples. Let me call these "expectations about how good apples will behave" to distinguish them from ranking criteria.

We have quite a number of such expectations. For example, we should expect that, if we apply our ranking criteria to a batch of apples and then put the apples on display in a supermarket under a sign "Your choice, 29¢ a pound," the apples we have classed as good will be among the first to disappear. We should expect that people would be willing to pay more for a good apple than for a bad one. And so on. We are willing to have some of these expectations frustrated, but not all of them at once. If all or most of them *are* frustrated, then we begin to think perhaps we are using the wrong truth criteria for the statement '*x* is a better apple than *y*.' And in particular, we would reject the suggestion that apples be classed in terms of better and worse on the basis of the time they left the tree on just these grounds.

It is such expectations that are generally used to criticize established criteria of goodness. If our school system is good, why is it that our A students cannot spell? Why is the drop-out rate among talented youngsters so high? If our trade policy is reasonable, why do we persistently have an unfavorable balance of payments? Classifications of goodness are expected to show certain relations to other, independent classifications of the same objects; and when they fail to, we begin to suspect that we are ranking things incorrectly at some point.

We may conclude, then, that goodness is not *a* property, it is not a *property*, it is not nonnatural, it is not indefinable, and its perception does not depend on a special kind of intuition. I hope, then, that in trying to construct a cogent argument against G. E. Moore, I have also been trying to construct a good one, because, as I said at the beginning, I think that the criterion of goodness in arguments *is* just their cogency.

Notes

1. In *Philosophical Studies* (Paterson, N.J.: Littlefield, Adams & Co., 1959), pp. 260-61 (italics omitted). Hereafter referred to as PS.

2. *Principia Ethica*, (Cambridge: Cambridge University Press, 1954), p. 41. Hereafter referred to as PE.

3. There are some exceptions to this generalization, of course, but I would urge that they exactly parallel the exceptions to Moore's statement about goodness. If one considers the duck-rabbit in Wittgenstein's book, one could say that sometimes it is a duck and sometimes a rabbit. But so far as one can say this, one can also say that it is sometimes good and sometimes not: it is a much more plausible duck than rabbit. Moore himself handles exceptions to the dependence criterion with the "principle of organic unities," which says, in effect, that what a thing *is* depends in part on its circumstances, and that it is *in situ* that things must be evaluated. This allows him to maintain the dependence criterion, but he does so in a way which depends on our ability to *reclassify* things as they shift circumstances.

4. There is a second, noncomparative sense of 'good' in which the reference class is thought of not as internally *ranked*, but as *subclassed* into "good" and "bad" (or into finer gradations). This second sense allows us to say that "while the Atlas is our best space vehicle, it is still a bad one." Moral goodness (as opposed to goodness of character) seems to be of this sort—one in which we have ranked *classes* of men or acts rather than ranked *men* or ranked *acts*.

5. Once more, I am concerned with the comparative sense of good, not with the subclass sense noted in footnote 4.

Four

ON THE NATURALISTIC FALLACY

George Nakhnikian

G. E. MOORE's now classic discussions of the naturalistic fallacy are frequently unclear and imprecise, and in certain crucial places they are misleading. A thorough documentation of these charges would require lengthy exegesis and digressions into metaphysics and theory of meaning. I shall dispense with both. Instead of dwelling on defects, I shall try to formulate clearly and defend what I take to be Moore's perfectly correct warnings against certain mistakes in moral philosophy.

In Chapter I of *Principia Ethica*, while discussing the naturalistic fallacy, Moore either directly or obliquely calls attention to six distinguishable errors:

(1) Failing to see that no definition can be a moral or evaluative assertion.

(2) Failing to see that no analytic moral or evaluative statement can be a moral or evaluative assertion.

Reprinted from H.-N. Castañeda and G. Nakhnikian (eds.), *Morality and the Language of Conduct* (Detroit: Wayne State University Press, 1963), by permission of the publisher. Copyright 1963 by Wayne State University Press.

(3) Misidentifying two different but co-extensive properties.

(4) Supposing that an expression E is synonymous with an expression E′, while in ordinary discourse "This is E but not E′" is not self-contradictory.

(5) Defining "good" in terms of the very properties we would invoke if someone wanted to know the reasons why *x* is good.

(6) Thinking that a definition of "good" is the ultimate support or justification for any of our evaluations.

One gathers from the way Moore writes that although every one of these errors is either the result of the naturalistic fallacy or leads to it, still none of them is *the* naturalistic fallacy. In one place Moore says, that *the* naturalistic fallacy, the root error, is failing to see that it is in principle impossible to give a *correct* definition of "good," a term Moore uses to refer to "that which is at the same time common . . . and peculiar" to all ethical judgments. But elsewhere Moore tells us that he will call "the naturalistic fallacy" the error of confusing good, which is not a "natural" object, with any "natural" object whatever. He goes on to add that even if no "natural" objects were involved in the definition, there would still be a fallacy in defining "good" at all, although in that case he would not call it "the naturalistic fallacy." Moore thus presents two different formulations of what *the* naturalistic fallacy is. One formulation identifies it as the attempt to define "good" at all. The other identifies it as the misidentification of goodness with some "natural" object. To complicate matters further, we have the list of errors, (1)-(6), some of which at least qualify as species of the generic "fallacy" of trying to define "good" at all. For if it is a fallacy to define "good" at all, then (4) and (5) are specific ways of committing it, provided that in (4) the expression being miselucidated is "good."

My main object is to support Moore to the effect that (1)-(6) are pitfalls to be avoided by anyone who tries to clarify the nature of evaluation and obligation. Along the way I shall be saying that Moore has not proved the impossibility of explicating "good" in naturalistic terms. The point is not new, but the way I shall be making it may be. Moore has three main lines of attack against the definability of "good." In one line of attack, he seems to imply that anyone who sees that (1)-(6) are errors will see that "good" is indefinable. Moore is right that (1)-(6) are mistakes; but he is obviously wrong in supposing that this fact implies the indefinability of "good." The second and third lines of attack relate to Moore's view of analysis. The "open question" argument comes in at this point.

Moore has two distinguishable conceptions of analysis: a phenomenological-atomistic one and a "linguistic" one. According to the phenomenological-atomistic conception, we are supposed to see, as a result of holding before our minds the object goodness, that goodness is simple, not capable of being broken up into parts, hence indefinable. This recipe is dialectically inconclusive. Even with the best will in the world, most philosophers would be nonplussed if invited to take a phenomenological "look" at goodness. And the atomistic part of the recipe is inapplicable in principle. The notion of absolute simplicity is nonsense. Simplicity is always relative to some respect. Indivisibility into parts is not a respect. We have first to specify the respect in which the parts are to be distinguished from the whole.

It is only when Moore departs from the phenomenological-atomistic recipe and turns his attention to the contours and nuances of the language of evaluation in which the word "good" plays so central a role that we return to the philosophical dialectic. This brings us to the second conception of analysis, a conception which I have called the "linguistic" one. The paradigm here is the analysis of being a brother into being a male sibling. Although Moore explicitly disavows that analysis is concerned with the elucidation of linguistic expressions, in practice he defends his analytic elucidations by appeal to the logic of ordinary discourse. What, after all, is our final justification for identifying male siblinghood with being a brother except that in fact the English word "brother" is synonymous with the English expression "male sibling"? This ultimate appeal to ordinary discourse underlies the "open question" argument. Is pleasure, after all, good? This is an open question in ordinary English. Is a brother, after all, a male sibling? This is not an open question. The fact that the first is an open question shows that "good" cannot be defined as pleasure. To suppose that "good," as ordinarily used, means pleasure is to commit an instance of the error listed as (4) above. Although Moore never to his own or to anyone else's satisfaction gave a precise specification of what a "natural object" or property is, he has in mind such things as pleasure, the greatest happiness of the greatest number, fitness to survive, etc., the sorts of things that are, roughly speaking, empirical entities. He uses the "open question" argument hoping to show that *no* definition of "good" is possible, hence no naturalistic definition is possible. His reason for this is inconclusive. In Chapter I, Section 13, (2) of *Principia*, Moore says that anyone who runs through a number of attempted definitions of "good" and sees, on the strength of the "open question," that none of them works will come to see that *no* definition will work.

If we adhere to Moore's strict sense of "linguistic" analysis, his conclusion that "good" is indefinable is correct, but his reason for thinking that his conclusion is true is invalid. A better explanation than Moore's for why the appeal to ordinary discourse will not give us any secure grounds for claiming that "good" means so and so, in contrast to the "brother"-means-male-sibling case, is that ordinary discourse is not as precise about "good" as it is about "brother." And for this very same reason, the "open question" argument cannot work wholesale. For it can work only in those cases where ordinary discourse is quite clear as to whether or not an expression of the form "This is P but not good" is self-contradictory. Thus, Moore's discussions concerning the naturalistic fallacy lead us to admit that elucidatory analysis, in the "linguistic" manner, will not yield a naturalistic definition of "good." But so far we have no reason to despair of giving a naturalistic *account* of goodness as distinguished from an analysis in the sense in question.

At this point I must say something about the distinction I have in mind between analysis and giving an account. The vogue in contemporary ethical theory has been to assume that the analysis of ethical and evaluative concepts, in the sense of explicating their contours and nuances in ordinary discourse, exhausts the legitimate work of the critical moral philosopher. Some of the air of triviality in strict analytical ethics is, I think, a reflection of this methodological assumption. Although I am an analytic philosopher and much of what I do is straightforward philosophical analysis, I am convinced that analysis alone is insufficient to get to the bottom of the perplexities of moral philosophy. Analysis, be it in the style of Moore, Russell, Austin, or Wittgenstein, is indispensable as a propaedeutic. It clears away the conceptual confusions that plague all of us, philosophers and non-philosophers. For example, the Moorean techniques are adequate for dispelling certain purely conceptual fallacies, the avoidance of which is a necessary condition of an acceptable theory of goodness. But I believe that analysis alone cannot decide the issue between naturalists and their foes. Is this an "open question": After all, is a thing good which is so constituted that it would reinforce the desires, sustain the interest, and occasion the satisfactions

and enjoyments of everyone who had a mature and comprehensive grasp
of that thing's scientifically discoverable and imaginatively explorable
properties and relations? An appeal to the logical contours of ordinary
discourse cannot settle the issue as to the openness of this question. If
we are inclined, as we are, to saying that a thing of that description
might, without contradiction, be said not to be good, we are also inclined in the opposite direction of wondering what on earth more goodness could be. This type of ambivalence is not uncommon. And we
cannot simply admit its existence in a given case and then drop the
subject. We need to explain in some not *ad hoc* manner what is going
on and what can be done to dispel the ambivalence.

At this juncture we could make a linguistic legislation. But this is
improper in the case of goodness, for we are confronted with a philosophical perplexity arising out of the imprecisions of everyday talk about
good and bad things. Any adequate account of goodness must accom-
modate the clearly discernible logical features of the ordinary use of
"good." Otherwise we have evaded the problem with which we started.
The obscurities of ordinary discourse cannot override what we can
clearly discern. To give an account of goodness, then, is to map out
the clearly discernible features of the logical contours of "good" without
being intimidated by the obscurities, and to justify the account by some
means other than the claim that everything in our account can be seen
to be an accurate transcription of everyday usage. This refusal to be
intimidated by obscurities and the manner of justifying our results distinguish giving an account from "linguistic" analysis.

To provide an account of goodness we begin by asking: What general principles or standards do we employ in deciding that our evaluations are not spurious? This is not a question that can be answered by
sorting out entailments, equivalences, synonymies, contradictions in ordinary discourse. It is a matter which presupposes clarity about substantive
matters, such as the fact that immediate likings, enjoyments, approvals
are not always sustained in the light of further experience and knowledge; that a fool's evaluations are not as trustworthy as those of an
informed and intelligent man; that evaluating is an activity possible only
to creatures who are rational and capable of conative responses and
affective states. In denying these facts, one would not be contradicting
himself or making unintelligible noises. He would be simply expressing
materially false beliefs. Those who recognize such substantive facts
would see that the legitimacy of evaluations is a function of their satis-

fying principles or standards validated by just those extra-linguistic facts. When Dewey characterizes his discussion of the nature of value as "the construction of good," he may be trying to convey that what he is doing is neither stipulative analysis nor analysis in the sense of describing ordinary linguistic usage. He may be trying to say that he is doing the sort of thing which here I am calling "giving an account." (This has to be stated with reservations because Dewey is not always too clear as to what he thinks he is doing. In fact, in "The Construction of Good" Chapter X of *The Quest for Certainty,* he says things which sound as if he were stipulating a meaning for "good" and justifying it on the grounds of its pragmatic utility.) An account of goodness in naturalistic terms would be neither a stipulation nor simply a description of how the word "good" is used in ordinary discourse. It would be a formula which specifies the principles or standards whose fulfillment is necessary and sufficient for correctly ascribing goodness to things. And to locate these standards it is not enough to examine the logical properties and relations of evaluative statements. We must also become clear as to certain relevant substantive facts. However, a detailed exploration of these issues is beyond the scope of this paper.

The other formulation of the naturalistic fallacy, that it is the misidentification of good and some "natural" object or other, is a hint worth clarifying and developing. I suggest in passing that (5) may be a first step toward unpacking Moore's hint. We would further need to study the logical status of the properties we would invoke in giving valid reasons for calling something "good." We would have to understand the ways in which these properties differ from goodness as well as among themselves. I shall not do anything along these lines in this paper.

I now begin my defense of Moore's warnings against (1)-(6).

In the last paragraph of Chapter I, Section 6 of *Principia,* Moore says that "propositions about the good are all of them synthetic and never analytic; and this is plainly no trivial matter. And the same thing may be expressed more popularly, by saying that, *if I am right,* then nobody can foist on us an axiom as that 'Pleasure is the only good' or that 'The good is the desired' on the pretense that this is 'the very meaning of the word'" (my italics). Just before this quotation, Moore states the main thesis, that "good" is indefinable. If we take the italicized phrase to be referring to that thesis, then the quotation gives an outline of an argument, later to be elaborated, for the thesis that "good" is indefinable. I have already argued that the argument is inconclusive against the possibility of a naturalistic account of goodness. However, it is true that if propositions about the good are synthetic, then nobody can state it as a principle that, e.g., pleasure and only pleasure is good, and at the same time defend it *as a moral principle* on the ground that "good" means pleasure. The argument proving the truth of *this* hypothetical is quite independent of the question whether or not "good" is amenable to a naturalistic account, although if the indefinability thesis were proved, the consequent of the hypothetical would be a corollary of it.

Moore says that the indefinability thesis "amounts to this: That propositions about the good are all of them synthetic and never analytic. . . ." By "amounts to" Moore seems to intend identity. If this is what he means, he is wrong. The indefinability thesis does not entail the syntheticity thesis. Even if "good" is indefinable, it is possible to formulate analytic statements "about the good," viz., the good is the good. Because Moore mistakenly thinks that indefinability implies syntheticity and also that indefinability is proved, he does not bother to argue independently for the proposition that assertions "about the good," which I take to mean evaluations, are never analytic. There is, however, a proof of this proposition. I shall give the proof immediately after this word of caution: The proof of the syntheticity of evaluations and moral assertions does not entail the indefinability of "good." "Propositions about the good" may be either evaluations or analytic statements. The fact that all evaluations are synthetic is consistent with the possibility that there are analytic evaluative statements which are not evaluations and whose analyticity is owing to a definition of "good."

Now for the argument that definitions and analytic statements cannot be moral or evaluative assertions or principles. This is in two steps. First, no definition can be of an evaluative or moral assertion. Second, no analytic statement can be an evaluative or moral assertion.

No definition can be a moral assertion. Regarding two expressions as being definitionally equivalent is tantamount to holding that whenever, and only whenever, the one expression is correctly used, the other may be used with equal propriety. Underlying this permissive rule is a stronger one to the effect that the two expressions must be used in accordance with the same set of rules. These remarks obviously do not provide anything like a complete analysis of definitions. For that we need a thorough investigation of what language rules are and what constitutes using two expressions in accordance with the same set of rules. I am simply assuming that what I have said about definitions is correct as far as it goes.

Moral assertions are also "rulish." A moral assertion must satisfy at least two conditions. It must mention an identifiable action and say of it that it ought to be done or that it ought not to be done. A moral assertion can be satisfied or violated. Secondly, a moral assertion should be capable of being construed as an answer to: "In these circumstances (actual or imagined), ought I or ought I not to do such and such?"

Although definitions and moral assertions are "rulish" in that they are all directly action-guiding, there is a crucial difference between them. Definitions are relative to a language. Whenever we invoke, report, or stipulate a definition, we let it be known that *if* or *as* one wants to speak correctly in a given language, one must use a certain expression of that language in accordance with the very same rules by which one uses another expression (of that or of another language). No moral assertion relates to a language in this way. A moral assertion formulates an unconditional requirement or an unconditional prohibition to do a certain act. Therefore, no definition can be a moral assertion. Hence, no definition of a moral expression can be a moral assertion.

Similarly, no evaluative assertion is relative to a language in the way that definitions are. An evaluative assertion must mention an identifiable entity and ascribe merit to it or rank it in order of merit relative to something else. Therefore, no evaluative assertion is a definition. Hence, no definition of an evaluative expression can be an evaluative assertion.

There is a similar sharp distinction between moral assertions and analytical moral or evaluative statements. Again, I shall formulate first the argument proving that no moral assertion can be an analytic moral statement. Its extension to evaluative assertions is easy.

Examples of analytic moral statements are:

(*a*) The wrongful killing of a human being is wrong.

(*b*) All wrong actions are wrong.

(*c*) All actions which everyone in circumstances C ought to do are actions which no one in circumstances C is permitted to refrain from doing.

I call such statements as these "analytic moral statements" because they are analytic statements containing words like "ought," "right," "permitted." It is evident that not all analytic statements can be construed as being alternative ways of invoking or reporting in the material mode a definition normally formulated in the formal mode. For example, if "The wrongful killing of a human being is wrong" were construed as being a definition of "wrong" in the material mode, the assertion that lying is wrong would be a misuse of language, which it is not in ordinary discourse. Because some analytic statements could not possibly be mistaken for definitions, to show that no analytic moral statement can be a moral assertion we need an argument independent of the one proving that no definition can be a moral assertion.

Recall that a moral assertion must satisfy at least two conditions. It must mention an identifiable action and say of it either that it ought to be done or that it ought not to be done. Moreover, it must be capable of being construed as an answer to: "In these circumstances, ought I to do or ought I not to do such and such?" Analytic moral statements fail to satisfy both of these conditions. Consider (*a*) "The wrongful killing of a human being is wrong." We might be tempted to think that (*a*) is telling us not to kill human beings wrongfully and that it is an answer to: "In these circumstances, ought I or ought I not to kill this or that human being wrongfully?" But what is killing a human being wrongfully? (*a*) does not say. The statement fails to mention an action which we can identify independently of judging it to be right or wrong to do. Otherwise put, an answer telling me that such killings of human beings as are wrongful are wrong does not tell me which killings it is that I am to refrain from doing. I cannot guide my actions by such a statement. Contrast this with (*d*) "Killing human beings is wrong." This is a moral assertion. It tells us that an identifiable action, killing a human being, is not the thing to do. It can also be construed as an answer to: "In these circumstances ought I or ought I not to kill this or that human being?" Kill one human being and you violate (*d*). You do what it prohibits. Kill as many people as you will, wrongfully or not. You are not doing anything (*a*) says you are not to do. All (*a*) says is that any killing of a human being you are not to do is an action you are not to do.

For similar reasons, no evaluative assertion can be analytic. Examples of analytic evaluative statements are:

(*e*) The good wines of France are good.

(*f*) All good things are good.

(*g*) If a thing is good, then it merits being sought, realized, and perpetuated.

Recall that an evaluative assertion must mention an identifiable entity and say of it that it has merit or rank it in order of merit relative to something else. No analytic evaluative statement can do either one of these things. Take (*e*), for example. It says that the meritorious wines of France are meritorious. But this does not tell us which French wines it is that are meritorious (have value). The statement fails to mention an entity that we can identify independently of judging it to be good. Contrast this with (*h*) "The wine in the cellar is good." This is a genuine evaluation. It tells us that a certain identifiable entity has value.

To sum up, an evaluative assertion must perform one of two related linguistic acts, neither of which is performed by analytic evaluative statements. Therefore, no analytic evaluative statement can be an evaluative assertion. In fact, no analytic statement whatever can be an evaluative assertion, but this needs no emphasis because no one would be tempted to confuse an evaluative assertion with an analytic statement which did not contain at least one value word.

Anyone who argued that pleasure and only pleasure is good because "good" means pleasure *might* be in a complete muddle if he were not on guard against (1) or (2) or both. If he thought that he was defending "Pleasure alone is good" as an evaluative principle, he would be contradicting himself. If we take " 'Good' means pleasure" as a definition, it cannot be an evaluative principle. Moreover, the definition entails that "Pleasure alone is good" is analytic. But the statement is being defended as an evaluative principle. Hence it is being defended as being at the same time analytic and non-analytic, which is self-contradictory. The trouble here is not that we have a faulty definition. Even if the definition were correct, this way of arguing would implicate us in logical absurdities. And this shows that if propositions about the good are synthetic, and we have seen that they are, then regardless of whether or not "good" (or "right") are indefinable, nobody can establish it as a moral or evaluative principle that all and only F are good (or right) on the ground that "good" (or "right") means F.

The next question that naturally suggests itself is this. Are there definitions of "good" which can be shown to be inadmissable? The errors numbered (3), (4), and (5) are directly concerned with this question. Even if "good" were definable, no definition of it could count as correct unless it avoided these particular errors. It seems safe to say that (3) is a description in "the material mode" and (4) is a description in "the formal mode" of one and the same error. For to confuse two different properties is tantamount to regarding as synonymous two predicates which are not in fact synonymous. Whichever way we put it, the error is egregious, and it is not peculiar to moral contexts. It can occur even when the misidentified properties and expressions are of the same type, both "natural" or both "nonnatural." In this generic form, the error is not interesting. Moore himself, in Chapter I, Section 12 of *Principia*, mentions them only to dismiss them without further ado. On the other hand, (5) is an interesting species of this error. It specifically involves at least one moral or evaluative property or expression. Any instance of (3), (4), or (5) can be successfully demolished by the "open question" argument.

The mistake in (5) would be to treat goodness as being on the same level of discourse as the properties of things we have to take account of correctly in judging that a thing does or does not have value. In short, to proscribe (5) is to lay down a negative condition for a satisfactory definition of "good." It does not provide a criterion of being a property which we have to take account of in judging that a thing has value in the sense of providing a test by which we could unerringly pick out from any context these properties of things. It simply rules out all definitions of "good" whose definientia list the very properties we would invoke if we had to give the reasons why X is good; and for a very good reason. If "X is good" is defined as "X is a, b, c, . . . n," then a, b, c, . . . n cannot be the properties we invoke to support our evaluation of X as good. If someone required to be shown why X is good, it would be no answer to tell him "because X is a, b, c, . . . n." To say that X is a, b, c, . . . n would be just another way of saying that X is good. This, however, does not imply that "good" is indefinable.

We now come to (6) on our list of errors.

In the first sentence of the last paragraph in Chapter I, Section 14 of *Principia*, Moore writes: "My objections to naturalism are then, in the first place, that it offers no reason at all, far less any valid reason, for any ethical principle whatever. . . ." He means to be attacking any ethical theory which defines "good" at all and uses the definition as the ultimate support for all evaluations. Now Moore is right when he suggests that justification by definition is a fatuous enterprise. But he seems to be arguing from this fatuousness to indefinability. This inference is invalid. First let us see why Moore is right, and then we shall see why his inference is wrong.

It is easy to see that justification by definition is fatuous. Consider this example. I am trying to show you that doing A is your duty. You are not convinced. But A *is* your duty, I say, because your doing A would contribute to the welfare of the community. But suppose that I define "A is your duty" to mean that your doing A will contribute to the welfare of the community. In that case, "A is your duty" is just another way of saying "Your doing A will contribute to the welfare of the community," and I have not provided a reason why doing A is your duty. In asserting "A is your duty" and "Your doing A will serve the welfare of the community" I have simply used two different expressions to say the same thing. This is illuminating only to those who need a lesson in language. It is of no help whatever to anyone who requires to be shown that doing A is his duty.

Moore says that naturalism—the view that "good" is definable—offers no reason whatever for any ethical principle. But ethics must provide valid reason for ethical truths. Therefore, Moore intimates, naturalism is false; "good" is indefinable. But all that Moore's argument against fatuous validation proves is that the *defining* property of goodness cannot serve as a *reason* why X is good. An ethical theory which defines "good" need not also use the defining property of goodness in this illegitimate manner. In other words, from the fact alone that an ethical theory has a definition of "good" it does not follow, *pace* Moore, that the theory makes nonsense of giving good reasons to back up evaluations.

The failure of Moore's charge that naturalism cannot offer any reasons for any evaluation or ethical judgment whatever leaves him only the "open question" argument. I have already given my reasons for saying that this works against definitions one at a time. It cannot prove that "good" is in principle inexplicable in naturalistic terms. This, however, is not the main point of this paper. My principal objective has been to argue on the side of Moore against those who might be tempted to commit errors (1)-(6).

PART TWO

MOORE'S ONTOLOGY

Introduction

IT IS FITTING to include in this collection a series of papers devoted to Moore's ontology. Moore has been widely renowned and hailed as a philosopher of common sense, as an advocate of philosophy as analysis, and as an epistemologist intensely concerned with such issues as the problem of perception. But it must be recognized that Moore was profoundly concerned with problems of ontology long before he achieved fame for any of the above-mentioned characteristics. And there is good reason to believe that he conceived of ontology as one of the most significant branches of philosophy. In his 1910-11 lectures, published in 1953 as *Some Main Problems of Philosophy*,[1] he writes: "The most important and interesting thing which philosophers have tried to do is no less than this; namely, to give a general description of the *whole* of the Universe," and he goes on to say that "*The first and most important* problem of philosophy is: To give a general description of the *whole* Universe."[2] In this work he considers and argues for and against various ontological alternatives and even gives ontological status to (among other things) an incredible variety of universals. And in this work, he ends up affirming that the universe contains "three different kinds of constituents," namely "(1) particulars, (2) truths or facts, and (3) universals," and that, although only particulars exist, nevertheless truths and universals "have *being* or *are.*"[3] In various other works, both earlier and later than the 1910-11 lectures, Moore considers and opts for other ontological alternatives and clearly exhibits a concern with problems of ontology. At a time when Moore is, by some, chiefly lauded for other reasons—his emphasis on ordinary language, and what not—it is important to emphasize this aspect of Moore's work. It is his status as an ontologist which in the eyes of many makes him one of the great philosophers of modern times.

In "Inclusion, Exemplification, and Inherence in G. E. Moore," (Essay 5 in this volume), Gustav Bergmann tackles the question as to what Moore meant by his famous distinction between natural and nonnatural properties, a distinction which plays an important role in Moore's *Principia Ethica*. The solution to the "riddle" was first put forth by Herbert Hochberg in "Moore's Ontology and Nonnatural Properties" (Essay 6 in this volume). Hochberg argues that the distinction between natural and nonnatural properties stems from an ontology to which Moore adhered at the time when he wrote *Principia Ethica* and (more specifically) that Moore's view regarding the nature of universals provides the ground for the distinction between the two kinds of properties. In "Mr. Hochberg on Moore: Some Corrections," John O. Nelson raises various objections to Hochberg's paper. And Professor Hochberg replies in "Some Reflections on Mr. Nelson's Corrections" (Essay 8).

In "Moore and Russell on Particulars, Relations, and Identity" (Essay 9), Hochberg examines certain arguments of Moore and Russell for the existence of particulars. He argues that neither of them proved that particulars—in the sense of what each meant by 'particulars'—exist, but that both proved the existence of particulars in some sense of that term.

Notes

1. London: Allen & Unwin, 1953.
2. *Ibid.*, pp. 1, 2. My italics for the first five words of the second quotation.
3. *Ibid.*, p. 372.

Five

INCLUSION, EXEMPLIFICATION, AND INHERENCE IN G. E. MOORE

Gustav Bergmann

GREEN AND GOOD are both simple properties. In this they are alike. Green is a natural property; good, a nonnatural one. In this they differ. That is the key formula of Moore's *Principia Ethica*. Take two green spots. Some philosophers hold that their both being green is accounted for by a single entity, green, which, in a sense to be specified, is a constituent of both spots. Such entities are called universals. The "properties" of the formula are universals. About that there is no doubt. A property that can be referred to by a compound expression such as 'green and square' is not "simple." One which in direct reference can only be named is simple. Much unpacking as that needs, it will do. And, again, there is no doubt, this is what Moore had in mind. What though did he mean when he called some properties natural; some others, nonnatural? There has been much doubt and a great deal of discussion. No satisfactory answer has come forth. Moore's dichotomy almost seemed a riddle. I shall here propose a solution of the riddle. For this choice of topic I have two reasons, one personal, one structural.

Reprinted by permission of the author and the editor from *Inquiry*, V (1962), 116-42.

I am your guest. A guest ought to put his best foot forward. One of the best things, if not the best, a philosopher can credibly say for himself is that he has found some younger men, willing to call themselves his students, who have grown up to make some substantial contributions. The basic idea for the solution of Moore's riddle is not mine. Rather, it is a substantial contribution of one of my most gifted students, Herbert Hochberg, who has elaborated it in the essay following this. This is the personal reason.

In what a great philosopher says there is a pattern. It all flows from one source, a few fundamental ontological ideas. In the light of this source and only in this light, it can all be understood. In this sense, ethics properly understood is but a corollary of metaphysics; and the heart of metaphysics is ontology. I want to drive home this point by showing that Moore's puzzling dichotomy can be understood only in the light of his ontology. That is the structural reason for my choice of topic.

To speak of Moore's ontology in the singular is misleading. There are at least two, probably more. An early version, explicitly stated in some papers published around the turn of the century, even though never mentioned in *Principia Ethica,* yet controls this book. That, specifically, is Hochberg's precious discovery. One later version is recorded in *Some Main Problems of Philosophy,* a course of lectures delivered in the 'twenties, published only in the 'fifties. This later and that earlier version throw much light upon each other. Speaking about them, I shall simply call them Moore's first and second ontology.

Moore always knew where he wanted to arrive. But, alas, he never found out how to get there. There are minds as well as bodies. Also, a mind may know a body, for instance, by perceiving it. If that is called realism, Moore wanted to arrive at realism. There are not only valuings but also values. Goodness, for instance, is in some things valued, not just in the minds valuing them. If that is called objectivism, Moore wanted to arrive at objectivism.

What does it mean for anything to be in a thing? One cannot answer the question without first answering another: What is a thing? The kind of answer required is, of course, an ontological assay. Before turning to Moore's early answer, some general remarks are in order.

Take two spots; one, green and square; the other, red and round. The green goes with the square, not with the red; the red with the round, not with the square. Hence, there must be something that makes these items go or hang together as in fact they do. In assaying that something there are two possibilities. Either the tie required is in the mind of the beholder. That is the road to idealism. Think of Kant's transcendental unity of apperception. Or the ties are in the things themselves. In this case an infinite regress threatens. What ties the tie to what it ties? The question reveals the threat. The only way out is to give ontological status to entities I call *fundamental ties* or nexus. A fundamental tie needs no further tie to tie it to what it ties.

Take now two green spots. There is identity as well as diversity to be accounted for. The two spots are identical in being both green. The universal accounts for the identity. They are different in being two, not one. The ontological assay must account for that difference. In traditional words, all philosophers embracing universals are faced with the problem of *individuation*. Basically, there are two ways of solving it. I shall call them A and B.

A. There is a kind of simples called individuals. In the example there are two, each spot being a complex containing one individual and the color. An individual once presented could not, if presented again, be recognized as such. That is why individuals are also called bare, or bare particulars. Their sole function, as it were, is to individuate. Accordingly, the spatial and temporal relations, assayed as relational universals, obtain among individuals and among them only. Space and time thus are assayed as being in essence relational. The nexus between individuals and universals is called *exemplification*. Individuals and universals belong to different types. That means, first, that of two entities of the same type, say, two individuals, none can exemplify the other. It means, second, that exemplification is intransitive; i.e., if α exemplifies β and β exemplifies γ then α cannot exemplify γ. The complex, finally, the individual exemplifying the universal, is of a third type. B. All simples are universals. The basic tie is *inclusion*.[1] A simple may be included in a complex. "Two" complexes are one if and only if they include the same simples. Individuation is achieved by a special class of nonrelational spatial and temporal universals. Call them here, there, now, then, and so on. One of the two spots, for instance, is a complex including green and there, the other, one including green and here. Space and time, one sees, are assayed as being in essence nonrelational.[2] Simples and complexes are of the same type. More poignantly, there are no types. Accordingly, if α includes β and β includes γ than α includes γ. This gambit cannot but remind one of Scotus', with the special class of space-time properties corresponding to his *haecceitates*.

Think of *cognoscere* and *recognoscere,* *erkennen* and *wiedererkennen.*
"What cannot be recognized cannot be known. Bare particulars cannot
be known. Hence, there are no such entities." That is the structural root
of the resistance again *A*-ontologies. At least, it is a very important root.
"Space and time qualities are not presented to us. Hence there are no
such entities." That is the structural root of the resistance against *B*-
ontologies. At least, it is a very important root. *A*- and *B*-ontologies must
both face the problem of relations. That is, they must in their respective
assays indicate the constituent or constituents which account for, say,
this spot being to the left of that. A consistent *A*-ontologist accounts for
it by a relational universal, exemplified by a pair of individuals. Exemplification, being either unary, or binary, or ternary, and so on, thus
becomes subdivided. But the *A*-ontologist needs, up to this point, no
other fundamental tie.

There is throughout the tradition a tendency to favor individuals over
universals, to deny the latter the same ontological status as the former.
One of its roots is the pattern according to which what exists is "in"
space and time or localized, in the sense in which the universals of
either *A* or *B* are not and the individuals of *A* are localized. In this
sense, in *B* nothing is in space and time. Rather, certain complexes are
individuated by the combination of spatial and temporal universals they
include. There is also a tendency to discriminate among universals, in
favor of nonrelational ones (properties, qualities), against relations. Its
root, somewhat inconsistently, is the same pattern as before. The relation, spanning this spot and that spot, is not localized. I say somewhat
inconsistently because, strictly speaking, no universal is localized in the
sense in which the individuals of *A* are. The inaccuracy testifies to the
strength of the tendency.

Put yourself now in the place of a *B*-ontologist clever enough to know
that relations must be given some ontological status. This spot is to the
left of that; this other to the left of that other; and so on. Clearly, he
must assay relations as universals. Equally clearly, he must tie the relational universal, say, being to the left of, to the two complexes of properties which in his assay are the two spots. But then, even more clearly
if anything, the relation, spanning both spots, is not included in either,
in the sense in which "its" properties are included in each. As far as I
can see, there is only one way out. Our *B*-ontologist must introduce a
second fundamental tie which in all respects is like relational exemplification, except that the exemplifying entities are not the bare particulars

of *A* but, rather, the complexes of *B*. Call this tie relational *B-exemplification*. Thus where the *A*-ontologist makes shift with one nexus, the *B*-ontologist needs two; inclusion in the spots, if I may so put it, as well as *B*-exemplification by the spots.

What exists is independent. Less radically, the more independent an entity is, the higher or fuller its ontological status. Throughout the tradition, this pattern has been as influential as any.[3] By it, our *B*-ontologist's assay of relations, while giving them some ontological status, still discriminates against them in favor of properties. For the relation to be exemplified, the two complexes of properties must be there. A property, say, green, does not so "depend" on another, say, square, in order to be individuated, which in *B* corresponds to its being exemplified in *A*. The analogy, such as it is, is, rather, to how the "ordinary" properties in a complex, the colors, shapes, and so on, depend for their "individuation" on those spatial and temporal properties which are as characteristic of *B*-ontologies as they are, alas, problematic. But, then, these peculiar properties are themselves nonrelational. This shows how relations "depend" on properties in a way in which properties do not depend on each other, or, if you please, depend only on each other.

Except for one feature, to be taken up presently, the *B*-ontology with relations I just described is G. E. Moore's first ontology. Its simples are all universals. Universals are of two kinds. Those of the first kind are included in complexes; those of the second, *B*-exemplified by complexes. The dichotomy coincides with another. All universals of the first kind are nonrelational; all of the second, relational. For one of the first kind to be a relation is, as we saw, counterstructural. What spans both spots cannot be included in either. But there is no structural reason whatsoever why there should not also be properties (nonrelationally) *B*-exemplified by complexes. Good as assayed in *Principia Ethica* is such a property. Or, to say the same thing differently, to be a nonnatural property is to be a nonrelational universal of the second kind (in a *B*-type ontology). That is Hochberg's thesis, his solution of the riddle. In his study he most ably defends it, as it must be defended, namely, by showing that it permits one consistently to make sense out of what Moore has said about nonnatural properties, in *Principia Ethica* and elsewhere. I shall in the rest of this paper stay with some points of general ontology.

If the issue is whether something is either "in" the beholder or "in" the thing beheld, universals of the second kind surely are "in" the thing.

Moore's assay of goodness thus achieves his objectivist aim. It discriminates nevertheless among natural and nonnatural properties in favor of the former. (That is one plausible reason for calling the latter nonnatural.) In the case of relations I just showed that by means of the independence pattern. One sees easily that what in this respect holds for relations also holds for nonnatural properties. The two are in the same boat, as it were. Considering the strong tendency to deny all ontological status to relations, that may be significant in itself. Some reflections show that it is.

In *A*-ontologies individuals and universals are two different ontological kinds, just as among universals properties and relations are two subkinds. But these kinds and subkinds all enjoy the same status. *A*-ontologists, that is, are free from the "nominalistic" tendency to discriminate against universals in favor of individuals and, among universals, against relations in favor of properties. Now there is *one* obvious sense in which to the universals of *A*-ontologies correspond, in *B*-ontologies, those and only those of the second kind. One may express this by saying that in *this* sense only the universals of the second kind are true universals. A true universal, then, is either a "nonnatural" property or it is "merely" a relation. The "nominalistic" tendency behind all that is unmistakable. In *another* sense which is equally obvious, properties of the first kind are universals. Considering that, ask yourself what the outcome will be if, in a philosopher who started as Moore did, the "nominalistic" tendency eventually prevails. Again, the answer is obvious, or all but obvious. The only universals, in *any* sense, that will be left in his eventual ontology will be either "nonnatural" properties or relations. We shall see that this is what happened in Moore's case. First, though, we must attend to that feature of his early ontology which so far has been ignored.

Believing, remembering, perceiving, and so on, are species of awareness. Epistemology or theory of knowledge is nothing but the ontological assay of the awareness situation. Realists have a tendency, easy to understand, of assaying the several species of awareness as relations, such that, when a mind is aware of something, say by perceiving it, perceiving is relationally exemplified by this mind and whatever it perceives. For a relation to be exemplified, the entities exemplifying it must be there (exist). For this spot to be left of something, for instance, the something must be there. Consider now a false belief. In this case what I believe is not there (does not exist). Nor is what I perceive, in the case of perceptual error. Yet there is, in either case, an awareness situation! Any relational assay of such situations must face the dialectical problem that presents. It may help you to recognize it if I remind you that Frege tried to solve it by giving ontological status outside of minds to what he called *Sinn*. Details apart, some British philosophers spoke instead of *propositions*. There are good reasons, one of which I shall eventually mention, for the belief that Moore's first ontology was above all designed to solve this problem. Later on, turning to ethics, he found in this ontology the ready means for achieving his objectivist aims. That shows how the several answers of a great philosopher all hang together, flow as they all do from the same source, a few fundamental ontological ideas.

In Moore's first ontology, natural properties fall into three subkinds. Two we have encountered. The third is the missing feature. Only one of the three is unproblematic. A natural property either is (1) what a moment ago I called an ordinary property, a color, a shape, a pitch, a loudness, and so on. Or it is (2) one of those "coordinate qualities," as one might call them, a here or a there, a now or a then. Between *A*- and *B*-ontologists at least, (1) is unproblematic. To *A*-ontologists, and not only to them, (2) is problematic. In the third category there resides in lonely splendor (3) the single entity which the young Moore calls *existence*. That (3) is problematic needs no argument. The job is, rather, to show accurately what the problem is. First, though, let us check how with (3) one can solve the problem of false belief, erroneous perception, and so on.

Return to the green spot. In the case of veridical perception, I perceive it and it is there. Or, rather, it is there, it exists, and I perceive it. In the case of perceptual error, though I perceive it, it is not there. Upon the relational assay, there must be, in either case, a complex to be perceived. Now the existing spot, in the case of, say, veridical perception, is assayed as a complex including some members of (1) and (2) and, in addition, the lonely member of (3), existence. In the other case, say, of perceptual error, the complex has the same members, except existence. That gives the idea. No doubt the problem is solved. Indeed one can hardly escape the impression of a construction *ad hoc,* the reason, or, at least, a very major reason for (3) being the felt urgency of the problem of false beliefs. The price paid for the solution is the new entity. Let us now look at it more closely.

Does existence exist? That is the question. Less dramatically, are we dialectically forced to acknowledge some such entity? Is it redundant?

Does acknowledging it inevitably lead to dialectical disaster? Ontological kinds do or may differ in ontological status. There is thus a range of possible affirmative answers. Existence may be assayed as a property among properties, it may be assigned a higher status, it may be relegated to a lower one. The one point I wish to make here is that Moore's answer in his first ontology is at the upper extreme of the range. Formally or officially, if I may so express myself, he makes existence a universal among universals, a natural property among natural properties, a simple among simples. Structurally, it is a very peculiar universal, just as Frege's True and False, though officially things among things, are two very peculiar things. The comparison with Frege, though, is too rough to be very illuminating. The one which serves best is with Thomas. Take a tree. As Thomas assays it, it has a nature and it has being. But its being is anything but one among the attributes in or of its nature. To use the traditional words, it is, rather, the divine fulguration creating the tree, endowing a mere nature with—Being. Moore's existence (3), though formally a property among properties, is thus structurally much more than just that, enjoys an ontological status much higher than that of a "mere" property. That Moore's first ontology is part Scotist in structure we saw before. Now we see that it is also part Thomist. Each feature corresponds to one of the two problematic subkinds of natural properties; existence (3) to Thomas' being, the coordinate equalities (2) to Scotus' *haecceitates*.

Some Main Problems of Philosophy is among all Moore's writings the one I love best and admire most. Yet it is, in the manner which is so characteristic of him, as inconclusive as any. In the concluding chapters, the second ontology is discussed, very accurately and in great detail. The discussion, call it the second, centers on the issue of universals. The middle chapters contain a discussion, call it the first, equally accurate and detailed, of the problem of false beliefs. I shall next give the gist of the second ontology, or, to say the same thing differently, of the second discussion.

Take once more two spots, one here, one there; both green; both round. Disregard all other "ordinary" properties they may or may not have. In Moore's first assay, of the *B*-type, each spot contains, in addition to the tie of inclusion, three universals; one, say, the one to the left, here, green, round; the one to the right, there, green, round. Green is one entity, contained in both spots. So is round. That is indeed what is meant by saying that upon this assay they are universals. In both spots, taken together, there are thus four universals: green, round, here, there. (With respect to the last two that is inaccurate. They ought to be replaced by classes of "coordinate qualities." But the inaccuracy merely avoids details which do not matter for what I am about.) These four are also simples. In the second ontology these four entities are replaced by six: this-here, this-green, this-round; that-there, that-green, that-round. This-green and that-green are two entities, not one. So are this-round and that-round. Also, notwithstanding the necessity of referring to each of them in English by connecting two English words through a hyphen, they are all simples. There being (in this case) six such simples is what is meant by calling each of them a *perfect particular.* So far, the second assay of, say, the left spot has thus yielded three perfect particulars, this-here, this-green, this-round. It also yields a fourth entity which is not a tie. This fourth entity is an *individual substance.*

The individuals of an *A*-ontology cannot be recognized. They are bare. An individual substance is not bare. It is a nature and it has a nature. 'Nature,' you will gather, has been used ambiguously. So perhaps I had better say, an individual substance is a *dynamic* nature and has a *definitional* nature. The former creates, or produces, and supports the latter. The ineradicable anthropomorphic flavor of these three notions, creation, production, support, is only too obvious. But it is not and could not be my purpose here either to criticize or to explicate completely these classical notions. I merely try to state intelligibly what I need. Four remarks should be helpful. 1. A Leibnizian monad is an individuated dynamic nature. 2. A definitional nature is the class of attributes the substance has "by its nature." These attributes are enumerated in what the tradition calls a real definition. That is why I chose the phrase, definitional nature. 3. I neglect here the classical distinction between attributes and accidents. 4. I am of course committing myself on Moore. But I neither need nor wish to commit myself here as to whether either the attributes or the accidents of any other philosopher are either universals or perfect particulars.

What is the nexus between an (individual) substance and one of its attributes? The affiliation between two items in a *B*-complex is symmetrical. To whatever extent the idea applies, they support each other mutually and equally. The substance supports the attribute, but not conversely. The nexus we are looking for thus is not inclusion. Exemplification, either *A* or *B,* is completely free of what is conveyed by the ideas of either creation or production. The nexus we are looking for thus is not exemplification. It follows that this nexus, the fundamental tie between substance and attribute, is *sui generis*. The tradition speaks of *inherence*. The attribute inheres in the substance. I shall use the traditional word.

The spot is a complex containing four entities which are not fundamental ties, one individual substance, three perfect particulars. The tie which makes them a complex is inherence. Each of the three perfect particulars inheres in the individual substance. This is not yet all of Moore's second ontology, but as far as the single spot is concerned, it is its gist. Three comments will illuminate its structure.

First. Remember the realism Moore always wanted to arrive at. To be consonant with this aim, an assay of the perceptual situation must do equal justice to two features. (1) In a very "close" sense of presentation, the properties of the body perceived are presented to the perceiving mind. (2) These properties are nevertheless "in" the body. 'Nevertheless' spots the tension between (1) and (2). The closer the presentation, the stronger is the pull on the properties away from the body, toward the mind, or, in the limit, into the mind. The more firmly the properties are anchored in the body, the more strongly they are pulled in the opposite direction. If, as in *B*-ontologies, the body is merely a complex of properties, there is danger that the pull toward the mind will prevail. Making the properties inhere in an individual substance lends them support against this danger. This, I submit, is the intellectual motive, or, at least, it is a very major intellectual motive for the appearance of individual substances in the second ontology. That also shows the exact sense in which in the second ontology individual substances do the job existence does in the first, which shows in turn that existence (3) is indeed a most peculiar universal. Presently we shall see that this universal, just because it was officially assayed as a nonrelational and natural universal, was in the second no longer available for that job.

Second. However problematic the idea of a perfect particular may be, such hyphenated expressions as 'this-green,' 'that-round,' represent it very aptly, neither adding nor subtracting anything to or from the problem. That is not so in the case of such expressions as 'this-here,' 'that-there.' They seem and in fact are redundant. Their verbal redundancy, it may seem, gratuitously adds to the problem. In fact, it is merely the symptom of a structural redundancy. In the first ontology such coordinate properties as here and there are needed to do the individuating job. In the second, where this-green and that-green are two entities, no special further entities are needed to do this job. That makes such perfect particulars as this-here, that-there structurally redundant. Since the second ontology, in this respect like the first, contains spatial and temporal relations, that raises a question. Why do these peculiar perfect particulars occur at all? Or, what amounts to the same, why did not Moore in the second ontology abandon the earlier nonrelational assay of space and time in favor of a relational one? The answer I propose is structurally enlightening. For one, the ontological status of relations in either ontology is not as good as that of natural properties in the first or that of perfect particulars in the second. For another, the better the ontological status a philosopher who wants to arrive at realism can assign to space and time, the closer he will plausibly think he has come to his goal. Take these two ideas together and you will see what I believe is the intellectual motive for the occurrence of those redundant perfect particulars in the second ontology. Another cause, if not motive, is that they are the successors, or, rather, the survivors of the spatial and temporal properties (2). I add, in fairness to Moore, that these peculiar entities are nowhere mentioned in *Some Main Problems of Philosophy*. But a nonrelational assay of space and time is most vigorously propounded throughout the book. And this assay cannot without those entities be reconciled with the second ontology.

Third. What exists is localized, is in space and time. We know the pattern and its power. In the second assay the constituents of the spot are one individual substance, three perfect particulars, and the nexus of inherence. Individual substances and perfect particulars are localized. The pattern has prevailed. Universals, not being localized, ought not to exist. That is the "nominalistic" urge. A philosopher feeling the urge, as Moore did, may yet know, as Moore also did, that one cannot get along without universals. The one thing he can do to satisfy the urge is to depress their ontological status. How that is done in the first ontology we have seen. As a result, all its true universals are either "nonnatural" properties or "merely" relations. In an ontology of the *B*-type, such as the first, this result is easily achieved. The goal of the second ontology is the same. All its universals ought to be either relations or, presumably, the nonnatural properties of *Principia Ethica*.[4] This time I call it a goal rather than a result, because in an ontology of perfect particulars it cannot be reached unless a certain difficulty has been overcome.

This-green and that-green are two entities, not one. That is half the gambit of perfect particulars. They are both simples. That is the other half. There is something in or about them which makes them two greens.[5] There is no such something in the case of, say, *a* green and *a* round. This something must be ontologically grounded, accounted for. That is the difficulty. For, since all greens are simples, the something cannot be a constitutent of any of them. That is indeed what is meant, or a part of what is meant, by calling them simples. The only way out is a relation of similarity exemplified by any pair of greens, any pair of rounds, reds, and so on. The idea is not new of course. New, or at least rare, is the candor with which Moore acknowledges that this relation must be given some ontological status. Thus the difficulty is overcome, the goal reached. Except presumably for nonnatural properties, the universals of the second ontology are all relations exemplified by perfect particulars; "ordinary" relations such as being to the left of, and, in addition, *similarity*.

Pick *a* green; no matter which. The *complex* property of being either identical with it or similar to it is coextensive with the A-ontologist's simple universal green. In this sense, as Moore knows and explains very well, there are universals in the second ontology. Why, then, we must ask, are his "nominalistic" sensibilities not offended by the occurrence of these complex universals. Notice that I speak of occurrence rather than of existence. The wording hints at the pattern in which I believe the answer lies. Only what is simple exists. This pattern, too, has been very powerful throughout the tradition. Taking it into account, we can now complete the inventory of the second ontology. Disregarding nonnatural properties, there are three kinds of simples, namely, in descending order of ontological status, individual substances, perfect particulars, relational universals. The fundamental ties among them are inherence and exemplification. Universals are exemplified by perfect particulars which in turn inhere in individual substances. It will be remembered that I took this ontology, which I call Moore's second, from what I have called the second discussion in *Some Main Problems of Philosophy*.

The first discussion centers around the problem of how to account for false beliefs within a relational assay of awareness. Moore with great accuracy and considerable detail explains first the problem, then the only solution he can think of.

There are things, e.g., Peter, facts, e.g., Peter's being blond, and propositions, e.g., the proposition that Peter is blond. If Peter is in fact blond, both the fact and the proposition exist; if he isn't, only the proposition does. What is believed is always a proposition. A belief is true or false depending on whether or not the fact that corresponds to the proposition believed exists. Propositions are very similar to those complexes of the first ontology which do not contain existence. I say very similar rather than the same because there is also a difference. Existence is, throughout the book, not only called a property but also treated as such. Or, at least, an attempt is made to treat it as such. But the similarity by far outweighs the difference. Let me describe this state of affairs by saying that the first ontology, of about 1900, is implicit in the first discussion, of the 'twenties. At the end of this discussion Moore tells us that since he cannot bring himself to countenance such entities as propositions, he must reject the solution, even though he knows of no other. In *Some Main Problems,* or, what amounts to the same, in the second ontology, the problem of false beliefs thus remains unresolved. Surely this is a striking instance of that inconclusiveness which is as characteristic of the man as are his candor, his accuracy, and his profundity.

Let me now make a schema. Throughout his career Moore thinks of awareness as relational. Throughout his career he has therefore a characteristic problem concerning false beliefs, perceptual error, and so on. In his first ontology the problem is soluble. In the second it is not. In the book in which he expounds the latter, Moore not only candidly tells us so but also expounds at great length, if only in order to reject it, a solution in which the first ontology is implicit. Remember now that I promised to give a reason for the conjecture that even though the first ontology subsequently provided him with the ready means for achieving his objectivist goal in ethics, that early ontology was above all designed to solve the problem of false beliefs. Look at the schema and you will see the reason. If you don't see it or if you do not think it is good enough, consider that not much really depends on whether a conjecture of this historical or, rather, biographical kind is held to be properly substantiated. My main purpose in advancing it was indeed structural. It helped me to show how in the thought of a great philosopher everything hangs together, everything depends on his answers to a few fundamental questions. Let me conclude with another lesson of this kind.

Throughout this paper I have not tipped my hand. At least, I have tried not to tip it. If I succeeded, you may wonder what my own views are. If you do, I am pleased to oblige. I am an A-ontologist; I am a realist; I am not an objectivist. I believe that we are dialectically forced to give existence some ontological status but that this status is neither that of a property among properties nor higher. All this, though, is beside the point. The point, or the lesson, is that I could say quite a bit about the problems without offering any solutions, and, if I succeeded, without even tipping my hand. That shows how very, very much of philosophy is dialectics and nothing but dialectics.

Notes

1. This is rough. The complex ought to be built up from what it includes by some tie or ties of "affiliation." For my limited purposes, though, the roughness helps a good deal without spoiling anything. Inclusion is, literally, one of Husserl's basic ties. The two with which Goodman begins are "affiliations."

2. Notice that I use 'relational' and 'nonrelational' instead of the conventional 'relative' and 'absolute.' There are good reasons for that.

3. See E. B. Allaire, "Existence, Independence, and Universals," *Philosophical Review*, LXIX (1960), 485-96.

4. I say presumably because these properties are not mentioned anywhere in *Some Main Problems*. But, then, neither is any problem of either ethics or aesthetics.

5. Neglecting shades, as I have throughout, or, what amounts to the same, using the adjective for just one shade, this use of the plural and the indefinite article is of course, as one now says, the grammar of perfect particulars. I have avoided it in all other contexts.

Six

MOORE'S ONTOLOGY AND NONNATURAL PROPERTIES

Herbert Hochberg

MOORE'S DISTINCTION between natural and nonnatural properties has never been clearly and cogently made. In this paper I will attempt to show that this distinction stems from an ontology to which Moore adhered at the time *Principia Ethica* was written. While the distinction itself may not be clarified, it will become clear why this is so and why attempts to deal with it which ignore Moore's ontology are hopelessly inadequate.

First, we shall consider the distinction as set forth in *Principia*. Next, on the basis of what Moore says there, a view as to the nature of universals will be attributed to him. This view will provide the ground for a radical distinction between natural and nonnatural properties, but it will not be clear why he holds to such a view in *Principia*. Finally, we shall consider a very early paper of Moore's written just prior to *Principia*. An analysis of this paper will reveal a rather strange and complex ontology implicit in it. This, in turn, will show: *(a)* the source

This is a slightly revised version of the paper previously published under the same title. Reprinted with revisions by permission of the author and the editor from *The Review of Metaphysics*, XV (1962), 365-95.

of the ontology of *Principia;* *(b)* why the ontology attributed to him in *Principia* does not jibe with other things he says; and *(c)* the origin of the notion of nonnatural properties.

The problem arises in a remarkable passage in *Principia.* There Moore writes:

> Can we imagine 'good' as existing by itself in time, and not merely as a property of some natural object? For myself, I cannot so imagine it, whereas with the greater number of properties of objects—those which I call the natural properties—their existence does seem to me to be independent of the existence of those objects, They are, in fact, rather parts of which the object is made up than mere predicates which attach to it. If they were all taken away, no object would be left, not even a bare substance; for they are in themselves substantial and give to the object all the substance that it has. But this is not so with good.[1]

In a criticism of this passage Broad argues:

> Now it seems to me that *every* characteristic of a natural object answers to Moore's criterion of non-naturalness and that *no* characteristic could possibly be natural in his sense. I do not believe for a moment that a penny is a whole of which brownness and roundness are parts, nor do I believe that the brownness or roundness of a penny could exist in time all by itself. Hence if I accepted Moore's account I should have to reckon brownness, roundness, pleasantness, etc. as *non-natural* characteristics.[2]

In a reply written almost forty years after the publication of *Principia Ethica,* Moore accepted Broad's criticism and acknowledged that his earlier account was "utterly silly and preposterous."[3] But Moore did not attempt to explain why he had made the distinction the way he did in *Principia.* Rather, by calling his earlier view "silly and preposterous" he seems to suggest that it was just a wild and spontanous notion he once had. But it goes deeper than that.

I. *Natural and Nonnatural Properties*

Natural qualities, Moore tells us, exist in time, are substantial, and are parts of natural objects. He further tells us that it is easy to say what sorts of things are natural objects. Minds, thoughts, and, for that matter, anything which may be said to exist is a natural object. Sometimes he uses the term 'object' to include both qualities and what we might call particulars. At other times qualities are spoken of as properties of natural objects rather than as objects themselves. All this might suggest that at this stage of his thought Moore, explicitly or implicitly, considered the property yellow in a particular yellow patch as something like an Aristotelian *this yellowness*. This would fit with its being considered as substantial, existing in time, and being *a part* of the yellow patch. (Hereafter, I will refer to such things as a *this yellowness*, a *this redness*, etc., as "simple particulars" or "simple objects.") In short, natural properties are, for Moore, construed nominalistically as simple particulars. An "ordinary" particular, like a yellow patch, would then be thought to be a composite substance containing simple substances, like this yellowness, as parts. Such simple particulars are not composed, in turn, of, say, a bare *this* and the property yellow. They do not, on such a view, seem to be composed of anything at all. In fact Moore tells us that there are no bare *thises*. A composite particular, like a yellow patch, is then made up only of simple particulars without any bare substantial element. As Moore says, these simple particulars would "give the object all the substance that it has." To say of a composite particular, say a yellow square named 'Paul,' that it is yellow would be to say either that Paul contains a particular yellowness or that a particular yellowness is a part of Paul. 'Contains' or, alternatively, 'is a part of' would then signify a relation that holds between two particulars—one composite and one simple. *Contains* holding between two particulars would then seem to replace *exemplification* holding between a particular and a universal in the analysis of assertions like 'Paul is yellow.'

At this point it will be necessary to specify some further terminology that will be used in the ensuing analysis. One basic division will be between ontological *entities,* on the one hand, and ontological *ties,* or structural relations, on the other. Such ontological ties hold between entities. *Exemplification* is an example of an ontological tie. The term 'entity' will apply to existents and non-existents. Thus an entity will have some ontological "status" even though it is not an existent object or thing. 'Object' and 'thing' will be reserved to indicate existents, and the former will be used to refer only to particulars, and not to universals. Simple particulars, as well as universals, will sometimes be called properties and sometimes simple objects, but such simple particulars will not be referred to as universals. With this in mind we may return to Moore.

We are not here concerned with all the difficulties of the view I attributed to Moore, but only with the possibility that Moore might have held such a view, albeit implicitly, in *Principia*. We can see why he might have been attracted to such a position. On the one hand he does not wish to accept bare substances, or bare particulars, in his ontology. One who holds to the existence of universals may be led into acknowledging bare particulars as well. For, holding to the existence of universals, one might feel required to acknowledge bare particulars or substrata to exemplify the universals and provide the basis for individuation. A yellow square would be "composed" (in some sense) of the universal yellow, the universal square, and a bare particular. Thus the rejection of bare particulars may lead one to reject universals.[4] On the other hand, Moore is apparently bothered by universals in their own right. This is made clear by what he says of natural properties in the passage cited above, as well as by what he later says in *Some Main Problems of Philosophy*. In this latter work he is trying to decide whether or not there are any universals like redness, whiteness, etc. In the course of his discussion he writes:

> And it *is* very natural to think this, it is very natural, for instance, to think of the universal 'pure red' as resembling particular patches of pure red in precisely the respect in which they all resemble one another. It is, therefore, important to realize that this cannot possibly be the case. And when this is realized, it does, I think, diminish the plausibility of the whole theory that there is any such thing. . . . The objection which I feel to the theory is simply that I cannot discover any such thing. I cannot discover that I ever have it before my mind.[5]

Even where he goes on to find a case where he can have a property or universal before his mind—

> This, therefore, would be an argument for supposing that the property common and peculiar to all *pairs must* consist in their possession of a universal . . . whereas, in the case of colours, there is no necessity to suppose this, since in their case the property common and peculiar to them all *may* be merely a disjunctive property defined by reference to immediate resemblance.[6]

—he proceeds to remind us of a distinction already made use of in *Principia*—the distinction between being and existing.[7] Universals, like those involved in our comprehension of numbers, and "truths"[8] may be said to *be* in some sense, but only particulars *exist*. Moreover, the attempt to define "properties" in terms of a relation of resemblance was even then a classical move in some nominalistic gambits. Moore's evident concern about universals, like redness, and his suggestion that even universals which *are* do not exist, reflect nominalistic leanings. Furthermore, like the nominalistically inclined classical empiricists, Moore tends to confuse a phenomenal quality, like yellow, with particulars that exemplify it, yellow patches. Such confusion is apparent in Moore's celebrated "The Refutation of Idealism,"[9] published in the same year as *Principia*. Also, Moore himself says, in the appendix added in 1952 to *Some Main Problems of Philosophy*, "I failed, for some reason or other, to see that the colour of a patch is not identical with the patch in question." [10] In the same appendix he mentions another mistake he earlier made:

> A second gross mistake which I made was that of supposing anybody to hold that, in a case where we see two patches of exactly the same shade of colour, or one patch of the shade in question, this shade of colour is something which we don't see. . . . Why should it not be the case (as I now suppose it to be) that whenever I see a white patch of one and the same shade of white all over, I *also* see that particular shade of white, *of* which that patch happens to be?[11]

His earlier view that perhaps one does not *see* the universal but only the particular patch may have contributed to his suspicions about the existence of such universals. Recall, in a passage cited above, his earlier statement to the effect that he cannot discover a universal like white "before" his mind. Yet in both *Principia* and *Some Main Problems of Philosophy* Moore is concerned to give some ontological status to universals. In this vein he holds that not all universals may be eliminated by definition and he does not doubt that there are, in some sense, relational universals. Thus one cannot simply classify Moore as a nominalist, for there appear to be strains of both realism and nominalism in his thought. Why this "double aspect" is there we shall soon see.

Moore does not construe nonnatural properties in terms of simple particulars. Nonnatural properties, unlike natural ones, are not substantial for him. Goodness would not then be construed in terms of simple particulars like *this yellowness*. Rather, goodness is a *bona fide* universal. This may be the simple but striking difference between natural and nonnatural properties. *Only nonnatural properties are universals*. Natural ones are not universals at all but are thought of in terms of simple particulars. In the phrase 'nonnatural property' the adjective 'nonnatural' would then be superfluous if one equated properties with universals. This conclusion, while perhaps startling, certainly points to

a distinction between natural and nonnatural properties and thus provides a partial explication of the adjective 'nonnatural.' Natural and
nonnatural properties are different kinds of entities in somewhat the
same sense that a realist might say that this chair is a different kind
of thing from any universal it exemplifies. The distinction is far-reaching.
For it would involve more than Moore's holding that there are at least
three different sorts of entities in his ontology—composite particulars,
simple particulars, and nonnatural properties or universals. Such an
ontology would also seem to require an additional fundamental tie
besides that which combines natural properties into complex objects of
which they are parts. One would not say that Paul is good by asserting
that Paul contains goodness. Rather, the composite particular Paul, if it
were good, would *exemplify* goodness. Perhaps simple particulars would
also. Exemplification would not hold between two particulars but
between a particular and a universal. This structural complication reflects
the basic ontological difference between goodness and simple particulars.
Moreover, there would also be two ways of combining terms to make
sentences. One way would involve a term referring to a particular and
a term denoting a nonnatural property or universal; the other would
involve two terms referring to particulars. In this latter case one term
would refer to a simple particular or natural property. Thus, as Moore
often said, 'good' would indeed be a predicate of a different *kind* from
'yellow.' If by 'predicate' one meant either a term that could occupy a
certain place in a sentence expressing an exemplification relation or term
that must occupy a certain place in a sentence expressing a containment
relation, then we would have two different kinds of predicates. Only
the terms of one kind, however, would denote universals. Thus in a
perspicuous language there would be a fundamental difference between
sentences like 'this is yellow' and 'this is good.' This reflects the difference
between the two fundamental ontological ties of exemplifying and
combining. But there is still a problem about the ontological status of
universals. Before considering it, we might note another facet of Moore's
discussion of goodness that jibes with the structural difference between
goodness and yellowness that we just considered.

Moore makes frequent and systematic use of the argument that
pleasure, for example, may not be identified with good, since we may
always ask if pleasure is good. This query may be raised against any
attempted identification of a natural property with good. To identify
pleasure with good is to assert that pleasure is identical with good,

where both 'pleasure' and 'good' are predicates. With 'P' and 'G' abbreviating 'pleasure' and 'good' respectively this would assert the identity statement 'P=G.' But in Moore's characteristic query, he is not asking if pleasure is identical with good when he asks if pleasure is good. Rather, he is asking if pleasure exemplifies goodness. And it is precisely because he holds such a query to be "significant" that he questions the identification. Thus he is concerned with a proposition of the form 'G(P).' Since a proposition of the form 'G(P)' makes sense, Moore concludes that 'P=G' is false. But since 'G(P)' makes sense, one may note that 'G' and 'P' must be terms of different logical types. Consequently, one may conclude that part of Moore's objection to what he calls the naturalistic fallacy rests on a claim that terms like 'G' and 'P' are of different logical kinds. If one considers pleasure to be a universal, rather than a simple particular, one could look upon goodness as a universal of a higher "type" than pleasure. However, a complication would result from the possibility of its applying to objects that exemplified pleasure, as well as to pleasure. But the logical difference between goodness and pleasure would also be preserved, without this complication, if pleasure were construed along the nominalistic lines we have been discussing, while goodness remained a universal. Speaking of pleasure would then always involve a reference to some particular, either simple or composite. These particulars in turn, could exemplify goodness. Hence, one could, as Moore argues, always sensibly ask if good is exemplified by pleasure (a simple particular) or by pleasant objects. On the other hand, any proposed identification of goodness with pleasure would then commit a logical blunder. For goodness and pleasure are just different sorts of things.

In saying all this I do not mean to attribute to Moore anything like Russell's theory of types, and I certainly do not wish to suggest that he rejects 'P=G' on structural grounds alone. I merely wish to suggest that his abrupt dismissal of all proposed naturalistic identifications of goodness with natural properties may stem, in part, from his feeling that there is structural difference between terms like 'good' and 'pleasure.' And this feeling is made quite explicit in the view that we considered.

All this does not, however, seem to fit with Moore's statement that even if 'good' were a natural object that would not alter the nature of the fallacy. It seems to be the same sort of fallacy that we would commit if we identified two natural objects like yellow and pleasure or an orange and yellow. Nevertheless, he does say that such a misidentification "with regard to good marks it as something quite specific." Hence the structural difference mentioned above is a possible ingredient in the specific case of the naturalistic fallacy. Furthermore, the problem of predication is clearly involved in the misidentification of two things, even natural ones, since one of the roots of the fallacy seems to be the confusion of the 'is' of predication with that of identity. We only say something significant by asserting that 'an orange is yellow' if we take the 'is' to be one of predication. Taking the 'is' to be predicative requires that the "objects" involved be of different "kinds." To predicate a natural property is to hold that the subject (the orange) *contains* a simple particular (the particular yellowness): to predicate a nonnatural property (good) is to hold that the subject exemplifies it. In either case the predicate is a different sort of thing than the subject, for in the first case it is a simple natural object and in the second case it is a universal. Thus misidentification of the kind involved in the fallacy Moore is concerned with involves a structural error—taking a subject and predicate to be the same sort of thing. The particular mistake in the naturalistic fallacy involves the predicate being a different sort of thing in that it is a universal or nonnatural property or nonexistent object. Thus Moore writes in *Principia:*

> The fact is that there is one type of proposition so familiar to everyone, and therefore having such a strong hold upon the imagination, that philosophers have always supposed that all other types must be reducible to it. This type is that of the objects of experience— of all those truths which occupy our minds for the immensely greater part of our waking lives: truths such as that somebody is in the room, that I am writing or eating or talking. All these truths, however much they may differ, have this in common that in them both the grammatical subject and the grammatical predicate stand for something which exists. Immensely the commonest type of truth, then, is one which asserts a relation between two existing things. Ethical truths are immediately felt not to conform to this type, and the naturalistic fallacy arises from the attempt to make out that, in some roundabout way, they do conform to it. It is immediately obvious that when we see a thing to be good, its goodness is not a property which we can take up in our hands, or separate from it even by the most delicate scientific instruments, and transfer to something else. It is not, in fact, like most of the predicates which we ascribe to things, a *part* of the thing to which we ascribe it. But philosophers suppose that the

reason why we cannot take goodness up and move it about, is not that it is a different *kind* of object from any which can be moved about, but only that it *necessarily* exists together with anything with which it does exist.[12]

There is, of course, more to the notion of the naturalistic fallacy than the purported mixing of the *is* of identity with that of predication. Questions like "Is this orange yellow?" or "Is pleasure good?" are significant since the subject and predicate terms mean different things and their meanings are independent. One thing that is involved in this is explained by the ontology that we shall see Moore adhered to at this period. Concepts are among the ultimate constituents of the world and they, like the propositions composed of them, are independent of the minds which grasp them. Being such they are seen to be simple or complex, many or one, by direct inspection or apprehension. Moore sometimes speaks as if the significance of a sentence is the test of whether two concepts are independent or not. But this is misleading on both structural grounds and in terms of what he explicitly says when arguing about 'good' and 'exists':

> For whatever we may have proved to exist and whatever two existents we may have proved to be necessarily connected with one another it still remains a distinct and different question whether what thus exists is good; whether either or both of the two existents is so; and whether it is good that they should exist together. To assert the one is plainly and obviously *not* the same thing as to assert the other. We understand what we mean by asking: Is this, which exists, or necessarily exists, after all, good? and we perceive that we are asking a question which has *not* been answered. In face of this direct perception that the two questions are distinct, no proof that they *must* be identical can have the slightest value.[13]

The sentences in question, like 'This orange is yellow' or 'Pleasure is good,' are significant precisely because we directly perceive that the concepts involved are distinct. Thus to settle a dispute as to whether the "fallacy" of misidentification is being committed the ultimate appeal must be to "reflection," a type of thought experiment. To decide whether the concept red is included in the concept of red square, or square in that of checkerboard, or whether the concept good is the same as the concept yellow, one reflects on what the terms mean and inspects the concepts. On the basis of such direct apprehension one rejects or accepts purported definitions (reflecting analyses) as

x is a red square = df. x is red and x is a square
x is good = df. x is pleasant and x causes no pain

or identities as

yellow = good

and

pleasure = good.

The rejection of the naturalistic fallacy thus ultimately rests on intuitively or immediately apprehending the distinction between concepts. This intuitive grasp also provides the basis for acceptable conceptual analysis. One may then speculate that some of the things that Moore later writes, which are among the founding stones of the ordinary language movement, stem from a dissatisfaction with such a basis for conceptual analysis. The test of (conceptual or) linguistic use and the appeal to the ordinary sense of an expression is a tempting substitute for conceptual thought experiments. The substitution is made especially easy if one begins to think in terms of two concepts being independent if certain sentences are significant, rather than vice versa. One will then be led to ask what is the test of significance. Use or the "ordinary sense" is a natural answer. Whether Moore actually made the transition is a moot point; that he influenced others to do so seems clear.

Even though Moore may treat natural properties like redness in terms of simple particulars, goodness is clearly a universal for him. What then is its ontological status? He tells us that good is a mere predicate (the universal, not the term) which attaches to objects but is not a substantial part of any object. He also tells us in *Principia* that good does not exist.

> Metaphysicians . . . have always been much occupied, not only with that other class of natural objects which consists in mental facts, but also with the class of objects or properties of objects, which certainly do not exist in time, are not therefore parts of Nature, and which, in fact, do not *exist* at all. To this class as I have said, belongs what we mean by the adjective "good." . . . the assumption that "good" *must* denote some *real* property of things . . . is mainly due to two erroneous doctrines, the first *logical,* the second *epistemological.*[14]

Here he asserts quite clearly the classical nominalistic doctrine that to exist is to exist in time and, consequently, that the property good does not exist. We then have a second notion involved in the concept of a nonnatural property. *Nonnatural properties do not exist.* The first notion was, to repeat that nonnatural properties are the only universals. From these two contentions it follows that universals do not exist. And this, we noticed, is a theme that Moore explicitly adheres to in 1910-11 in *Some Main Problems of Philosophy.* But in *Principia,* as in this later work, he distinguishes between *being* and *existing.* Good *is* somehow, even though it does not *exist.* Moore thus explicitly recognizes two sorts of entities—existents and nonexistents. Within the first category we have composite particulars and simple particulars. In the second, there are properties and apparently, from the cited passages, certain individuals or particulars as well. Thus the phrase 'kind of entity' takes on two meanings for Moore. There are two "kinds of entities" in the sense of particulars and universals. There are also two "kinds of entities" in the sense of existents and nonexistents. Thus we have four possible kinds of entities: existent particulars, existent universals, nonexistent particulars, nonexistent universals. But in *Principia,* only three of these possibilities are realized. For there are no existent universals. Hence, non-existent universals are exemplified not only by nonexistent particulars, but by existent ones! Thus there is an ontological tie between existent and nonexistent entities. That existent particulars exemplify existent universals is a familiar philosophical theme. That there are no universals for particulars to exemplify is another. But Moore's view is neither of these, for his nominalism (i.e., his contention that universals do not exist) is tempered by the addition of universals, as nonexistent entities, to his ontology. A classical realist would hold that a particular which is in time, exemplifies a universal which is not. Like the realist, Moore retains the exemplification relation and the atemporality of universals, but, identifying, like the nominalist, *existing* with *being in time,* Moore contends that exemplification holds between an existent and a nonexistent. This explains why he speaks of good as a "mere predicate." But such a view itself requires explanation. And this returns us to Moore's view that an (existent) composite particular contains its natural properties rather than exemplifying them. This, of course, is the nub of Moore's nominalistic leanings in *Principia,* since it is plausible to hold, once one has replaced *exemplification* by *contains,* that parts and wholes are the same *sorts of entities* in both senses of that phrase. For it might seem strange to say either that a real thing has unreal parts or that *part* of a substantial particular object is not itself a substantial particular object. This much would seem to be involved in the use of *contains* rather than *exemplification*. Thus we must ask two further questions. Why does Moore think in terms of contains at all? And, second, once he replaced *exemplification* by *contains* for natural properties, why does he retain exemplification for nonnatural ones? To put it another way, why does not a composite particular *contain this goodness* as it *contains this redness?* Or, to put it still differently, why does he not construe the so-called nonnatural properties, like goodness, in terms of simple particulars? Moreover, a number of further questions arise concerning simple particulars (natural properties). Since simple particulars are temporal entities, how are they related to temporal properties? That is, are temporal properties nonnatural properties, and hence nonexistent universals, which are exemplified by simple particulars, or are temporal properties themselves natural properties and thus also to be construed in terms of simple particulars? Further, do two yellow patches contain the same *this yellowness* or would there be more than one such simple particular? And, if the latter, in virtue of what are they both yellowness? Yet there are no explicit answers to these questions in *Principia*. Before they are considered, one further complication in Moore's ontological views is relevant here.

Sometimes Moore suggests that simples only are real, while composites are simply collections of simples. Thus simple particulars would be, ultimately, the only existent entities. But in *Principia* Moore consistently uses 'real' as synonymous with 'being in time,' rather than with 'simple' or 'simple and in time.' Thus natural objects which are composites are existents in the sense of being *natural* or *temporal*. For Moore does not seem concerned with the ontological theme of simplicity in *Principia,* aside from his concern with the simplicity of goodness. Nevertheless Moore is ultimately concerned with simplicity, and we shall see some further complications when that concern is blended with his view that an existent is in time.

II. Concepts and Objects in Moore's Ontology

In Moore's 1899 paper "The Nature of Judgment," we find not only the origin of the ontology I attributed to *Principia* but a basis for answering the questions raised at the end of Section I. In that paper Moore tells us that a *concept* is not something mental but "what Mr. Bradley calls a 'universal meaning.'" In short, concepts are objective universals and not "subjective ideas." Among concepts we find *red, this,* and *now.* Propositions are composed neither of words nor of thoughts but of concepts. Concepts may also be objects of thought. But this merely means that they come into a relation with a thinker and are not dependent upon such a thinker. Further, concepts are incapable of change and hence are immutable. Existence, we are told, is also a concept. And, moreover, everything that exists is composed of concepts. Objects, as well as propositions, are thus composites of concepts. In this vein Moore asserts, "It seems necessary then, to regard the world as formed of concepts."[15]

What Moore seems to have in mind in stating all of this is the following view. Recall the square yellow patch named 'Paul.' The *concept of Paul* is a complex concept composed of simple concepts like yellow and square. The object named 'Paul' is also a complex of concepts. It is composed not only of the concepts contained in the *concept of Paul* but of existence as well. Each of these complexes of concepts also contains a relation in which its constitutive concepts stand. It is not quite clear whether these relations differ in the case of objects and concepts of objects, but at times Moore suggests that they do.[16] Let us then refer to the relation involved in the concept of Paul by the term 'R_1' and to that relation in the object Paul by the term 'R_2.' Also, it is not exactly clear whether the object Paul is made up of the concept of Paul and the concept of existence in the relation R_2 or whether the object Paul is composed of the constituent concepts of the concept of Paul together with the concept existence in the relation R_2. The difference would be that in the former case the relation R_1 would also be involved in the structure of the object, whereas in the latter case it would not be. Aside from the difference between R_1 and R_2 objects would differ from concepts of objects in that the former would contain the concept *existence,* while the latter would not. Propositions, too, are complexes of concepts in a relation. Thus Paul, the concept of Paul, and propositions about Paul are all composed, ultimately, of concepts; and existents are those entities which "contain" the concept existence. Since both Paul and the existential proposition 'Paul exists' contain exactly the same concepts Moore is driven, perhaps by ontological parsimony, to identify them: to identify objects with true existential propositions.

> Even the description of an existent as a proposition (a true existential proposition) seems to lose its strangeness, when it is remembered that a proposition is here to be understood, not as

anything subjective . . . but as the combination of concepts which is affirmed.[17]

Whatever his motive Moore achieves considerable ontological parsimony. For, in effect, objects, facts, and propositions, are identified. Just as an object is identified with a true existential proposition, facts are dispensed with as the grounds of truth for propositions. What makes a proposition true is an internal character of it, not its relation to a fact or something else. Thus the relation that combines concepts into objects is also the relation that combines concepts into true existential propositions. A true nonexistential proposition is not an object in virtue of its not containing existence. A false existential proposition is not an object in virtue of its constituent concepts being combined by a different relation than that involved in a true existential proposition. Hence two features are crucial for an entity's being an object: it must contain the universal existence, and thus be complex, and its constituent universals must be combined by a special relation (the true-making, object-making relation). R_3, the proposition-making relation, really dissolves into two relations: one of them is R_2 which combines concepts into true propositions. When the true proposition is an existential one the proposition is an object. The second relation, call it R_f, combines concepts into false propositions.[18] But then a sentence will signify one propositional entity if it is true, an entity involving R_2, and another propositional entity if it is false, one involving R_f. Hence, if propositional entities provide the meaning for sentences just as concepts provide the meaning of terms, a sentence would mean one thing if it were true and another thing if it were false. This is not the only awkwardness of Moore's view. Identifying existential propositions with objects requires one either to take some propositions as temporal or objects as nontemporal. Thus either objects will not exist in (or at a) time or existential propositions will.

Moreover, since the combining relation plays the role it does, Moore need not identify existential propositions with existents. He could distinguish complexes of concepts which contain existence and involve the relation R_2 (the "object" relation) from complexes of the same concepts in a further relation, say R_1, which constitute a true existential proposition. Thus he could separate existent objects from true existential propositions. This would in effect involve him in having both propositions and facts. For, as we shall see, his objects, as complexes of concepts, structurally resemble facts, and an ontology embracing facts and propositions is something Moore consciously seeks to avoid later in

Some Main Problems of Philosophy. But there he seeks to avoid propositions in favor of facts. Aside from parsimony, there is another reason why Moore may identify existent objects with existential propositions. All of the R's give rise to complexes which "contain" their constituent concepts. Hence all these relations may be confused with a relation of containment. Since an existent is what *contains* existence, it might then seem natural to hold that any complex of concepts which "contains" existence is an existent. (If consistent, one would not then balk at false existential propositions.) Thus the notion of *containment* may provide a basis both for the fusing of the various R's and for Moore's consequent belief that some propositions are existents. If one confuses the R's with each other and with *contains*, we should not be surprised if he identifies objects with true existential propositions. It is interesting to recall here that Moore once recounted a nightmare in which he could not distinguish propositions from tables.

Let us assume that Paul has no other properties than being yellow and square. He would then be composed of the concepts *yellow, square, now*, and *existence* (and perhaps also *this*), in the relation R_2. To "picture" Paul's structure, we might use the following complex sign:

(a) R_2 (yellow, square, now, existence).

Similarly, the concept of Paul might be signified by

(b) R_1 (yellow, square).

Recall that Paul might be considered to be composed of *his concept* together with *existence* (and *now*). On this alternative Paul would be represented not by (a) but by

(a') R_2 (R_1 [yellow, square], now, existence).

In either case, (a) or (a'), we can see in what sense Paul is ultimately composed of simple concepts. The inclusion of the concept *now* also shows the temporal character of existent objects.

At this point two alternative interpretations of what Moore says are open to us. We may consider him to hold that there is one relational notion *contains*, which is not a concept among concepts, but which relates any complex of concepts to any constituent of that complex. Thus statements asserting that a certain complex concept contains a constituent *x* and that a certain proposition contains a constituent *y* would both involve the same sense of 'contains.' But the constituents in both cases would be "tied" together to make the different complexes by different relations—relations other than containment—R_1, R_2, etc. These R's, rather than "contains," constitute the ontological ties. Hence they are not concepts, though Moore does sometimes unwarily speak of such relations as if they were concepts among concepts.[19] This contrasts with one who, not holding to the containment pattern, thinks in terms of bare particulars *exemplifying* universals. For this latter pattern does not involve one in speaking of wholes which contain parts unless he distinguishes the particular yellow square, as a composite of a bare particular (or substratum) and the universals the substratum exemplifies, from the bare particular "in" the composite. The former "particular" would then "contain" the latter as well as several universals.[20] But the whole which is a complex of concepts connected by one of the R's is related to each of its constituents in that it *contains* them. One who embraces this pattern thus seems to require, in addition to the R's, the containment relation. For the R's relate parts to each other to form the whole; they do not, in turn, relate the whole to each part. The containment pattern thus seems to involve one with two sorts of relations. In the case of exemplification one does not require a further relation. For what is connected by exemplification to the universal to form a "fact," and what is spoken about in a sentence that ascribes the universal to something, is, in both cases, the same bare particular. A corresponding need for a further relation could arise if one included facts as further entities in one's ontology and then wished to assert that such facts *contained* universals as constituents. For then one would speak of a certain whole, the fact, and not of a bare particular as being connected with a universal, and this would certainly involve a different relation than exemplification. In the containment pattern the subject of that relation is always a composite of related concepts. Hence such subjects have a factual aspect; they are, as it were, facts compressed into objects. This contrasts strongly with the case of a bare particular's exemplifying a universal in the exemplification pattern. For there, there is a clear distinction between the bare particular and the fact to which it gives rise by exemplifying a property. Thus one may notice, perhaps uncomfortably, that by using *contains* there seems to be a redundancy in assertions like 'Paul is yellow.' Since yellow is contained in the concept of Paul and in Paul, this is like saying that a complex of concepts, of which yellow is one, contains yellow. Thus, upon analysis, sentences like 'Paul is yellow' may, by the use of *contains*, turn out to be analytic. All of this is perhaps what attracts some to bare particulars and the ontological tie of exemplification.

If one accepts both the R's and *contains,* he may, however, point out that the R's, rather than contains, are the fundamental ties of the pattern since they unite concepts into composites. This may lead one to propose an alternative interpretation of what Moore says. On the one hand it might be suggested that to say 'Paul is yellow' is not to say that 'Paul contains yellow,' but that certain concepts (the others which make up the concept of Paul) stand in a certain relation, R_2, with yellow. Alternatively one may say that 'Paul contains yellow' but hold that 'contains' does not reflect any tie between entities. The use of 'contains' merely reflects the view that yellow is tied to other concepts to constitute Paul. Hence "contains" merely reflects, in language, that one of the R's obtains (or is purported to obtain) in the world among certain concepts.

In connection with all this we might note that *(a),* above, may alternatively be considered a sentence stating that certain concepts are "tied" by R_2 or a sign referring to Paul. This reflects, again, the factual "aspect" that objects take on in the containment pattern. Even though Moore suggests otherwise, in neither case must R_2 be thought of as a relational concept. For then one either falls heir to a Bradleian type regress or lapses into the exemplification pattern by holding, in effect, that the other concepts exemplify a concept (albeit relational) among concepts. Be that as it may, the twofold way in which *(a)* may be considered leads to a problem which brings us to the heart of Moore's pattern. To get to that problem, consider the sentence 'Paul is yellow.' We may transcribe this sentence by

(α) Paul C yellow,

where 'C' stands for 'contains.' *(α)*, if true, would also give rise to a propositional entity denoted by

(c) R_t (the concept of Paul, yellow)[21]
and an object, Paul, denoted by *(a)* or *(a′)*. (Hereafter *[a′]* will be used, since the distinction, once seen, may be forgotten for the ensuing discussion.) The sentence *(α)* would then be true if there is a certain propositional entity (which, by the way, is what is true for Moore, since he thinks of propositions, rather that sentences, as being true or false) denoted by *(c)*. Likewise, if we are talking about an object the truth of the sentence, or proposition, would indicate that the object contains

yellow. The same would hold for existential propositions. To say that Paul exists would be to assert

(β) Paul C existence.

This would be the case if there were an entity denoted by

(d) R$_2$ (the concept of Paul, existence),

an existential proposition or object, i.e., Paul. All this shows why Moore sometimes expresses the fact that an object exists in terms of the object's containing existence and other times by stating that the concept of the object stands in a certain relation to existence.[22] For *in* the existent object we have the concept of it and existence in the relation R$_2$. This, of course, fits with what was said above about the twofold way one may look at expressions like *(a)*, *(b)*, *(a′)*, etc. If we take them as signs referring to objects (or as signs reflecting the structure of objects) we would use them as subjects, in a perspicuous language, of sentences stating that what they refer to *contains* something. If we take them as sentences, they may be used to state that concepts stand in certain relations. Moore speaks of them in both ways. But the use of these alternative phrasings brings us to the problem I mentioned. Actually, the problem does not arise directly in the case of an object like Paul. But suppose we wish to say that the simple concept red exists. One might think that this would be asserted by holding that red and existence stand in the relation R$_2$. But then what exists is not the concept red but a composite composed of *red, existence*, the relation R$_2$, and *now*. Speaking in terms of containment makes it even clearer, for only composites can contain anything. Hence, a simple concept like red could not be said to contain anything. *Red cannot then exist,* if the existents contain the concept existence. But Moore speaks of the existence of red. Sometimes he seems to mean a particular red patch. But some other times he may mean something else.

> It was pointed out that a pure existential proposition could only assert the existence of a simple concept; all others involving the *a priori* concepts of substance and attribute. If now we take the existential proposition "Red exists," we have an example of the type required. It is maintained that, when I say this, my meaning is that the concept "red" and the concept "existence" stand in a specific relation both to one another and to the concept of time. I mean that "Red exists now," and thereby imply a distinction from its past and future existence.[23]

Here Moore does not appear to be talking about red patches but about the simple concept red. Yet concepts, recall, are immutable. Hence, there is no need, if we are talking about a simple concept, to distinguish its present, past, and future existence. And, as we just noted, the simplest existent still could not be a simple concept. We could, however, have a complex of concepts composed of the concepts *red, existence,* and *now* in the relation R_2. Such an object would be denoted by

(e) R_2 (red, existence, now).

This object would not be a red patch, since it would have no shape or other property. But neither would it be the concept red, which it would, however, *contain*. Moore may be confusing such an object with the concept red. This confusion could be aided by his sometimes speaking of existents in terms of their concepts standing to existence in the relation R_2. But even so, if we render 'Paul exists' by 'The concept of Paul stands in the relation R_2 to existence,' what then exists (if the sentence is true) is Paul, not his concept. That is, the object Paul exists. However, in the case of Paul, there is clearly a difference between the object and the concept of it. But Moore does not think in terms of the *concept of red*. He speaks of the *concept red*. There is no distinction between the universal red and a concept of it; to say that red is a concept is to say that it is a universal. But the concept of Paul is not a universal like red. Hence, when one says that red exists, it might be natural to think that one is talking about the concept, especially if one thinks in terms of the concept standing in relation to existence. But on Moore's analysis of existents, when one says that a concept stands in the relation R_2 to existence, one does not assert that the concept exists. Rather, what exists is what the concept is "the concept of," an object or existential proposition. Thus, just as when we say Paul exists we are not talking about the concept of Paul, when we say that red exists we cannot be talking either about the concept red or about a red patch.[24] Instead we would be talking about a third thing. This third sort of thing, denoted by (e), we will call a 'simple object.' Thus to a nonexistent simple concept there would seem to correspond an existent simple object (or simple existential proposition). The latter is simple first, in that it contains no object and, second, in that besides existence and a temporal concept it contains only one simple concept. It is not simple in that it contains concepts. One may note a similarity here between such concepts and simple objects and Frege's concepts and concept correlates. Being existent temporal objects, such simple objects may be considered to be substantial or particular. Hence, such simple objects may be confused with particular patches. Since we have already noted why Moore may confuse simple objects with simple concepts, such simple objects may provide, in turn, the bridge for the confusion of simple concepts with particular patches, of red with a red patch. Be that as it may, with the appearance of such simple objects, we may look upon a sentence like 'Paul is yellow' in a different light. Instead of holding that Paul contains yellow, one might suggest that Paul contains a simple object denoted by 'R_2 (yellow, existence, now),' which will be abbreviated by 'yellow$_1$.' Thus Paul, being substantial, would be made up of, or contain, substantial parts. The sentence 'Paul is yellow' would then be transcribed by

(γ) Paul C yellow$_1$.

Since (γ) provides a basis for thinking of a composite substance like Paul as being composed of substantial parts, it reflects the point we noted much earlier that objects contain entities that are both substances and existents. In turn this may be taken to indicate a sort of Aristotelian nominalism or conceptualism in Moore's 1899 paper. We thus have a link with what Moore says in *Principia*. More about this shortly.

The simple object yellow$_1$ might also be said to *contain* the concept yellow, just as Paul *contains* yellow$_1$. But about this we should note two things. First, as holding between Paul and yellow$_1$, C connects two entities both of which are particulars and existents. But as holding between yellow$_1$ and yellow, it holds between an existent and a non-existent. For concepts, recall, cannot be existents. This suggests that we might distinguish the sense in which Paul contains yellow$_1$ from that in which yellow$_1$ contains yellow. In other words, simple objects "contain" simple concepts in a different sense from that in which complex objects "contain" simple objects. Thus an ontology recognizing complex objects, simple objects, and concepts might acknowledge two distinct senses of 'contains.' This second relation holding between yellow$_1$ and yellow will be designated by 'C*.'[25]

Second, both C and C* are ordered relations. If we consider the first place in a sentence containing either C or C* as the subject place and the second place as the predicate place, then we see, first, that 'yellow' will not occur in the subject place of a sentence expressing a "containing" relation (in either sense); and, second, that 'yellow$_1$' can occur in either place. It will occur in the subject place in a sentence like 'yellow$_1$ C* yellow,' and in the predicate place in 'Paul C yellow$_1$.' The first point shows, again, why yellow cannot be said to exist; the second point shows in what sense simple objects like yellow$_1$ might be considered to be properties. Also, if we distinguish C from C* we could not have a sentence like 'yellow C* existence' or 'yellow C existence,' but we could have 'yellow$_1$ C* existence.' It is also noteworthy that while yellow$_1$ is the relevant existent, the concept yellow is what stands in the relation R$_2$ to existence. But if one thinks in terms of a sentence like 'yellow R$_2$ existence' or 'R$_2$ (yellow, existence)' as stating this fact, we can see why he may confuse yellow with yellow$_1$ and R$_2$ with C.

A question also arises as to whether there is a plurality of simple objects like yellow$_1$ associated with a simple concept like yellow. If there is, then we clearly have a view very much like an Aristotelian type of nominalism. For then one may hold that the simple object, say yellow$_1$, contained in one yellow patch is different from that, say yellow$_2$, in another yellow patch. Alternatively, if one holds that there is only one such simple object which is contained in all yellow patches, then we have a view somewhat like the extreme "Platonism" of William of Champeaux. To hold to such an entity in addition to the concept yellow would indeed seem pointless, since one would then have not only a universal concept but also a universal particular, whatever that would mean. As Moore's discussion is neither clear nor detailed, one can only attribute views to him. But this version of extreme realism does not at all seem to be what is involved, even implicitly, in his discussion. The only reason one might have for considering it at all is that Moore does not include either the concept *this* or a spatial concept in a simple object like yellow$_1$. One reason for this might be, again, his fusing simple objects with simple concepts. Yet he might have intended to include a spatial concept in a simple object like yellow$_1$. Thus, when he says

> If now we take the existential proposition "Red exists," . . . my meaning is that the concept "red" and the concept "existence" stand in a specific relation both to one another and to the concept of time.[26]

he may simply have neglected to include a spatial concept. For he later says:

It seems rather to be this: That time alone is sufficient for some sort of experience, since it alone seems to be involved in the simplest kind of existential proposition, e.g., "Pleasure exists"; and that again time and space together will suffice to account for the possibility of other pieces of knowledge.[27]

A simple object containing the concept *red* might then differ from a simple object which contains the concept pleasure, in that the former also includes a spatial concept whereas the latter does not. For the former, unlike the latter, may be thought to be in space. But in neither case does Moore include the concept *this*. This seems to be due to his reserving that concept for those cases where we would use a phrase like 'this paper.' For he holds that the simplest kind of existential proposition need not involve the concept of substance, and the inclusion of the concept *this* would seem to do just that.[28] Even without the inclusion of spatial concepts or the concept *this* in simple objects, the fact that simple objects contain temporal concepts would seem to indicate that there would be a plurality of such objects containing the concept yellow.[29] All the simple objects containing the concept yellow would then be yellow in virtue of the concept yellow contained in them.

Concerning the attribution to Moore of an ontology embracing such simple objects, we might note what he says in his 1901 paper, "Identity."

> On the other hand, we have accepted the principle frequently implied in Plato that the idea in a thing may be different from the idea in itself; and we have still to see whether there is any insurmountable objection to this view.
>
> The view we have accepted is that in some cases where two things are truly said to have a common predicate, there exists in each a predicate exactly similar to that which exists in the other, but not numerically identical with it. And I confess I see no objections to this view, except what seem to rest on a bare denial of the difference between conceptual and numerical difference. These two exactly similar things are, I may be told, identical in content: exact similarity means identity in content. I admit that they are so. In that case, my adversary may retort, they are the same thing; there is no difference between them: there are not two but one. But this is merely to beg the point at issue. What I have urged is that many of our judgments plainly imply that there may be two things, things having a kind of difference which I call numerical, which yet have not another kind of difference which I call conceptual. And I explain the phrase, identity of content, as applying only to two such things, which have no conceptual difference. The two things are, I admit, in one sense

the same; but that they are not therefore also *one* and the same is just what I have tried to show.[30]

Here Moore explicitly leans to the immanent characters of Plato as distinct from the transcendent forms. The *tallness in Phaedo* is distinct from, though conceptually related to, the form *tallness*. *If such immanent characters are considered to be substantial*, as they are in *Principia* and in "The Nature of Judgment," *we have the simple objects of Moore's ontology*. Notice too how the simple objects easily provide him with the distinction he asserts between numerical and conceptual identity. Yellow$_1$ and yellow$_2$ would be conceptually identical, in that both are simple objects containing the concept yellow. Yet they are numerically different, in that yellow$_1$ is not the same simple object as yellow$_2$. Thus what he says in his paper "Identity" jibes with the above interpretation of the ontology of his 1899 paper. However, in the 1901 paper the connection between yellow$_1$ and the universal yellow is no longer that of containing. Rather, the former now "exemplifies," or stands in a basic asymmetrical relation to, the latter.[31] The simple objects now seem to be simple in that they do not contain anything, though they may be thought to be complex in that they are numerically different from but conceptually identical with all other simple objects exemplifying the same universal.

The ontology of the 1899 paper may then be summed up as follows: There are two kinds of entities, existents and nonexistents, and several ontological ties, the R's. All existent entities are made up ultimately of simple concepts which are nonexistent. Also, all other nonexistent entities are likewise reducible to simple concepts. The category of existent entities includes simple objects, like yellow$_1$, and complex objects, like Paul, all of which are existential propositions. In addition to simple concepts, the category of nonexistent entities includes nonexistential propositions and complex concepts like the concept of Paul. With such an ontology we can understand why Moore must sooner or later explicitly distinguish between being and existence. For his ontology includes a variety of nonexistent entities among which are the "ultimate" ingredients of the universe. This, in its way, seems to reduce the importance of the notion of existence in Moore's ontology, and, as we saw, he does distinguish, in *Principia*, between being and existence. We can now see the root of the view, expressed in *Principia*, that universals do not exist and, hence, the basis of the ontology implicit in those strange passages cited from *Principia*.

III. Contains, Exemplification, and Goodness

Moore's ontology, then, includes existent objects "constructed" of non-existent concepts. He also tells us that concepts are not adjectives but substantives:

> A concept is not in any intelligible sense an 'adjective,' as if there were something substantive, more ultimate than it. For we must if we are to be consistent, describe what appears to be most substantive as no more than a collection of such supposed adjectives: and thus, in the end, the concept turns out to be the only substantive or subject, and no one concept either more or less an adjective than any other.[32]

Since substantial objects are composed of concepts, Moore apparently thinks that such objects cannot be more substantial than concepts. That concepts or universals *depend* upon objects that exemplify them is a familiar ontological theme of nominalistically inclined philosophers. It reflects the idea that what exists, ultimately, is independent. But for Moore, objects depend on concepts in that they are composed of concepts. We shall shortly see how the notion of "dependence" enters into Moore's conception of goodness and into his variation of a view having particularized properties or, as some call them, perfect particulars. Here we see not only the importance of the ontological themes of simplicity and independence for Moore (for simple concepts, the ultimate ingredients of the universe, are both simple and independent), but also why he may confuse concepts with their simple objects as a consequence of his considering substantial objects to be composed of simple concepts. Moore has two notions of a "substantive." First, a substantive is an existent and, hence, temporal object. Second, a substantive is an "independent" entity, a subject, on which adjectives "depend." Since simple concepts are the entities on which all others "depend" he may think of them as substantial existents. If he then confuses the two notions of a "substantive," he could explicitly confuse simple concepts with their simple objects. This would explain why he says what he does in *Principia*. Properties like yellow in *Principia* are thought of partly as the concepts and partly as the simple objects of the 1899 and 1901 papers. When he speaks in *Principia* of natural properties as existing independently in time, he is really speaking of simple objects like $yellow_1$ as properties. We can then see why one might think of Moore as a realist in *Principia* and yet be puzzled by his speaking of properties as temporal substances and of universals as nonexistents but as having "being." For once one has fused simple objects with universal concepts, what one says will indicate both realism and nominalism.

Before considering how goodness fits into all this, we might note a further classical ontological theme embodied in Moore's discussion. Objects, like Paul, are thought of as composed either of the concept of Paul together with existence (in the relation R_2) or of the simple concepts which make up the concept of Paul together with existence (in the relation R_2). One may then think of Paul as somehow made up of his concept together with existence. This is certainly reminiscent of those who held that existents were composites of essence plus existence.

We have seen the answer to the first question asked at the end of Section I, "Why does Moore think in terms of contains rather than of exemplification in *Principia*?" We have also seen the answers to the questions raised there about "simple particulars" in view of the discussion of the simple objects of the 1899 paper. We will now proceed to the second question: "Why is goodness different from redness and yellowness in that it is exemplified by, rather than contained in, objects?"

In the 1899 paper Moore held that no one concept is "either more or less an adjective than any other." Clearly he had not yet formulated his later view about goodness. Goodness was thus grafted onto an earlier ontological framework. While this marks goodness as a sort of intruder into Moore's ontology it does not explain why he fitted it in the way he did. But there are several reasons that do.

First, Moore does not think of goodness as an "empirical" property in that it is not sensible or an object of perception. In this sense it is more like mathematical properties than like red. In the 1899 paper he seems to have distinguished empirical concepts as those which can exist in time.[33] Fusing these two senses of 'empirical' may have contributed to his view that goodness cannot exist in time, and hence cannot be a substantial part of objects. Consequently, the concept good would not correspond to simple objects as yellow does to $yellow_1$, etc. Thus good objects would have to exemplify goodness rather than contain a simple object like, say, $goodness_1$. Since Moore already recognized entities like numbers which did not exist in time and which were not objects of perception, he already had a category in which to place goodness in *Principia*.

Second, recall the difference between 'G = P' and 'G(P)' that we discussed earlier. Moore is preoccupied by the notion that one can always ask of anything other than goodness, "Is it good?" But if goodness were contained, rather than exemplified, we could not significantly ask of a simple property like red or pleasure if it were good, for we would be asking if these simple qualities contained goodness, yet simple qualities do not contain anything at all. Moreover, even simple objects like yellow$_1$ could not contain goodness. Thus one could ask only if these simple qualities were identical with goodness. But this is not what Moore believes he is asking, and hence one must speak of goodness being exemplified rather than contained.

Third, recall Paul, the square yellow patch mentioned above. Suppose Paul also contained a particular goodness as he contains yellow$_1$ and, say, square$_1$. There would still be a difference. If we "took away" the particular goodness we would still have an ordinary composite object that was a square yellow patch. But if we "took away" either the particular yellowness or the particular squareness of the patch, we would not have an ordinary composite at all. For square patches must have a color, and colored patches require a shape. We just could not have a good square or a good yellow thing where the first had no color and the second no shape. This could lead one to think that goodness should not be considered a substantial part of Paul in the way in which yellowness and squareness are such parts. If we recall one of the passages from *Principia* cited above, it does seem that Moore thinks along this line. Note that one is not merely saying here that Paul would be a different object without a particular yellowness but that there could not be the same sort of object, an ordinary composite object. To see this, suppose again Paul to be composed only of the concepts yellow, square, existence, and now. To withdraw yellow would leave something composed of square, existence, and now. This would be the simple object square$_1$. We no longer have a composite particular square patch. However, if Paul also contains goodness and it is withdrawn, we would still have a particular square patch, albeit not a good one. One may then hold that it is not the same square patch since its goodness is somehow "intrinsic" to it; but it would still be a square patch—a particular composite object. Hence it would be the same sort of thing, in that sense, as a good square patch. Not being a substantial part of Paul, goodness must then attach to the object as a mere adjective or predicate, for this seems to be the only alternative.[34]

Fourth, the notion of whole and part may enter in yet another way. Moore holds that the goodness of certain "organic" wholes is not reducible to the goodness of their parts. One cannot help but wonder if his concern with this point contributes to his refraining from thinking of goodness as a "part" of a complex object in the sense of being contained in it.

Fifth, some philosophers have held that universals are *dependent* on the particulars which exemplify them. Moore suggests this theme when he speaks of good as an adjective or "mere predicate." Whatever else is involved in this view, it certainly suggests the point that somehow the existence, or perhaps the being, of a universal requires the existence of an exemplifying particular—a substance. We noticed above Moore's concern with the adjectival nature of universals or concepts. He also thinks of goodness as being *dependent* on natural qualities. He thinks of it as dependent in two ways. First, he seems to hold that goodness is dependent in the sense that if an object exemplifies goodness then it must have, or must be conceived as having, other properties. This is not to say that from its being good one could infer that an object had *certain specific* characteristics (this he expressly denied), but merely that it must have some other characteristics besides goodness. Second, goodness is dependent in the sense that an object's being good follows from the fact that it possesses certain natural properties. But Moore thinks of natural properties as substances. This may well provide a ground for his mixing these various senses of "dependent." Goodness, then, being dependent on the substantial natural properties, would not itself be thought of as substantial. Hence it becomes *dependent* in the sense of being a mere adjective or universal. Moore's ontological views provide a natural basis for his mingling these senses of "dependent." If goodness were like yellowness, then there would be a simple object denoted by 'R$_2$ (good, existence, now),' i.e., good$_1$, the particular goodness in, say, Paul. We would, in Moore's terminology, have a substantive existent goodness without there being any natural properties like yellow, pleasure, etc., to be "dependent" on. Goodness would then be "independent" like yellowness. And, if "independent," it could be conceived of as existing by itself in time. But Moore believes goodness to be "dependent." Hence, there cannot be a simple object like good$_1$, and goodness cannot then be spoken of as being contained in composite objects.

We see then how Moore's 1899 paper provides the basis and explanation for the ontology of *Principia*. Moore might be thought to have nominalistic leanings, in that *(a)* he has simple objects; *(b)* concepts are nonexistents; and, most important, *(c)* in *Principia* he apparently confused some concepts with simple objects. This confusion, in turn, explains his attempt to distinguish natural from nonnatural properties. In the case of concepts like yellow we have a concept, simple objects, and complex objects. *Nonnatural* properties (concepts) *have no simple objects.* Hence there is nothing to confuse them with. Thus he speaks of them as genuine universals. But not being confused with simple objects, they are, in nominalistic fashion, classified as nonexistents. Without this confusion between concepts and their simple objects, Moore would have to recognize two kinds of concepts: those which had simple objects and those which did not. Both kinds of concepts would be nonexistents, though, being entities, *they* would *be* in some sense. Thus the difference between natural and nonnatural properties (concepts) would not be that the first are existents while the second are not; rather, it would be based on the existence of correlated simple objects for the natural ones. The introduction of such "nonnatural" concepts gives rise to yet a further ontological tie, namely, exemplification. For when we say of a composite natural object that it is red we are saying that it contains (C) a simple object which, in turn, contains (C^*) the concept red. But to say of either a simple or a composite object that it is good is to say that it exemplifies goodness. Thus, with concepts like goodness introduced, Moore's ontology embraces the R's and exemplification.

Three further points may be made about Moore's ontology. First, Moore clearly recognizes the inadequacy of an ontology which accepts simple objects but not universals. For without the universal concepts one could not say what made yellow$_1$ and yellow$_2$ both yellownesses. Yet even though he has simple objects his ontology is an original variant of an Aristotelian "conceptualism." For the simple objects do not "fall under" mental concepts; rather, they are composed of concepts which are clearly not mind-*dependent* but are the ultimate *independent* entities. In this sense Moore, far from being a nominalist, may be thought of as an extreme realist in 1899. Even when his view changes, in the 1901 paper, universals are independent mind-transcendent entities exemplified by, rather than part of, simple objects, like yellow$_1$, which are parts of ordinary objects like Paul. Since the 1901 paper appears just prior to *Principia,* it seems obvious that the simple objects of 1901 become the natural properties of 1903. But in 1903 the universal concepts exemplified by such simple objects (in 1901) are ignored or confused with their exemplifications. Hence, in *Principia* the particular simple objects or natural properties *combine* by a tie to constitute a natural complex object, like Paul. By contrast, a nonnatural property or universal, like. goodness, is *exemplified* by such a complex. Thus the natural properties of an object are particulars which are parts of the object, while non-natural properties are "adjectives" of such complex objects. The two kinds of properties thus involve two kinds of ties in the implicit ontology *of Principia.*

Second, nonnatural concepts like goodness are already foreshadowed in the 1899 paper. There, *truth* is considered a property of propositions. Moore does not go into any details concerning the connection between the property truth and true propositions, but it would seem to be that of exemplification rather than contains. Hence, *truth* would be a non-natural property like goodness. The only basis for considering *truth* to be contained in true propositions would be if one confused this property with the relation R_t and considered the latter, as Moore does, a *constituent* of a true proposition. But if one does not make this con-fusion, the relation R_t may be considered the "true-making" element of true propositions, just as good objects would have "good-making" characteristics *contained* in them.

Third, one might seek to simplify Moore's ontology by holding that composite objects contained, not simple objects, but concepts. One would not then require simple objects at all and would require only one sense of contains. But this would require abandoning the notion that "natural properties" were *substantial, temporal* existents.[35] One would then simply say that there were two basically different ways in which objects combined with concepts. The only difference between natural and nonnatural properties would then lie in their different ontological ties to objects. Natural properties would combine with each other, via the R's, to form complex concepts and objects, while nonnatural prop-erties would be tied to such complex wholes by exemplification.[36] Natural properties would then be parts of objects while nonnatural ones were "adjectives" of such objects. Here we may recall that, since objects are existential propositions, all this fits with the concept "truth," like "good," being a nonnatural adjective. In a clear sense, however, the crucial difference between natural and nonnatural properties would be that the former were internal (intrinsic) and the latter external (extrinsic) to objects.[37] Both kinds of tie, the R's and exemplification, would be ultimate, and one could not say anything more to "explain" the difference between natural and nonnatural properties.[38]

In "The Conception of Intrinsic Value" of 1922, Moore once again tried to distinguish between natural and nonnatural properties. He there held that a nonnatural property like good, while depending on the "intrinsic nature" of an object in the sense that no two objects could be "exactly alike" in natural properties if one of them had such a nonnatural property and the other did not, was not one of the properties one would list in a complete *description* of the object. But he does not tell us, as he admits he cannot, what distinguishes a descriptive property from a property like good. One might then notice that in this later essay the properties Moore considers to be intrinsic descriptive properties are those he once considered to be substantive parts of objects. A possible verbal bridge between the label "descriptive property" and the notion of being a part of an object may be provided by Moore's thinking that to describe something intrinsically is to say what it is. And this is what one would naturally say one does when one lists the parts which an object contains. Also, we may note that in the 1922 paper Moore distinguishes two kinds of necessity: one kind of necessary connection links intrinsic natures with nonnatural properties, the other connects such natures with natural properties. Thus the distinction between a natural and a nonnatural property is made to rest on there being two kinds of necessary connection, where formerly, as we saw, the distinction depended on there being two ontological ties, exemplification and some combinatory tie. That Moore still adheres to this structural pattern in 1922 shows how deep the matter lies in his thought.

Notes

1. G. E. Moore, *Principia Ethica* (Cambridge: Cambridge University Press, Cambridge, reprinted 1954), p. 41.

2. C. D. Broad, "Certain Features in Moore's Ethical Doctrines," in Paul A. Schilpp (ed.), *The Philosophy of G. E. Moore*, (Evanston, Ill.: Northwestern University Press, 1942), p. 59.

3. G. E. Moore, "A Reply to My Critics," in Schilpp, *op. cit.,* p. 582.

4. Moore resolves the problems about bare substances and individuation not by rejecting universals but by introducing simple particulars and universals with the former exemplifying the latter. See G. E. Moore, "Identity," *Proceedings of the Aristotelian Society,* (1901). But as we shall see considerable confusion attends his discussion of "properties" as "natural" and "non-natural."

5. G. E. Moore, *Some Main Problems of Philosophy* (London: George Allen & Unwin Ltd., second impression, 1958), p. 361.

6. *Ibid.,* p. 368.

7. *Ibid.,* pp. 372-73.

8. Moore distinguishes *truths,* not the universal *truth,* from existent particulars and from nonexistent universals. Perhaps, on analysis, these would turn out to be nonexistent particulars, since he classifies them, along with universals, as nonexistents. In that case, while all existents would be particulars, not all particulars would be existents. The distinction between existent and nonexistent particulars would undoubtedly be based on the "fact" that nonexistent particulars, like universals, would not be temporal entities (*Ibid.,* p. 372).

9. "The Refutation of Idealism," reprinted *in Philosophical Studies* (London: Routledge & Kegan Paul, 1922). See pp. 17-19.

10. *Some Main Problems of Philosophy,* p. 374.

11. *Ibid.,* p. 375.

12. *Principia Ethica,* p. 124. This quotation makes it crystal clear that one ingredient in the naturalistic fallacy is mistakenly taking a property to be natural, an existent particular, when it is really nonnatural, a nonexistent universal.

13. *Ibid.,* p. 126.

14. *Ibid.,* pp. 110, 140.

15. G. E. Moore, "The Nature of Judgment," *Mind,* XXX, (April, 1899), 182. The ontological status of mind is not discussed by Moore in this paper, unless one considers the general statement that all existents are composed of concepts to be a "discussion." But such a "view," aside from any question as to what it could mean, does not jibe with other things Moore writes at this period.

16. *Ibid.,* pp. 182-83.

17. *Ibid.,* p. 183.

18. *Ibid.,* p. 180.

19. *Ibid.,* p. 181.

20. For a comparison of a containment pattern with an exemplification pattern and a discussion of issues that are not taken up here see H. Hochberg, "Universals, Particulars, and Predication," *Review of Metaphysics,* XIX (1, 1965).

21. 'R_t' is used to indicate the relation combining concepts into a true nonexistential proposition, irrespective of whether it is in keeping with Moore's intent to identify that relation with R_2.

22. Moore, "The Nature of Judgment," pp. 180-81, 183, 189. Moore does not use the term 'contains,' but speaks of concepts being combined with each other.

23. *Ibid.,* pp. 189-90.

24. At one point Moore says, "I endeavor to show, what I must own appears to me perfectly obvious, that the concept can consistently be described neither as an existent, nor as part of an existent" (*ibid.,* p. 181). But just as the first

part of his statement (that concepts cannot be *described* as existents) should not be taken as supporting my point that concepts *are not* existents for Moore, the second part, that concepts cannot be *described* as parts of existents, does not weigh against the contention that they are, for Moore, parts of existents. For taking this statement in its context reveals that Moore is arguing that concepts are more basic than existents and, hence, what concepts are cannot be explained by a consideration of the nature of existents.

25. The distinction between C and C* is suggested simply to contrast Moore's with more traditional variants of the containment pattern. In them, Paul contains yellow$_1$, the latter does not contain, as a part, the concept yellow but "falls under" it. Here we clearly have a further tie connecting the simple particular with a concept.

26. "The Nature of Judgment," p. 189.

27. *Ibid.*, p. 191.

28. Moore is not accepting a bare substance in his acknowledgment of the concept *this*. For concepts are not substances. His distaste for bare substances could be shown by his not acknowledging simple objects constructed from the concept *this* in the sense in which yellow$_1$ is constructed from yellow and the quotation cited earlier in note 1.

29. This is not to say that problems would not arise in trying to distinguish simple objects constructed from the same concept on the basis of time alone. Also, it is quite unlikely that the concepts *now, was* and *will be* will prove adequate for dealing with the philosophical problems involved in time and change. But again, our concern here is not to attempt to make Moore's ontology adequate. We might note that if one attempts to solve the problem of individuation, within Moore's pattern, in terms of different objects containing different spatial and temporal concepts, then one accepts a view reminiscent of the *haecceitas* of Scotus. On the other hand, if one sees the solution to the problem of individuation to lie in there being different existent simple objects (yellow$_1$ as opposed to yellow$_2$, for example), then one adopts a view patterned after Aquinas' *principium individuationis*.

30. Moore, "Identity," pp. 111-12.

31. For a detailed discussion of Moore's paper "Identity," see my "Moore and Russell on Particulars, Relations, and Identity," in this volume.

32. "The Nature of Judgment," pp. 192-93. This quotation reveals the discrepancy between the 1899 and 1901 papers. In the latter the substantive parts of objects are clearly "simple objects" or particularized properties, yellow$_1$, etc., and not universal concepts.

33. *Ibid.*, p. 187.

34. In view of some of the things Moore says in "The Conception of Intrinsic Value" (in *Philosophical Studies* [London: Routledge & Kegan Paul, 1922]), the "withdrawal" of the goodness from a good object would also necessitate the "withdrawal" of those natural properties with which it was intrinsically or necessarily connected. Thus, as he puts it, one could not have two natural objects "exactly alike" in natural properties but differing in value. Hence the withdrawal of Paul's goodness would also necessitate the withdrawal of at least one of his natural properties, say his yellowness. Without his being good Paul would not then be yellow. But the point is that we would not then have a yellow square owing to its not containing yellowness, even though the yellowness would be withdrawn because of its intrinsic connection with goodness. In any case to speak of "taking away" or "withdrawing" properties, as Moore does, is to speak metaphorically. In short, the above discussion merely

reflects the simple and obvious point that natural properties can combine into objects without goodness, but goodness "requires" natural properties for there to be a good object. This involves the *dependent* nature of goodness, which is discussed further below.

35. In terms of the 1901 paper Moore would not accept such a modification, since it would, for him, amount to the denial of particulars and numerical difference. The 1901 paper marks the explicit recognition of simple objects which are implicit in the 1899 paper and function in a confused way in *Principia*. For in the latter they are confused with concepts, and this confusion is the basis for the way he puts the distinction between natural and nonnatural properties.

36. There would be no reason why complex wholes other than objects could not also exemplify the nonnatural property goodness. Thus the concept of a nonexistent object might do so. This would be a way of enabling us to say of a nonexistent that *it* is good or, perhaps, that it would be good were it to exist. It is here relevant to recall Moore's concern with separating ascriptions of goodness from questions of existence.

37. For a discussion of such uses of 'external' and 'internal' see H. Hochberg, "Universals, Particulars, and Predication."

38. To avoid unduly complicating the discussion, I have not considered an ambiguity that arises in treating an object like a yellow square as a composite of $yellow_1$ and $square_1$. Taking 'R_2 (yellow, existence, here, now)' and 'R_2 (square, existence, here, now)' to designate these simple particulars, we can use, with '$+$' indicating a further tie combining simple particulars,

(1) R_2 (yellow, existence, here, now) $+$ R_2 (square, existence, here, now)

to picture the composite particular. But this may appear overly complex, since

(2) R_2 (yellow, square, existence, here now)

would offer a simpler picture. Yet this latter picture would not show $yellow_1$ and $square_1$ to be constituents, though it would show what universal concepts were ultimate constituents. Thus, if we take both (1) and (2) to reveal aspects of the analysis of the complex object we should add

(1) $=$ (2)

as a sort of implicit principle of Moore's schema reflecting the fact that the complex object may be construed or analyzed in one of two ways in terms of the ontology of the 1899 paper. Thus, when I spoke earlier of withdrawing a natural property, it seems closer to Moore's thought to picture such "withdrawal" by taking 'R_2 (square, existence, here, now)' from (1) rather than 'square' from (2). *Principia*, recall, appears after the 1901 paper "Identity." In this paper, as I mentioned earlier, Moore holds that an object like a yellow square would be composed of particular properties $yellow_1$ and $square_1$, but these are not held to be composed of universal concepts. Hence to withdraw *the yellowness* of an object is to withdraw something like $yellow_1$ and not the universal yellowness which $yellow_1$ exemplifies. This, of course, fits with the fact that in *Principia* the universal yellowness apparently disappears in favor of the particular yellownesses. This is why *the yellow* of a yellow square is called a "natural" property. The origin of the notion of a natural property thus lies in the earlier distinction between and later confusion of yellowness and $yellow_1$.

Seven

MR. HOCHBERG
ON MOORE:
SOME CORRECTIONS

John O. Nelson

IN HIS ARTICLE, "Moore's Ontology and Nonnatural Properties," (above, pp. 95-127), Mr. Herbert Hochberg suggests that Moore is essentially a nominalist (p. 97), and he suggests that Moore's nominalism (as he calls it) has its origin in the ontology of Moore's 1899 paper, "The Nature of Judgment" (pp. 95, 106). Neither Hochberg's interpretations of "The Nature of Judgment," nor his suggestion that Moore is a nominalist, which he bases largely on them, are at all credible. This paper will be devoted to showing that they are not.

"The ontology of the 1899 paper may then be summed up as follows," says Mr. Hochberg (p. 117). "There are two kinds of entities, existents and nonexistents. . . . All existent entities are made up ultimately of simple concepts which are nonexistent. Also, all other nonexistent entities are likewise reducible to simple concepts. The category of existent entities includes simple objects, like yellow$_1$, and complex

Reprinted by permission of the author and the editor from *The Review of Metaphysics*, XVI (1962), 119-32. Page references and some spellings have been changed to conform with Mr. Hochberg's essay as reprinted in this volume.

objects, like Paul, as well as existential propositions. In addition to simple concepts, the category of nonexistent entities includes nonexistential propositions, and complex concepts like the concept of Paul." By "simple object," Hochberg means any complex of concepts in which a single adjectival concept, like red or yellow, is tied together by some ontological relation, R, involving containment, with the concepts *existence* and *now*. Any such composite, denoted by the words, e.g., R_2 (red, existence, now), R_2 (yellow, existence, now), etc. or by the words "red_1," "$yellow_1$," etc. (as opposed to "red," "yellow," etc., which are used without subscripts to designate the simple concepts of red, yellow, etc.), is a particular, since it has (i.e., it contains) temporal existence. Every complex composed of simple objects and only such complexes are likewise particulars, in contrast to simple or complex concepts, which are universals (pp. 106-15). Thus, as Hochberg interprets him, Moore in "The Nature of Judgment" denies existence to universals, while maintaining that particulars, and only particulars, exist.

Now this analysis does make it appear that Moore is essentially a nominalist. For traditionally nominalists are just those who have maintained that only particulars exist. If Hochberg is correct, however, Moore—to be consistent—must maintain these further doctrines. (1) He must maintain that every existential assertion is either self-evidently and necessarily false, or self-evidently and necessarily true. Suppose, for instance, that I assert, "There exists a spider in the house next door." According to Hochberg's interpretation of "The Nature of Judgment," in making this assertion I must either be referring to the concept, spider-in-the-house-next-door, or the particular object, spider-in-the-house-next-door. If I am referring to the former, my assertion is on the face of it false, since concepts do not exist. On the other hand, a particular consists, by Hochberg's definition, of a set of concepts, including the concept, existence. Now the way Hochberg argues (as the purported spokesman for Moore), if and only if a composite containing the concepts *existence* and *now* occurs, do we have a particular, and we have a particular just because such a composite has (contains) temporal existence. Consequently, if what I am asserting above is that a particular object exists, then I am asserting a necessary and self-evident truth. (2) Moore must also, on Hochberg's interpretation, maintain that a concept or universal cannot exist in parts of time, because it would then be a particular and not a universal. (3) Finally, Moore will have to maintain that existence somehow arises out of nonexistence and temporal particulars out of nontemporal universals. This follows from the claim (which Hochberg puts in Moore's mouth) that all existent entities are made up ultimately of simple concepts which are nonexistent and nontemporal.

Now in fact there is nothing in the text of "The Nature of Judgment" to support the view that Moore maintains (1), (2), and (3) above. On the contrary, there is a good deal of textual evidence that contradicts those claims. For instance, while Moore does seem to want to maintain that in some degree all existential propositions are necessary, he does not maintain that they are necessary because existence comprises part of the essence of all particulars, but because all existential or empirical propositions make some implicit reference to time or space.[1] Moore here must be understood to be arguing in the manner of Kant (to whom, indeed, he specifically refers). Thus, he argues that the proposition, "This body is heavy," involves necessity in its meaning because it predicates an attribute of a substance and *that* is a necessary relation, i.e., attributes must be predicated of substances and not the other way around (*NJ*, 87). Whatever one may think of the validity of this argument of Moore's, it is surely not an absurd argument, as would be the argument that Hochberg implicitly ascribes to him, that every existential proposition is necessarily true because particulars contain existence as a part of their essence. Moore, in fact, ostensibly repudiates any such theory as the latter. For one thing, he holds that some existential propositions, i.e., *purely* existential propositions like "Heaviness exists here and now," involve no necessity in their meaning *if* we ignore their temporal implications (*NJ*, 186, 188). For another thing, he asserts that an existential proposition can be false: ". . . whereas with an existential proposition it may be true that this exists now, and yet it will presently be untrue that it exists" (*NJ*, 188).

Just as certainly as "The Nature of Judgment" resists any such interpretation as that contained in (1) above, it resists any such interpretations as those contained in (2) and (3) above. Moore, for instance, *explicitly* maintains that some concepts exist in parts of time. He *says*, "Empirical concepts are those which can exist in parts of time" (*NJ*, 187), and later, ". . . an empirical concept is to be defined, not as a concept given by experience, since all concepts are so given, but as one which can exist in an actual part of time . . . a simple concept cannot be known as one which could exist in time, except on the ground that it has so existed, is existing, or will exist" (*NJ*, 189). In these passages

Moore is answering one of the main questions that he has set himself in "the Nature of Judgment," namely, how to clarify Kant's distinction between empirical and *a priori* propositions. The answer he gives is in precisely the above terms: empirical propositions are merely those propositions that contain empirical concepts, i.e., concepts existing in parts of time; *a priori* propositions are those that do not contain empirical concepts but only *a priori* concepts. Surely, therefore, Moore cannot mean to agree to (2) above, or (3) either.

But if the text of "the Nature of Judgment" so plainly contradicts (1), (2), and (3) above, either we must reject Hochberg's over-all interpretation of the paper, or we must suppose Moore to be guilty of the most colossal inconsistencies. And before we do that, we shall certainly want to see just what evidence or arguments Hochberg provides for his claims that (1) Moore in "The Nature of Judgment" holds that only particulars exist and universals do not and (2) that Moore's ontology of 1899 and afterwards is essentially nominalistic.

As far as I can make out, there are four main arguments or considerations which Hochberg appeals to in support of the above claims. For purposes of reference, I shall refer to these arguments or considerations by the letters A, B, C, and D.

A. Hochberg sometimes argues that a simple concept cannot exist according to Moore's ontology of 1899, because to say that it existed would be to say that it contained the concept existence, but if it contained the concept existence, then it could not be simple. His exact words are, "But suppose we wish to say that the simple concept red exists. One might think that this would be asserted by holding that red and existence stand in the relation R_2. But then what exists is not the concept red, but a composite composed of *red, existence,* the relation R_2, and *now*. Speaking in terms of containment makes it even clearer. For only composites can contain anything. Hence, a simple concept like red could not be the subject of a containing relation. *Red cannot then exist,* if one thinks of existents as containing the concept existence" (p. 112).

B. Hochberg takes Moore's analysis of existents to say that what exists is not a concept, whether simple or complex, but what a concept is *of,* and that what a concept is *of* is a particular. Again, I append Hochberg's exact words: "But on Moore's analysis of existents, when one says that a concept stands in the relation R_2 to existence one does not assert that the concept exists. Rather, what exists is what the concept is 'the concept of.' Thus, just as when we say Paul exists we are not talking about the concept of Paul, when we say that red exists we cannot be talking either about the concept red or about a red patch. Instead we would be talking about a third thing. . . . Being an existent temporal object, such an entity may be considered to be substantial or particular" (pp. 113-14).

C. Hochberg contends that Moore cannot be supposed to hold that concepts exist, because then there would be a needless and absurd duplication of objects in his ontology. Says Hochberg, "Alternatively, if one holds that there is only one such simple object which is contained in all yellow patches, then we shall have a view somewhat like the extreme 'Platonism' of William of Champeaux. To hold to such an entity in addition to the concept yellow would indeed seem pointless since one would then have not only a universal concept, but also a universal particular—whatever that would mean. As Moore's discussion is neither clear nor detailed, one can only attribute views to him. But this version of extreme realism does not at all seem to be what is involved, even implicitly, in his discussion" (p. 115).

D. In some measure at least, Hochberg's claim that Moore is a nominalist rests upon the interpretation that he gives the disjunction, existent or nonexistent. This interpretation accords with the nominalist view that the major ontological division is between existence and nonexistence the major ontological division is between existence and nonexistence.

Let us now examine A, B, C, and D with the aim of determining to what extent those arguments reflect Moore's thoughts in "The Nature of Judgment." We shall see, I think, that they are almost completely without textual support and reflect Hochberg's own philosophical views, or at least his views as to what Moore ought to have said, rather than what Moore actually did say in that paper.

Argument A. This argument rests upon interpreting the ontological tie between concepts in terms of the relation of containment. The simple concept red cannot exist, because in order to exist it would have to contain the concept existence. But does Moore ever maintain that the ontological tie between concepts is that of containment? Hochberg himself admits that Moore does not. The terms Moore uses in "The Nature of Judgment" are "connexion" ("connexion of concepts," *NJ*, 179), "conjunction" ("conjunction of concepts," *NJ*, 179), and "combination" (*NJ*, 180, 181, 183). These terms suggest that the attribution of existence to something, X, requires only that the concept existence be connected (conjoined, combined) with X; not that it be contained in X. Nor is it one of the doctrines of "The Nature of Judgment" that simple concepts cannot be connected with other concepts. On the contrary, it is an essential part of its thesis that they can be and are.

What might seem to support Hochberg in the present instance is the passage where Moore states that "a thing becomes intelligible first when it is analysed into its constituent concepts" (*NJ*, 182). For immediately afterwards, Moore goes on to say that "the opposition of concepts to existents disappears, since an existent is seen to be nothing but a concept or a complex of concepts standing in a unique relation to the concept of existence . . ." (*NJ*, 183). In the light of the first passage, the second would seem to say that to call *anything* existent is to imply that it is a composite, one of whose constituents is the concept existence. But if Moore in the passages quoted had meant to propound such a doctrine, then one should have to suppose that in the first sentence quoted he is maintaining that only composites are intelligible, and that is obviously not his contention at all. What seems, rather, to be the case, is that Moore is implicitly drawing on the following distinction, which he makes explicitly at the end of "The Nature of Judgment" as well as throughout *Principia Ethica*. That distinction is between substantives (things) and adjectives (properties, qualities). For instance, in the *Principia* goods (substantively considered) are definable; they are composites, one of whose constituents is good (adjectively considered). But good (adjectively considered) is simple and undefinable. Thus good (adjectival) cannot contain other objects or properties, though it can be connected or attached to them, and when it is, we call them *good.* For example, we may call the simple natural quality of pleasure *good.* In the passages quoted above from *NJ*, 182 and 183, Moore is obviously using the term *an existent* in the way in which he uses the term *good* when speaking of *a* good. He is using it as a substantive; this is indicated by the indefinite article *an.* But because Moore maintains that *an* existent (substantive) is a composite, containing the concept existence, it does not follow that he may not also maintain that existence (adjectival) can be connected with simple concepts, and that in such cases the latter may be said to exist or to be existent, just as pleasure in the *Principia* is said to be good. That Moore does maintain something of this sort is confirmed by the fact that he does explicitly maintain in "The Nature of Judgment" that simple concepts, such as the concept red, exist, and indeed exist in parts of time (*NJ*, 191).

Argument B. The entire force of this argument rests (1) upon distinguishing between a concept and what the concept is of, and (2) maintaining that what a concept is *of,* is (in some sense exclusive of universality) a particular. Now this may be Hochberg's own view of the nature of concepts, and he may be perfectly correct in holding it. It is, however, hard to see what grounds he finds for it in Moore's "analysis of existents" in "The Nature of Judgment." Moore nowhere in that paper holds that what exists is what a concept is "the concept of." Indeed, he could not hold any such doctrine without falling into the most palpable inconsistency. For in "The Nature of Judgment," concepts are the ultimate ontological entities. There *is* nothing beyond concepts. They are the stuff out of which all else is composed. Thus, they cannot be *of* some "third thing." One can only assume that Hochberg is reading into Moore's theories a psychological view of the nature of concepts. But one of the very things that Moore is most concerned to attack in "The Nature of Judgment" is psychologism in philosophy (see *NJ,* 178). As part of this attack, he maintains that concepts are objects existing absolutely independent of mind, and that, indeed, everything else resolves into complexes of these nonpsychological entities, including mind itself (*NJ,* 179, 182, 192-93).

Hochberg's second apparent assumption in argument *B,* that there are, according to the ontology of "The Nature of Judgment," absolute particulars—that is, particulars that contain no universality in their composition—is equally untenable. Moore makes a point of arguing that the question which empiricists find so difficult to answer, "How do we get from particulars to universals?" is easily answered if instead of deriving universals from particulars we derive particulars from universals. And this we can do, he argues, by considering material diversity as resulting from the different relations in which common concepts composing various things or complexes stand to other concepts. "The material diversity of things, which is generally taken as starting-point, is only derived; and the identity of the concept, in several different things, which appears on that assumption [i.e., the empiricist's assumption] as the problem of philosophy, will now, if it instead be taken as the starting-point, render the derivation easy. Two things are then seen to be differentiated by the different relations in which their common concepts stand to other concepts" (*NJ,* 182). In short, according to the ontology of "The Nature of Judgment," there really are no absolute particulars. There are only universals and combinations of universals which are simply *less* general than the universals themselves—that is to say, *relative* particulars.

Argument C. In this argument, Hochberg again seems to impose his own philosophical conceptions upon Moore's text in "The Nature of Judgment." How else does he pass from the antecedent, "if one holds that there is only one simple object which is contained in all yellow patches," to the consequent, "one would then have not only a universal concept, but also a universal particular"? Hochberg passes to this consequent on the assumption that "the simple object which is contained in all yellow patches" is something different from the concept yellow. Here, he may again be thinking of concepts in psychological terms. But Moore is not. In "The Nature of Judgment" it is quite clear that Moore does hold that there is a simple object which is contained in all yellow patches, and he holds that this simple object is the concept yellow. Furthermore, he holds that this simple concept yellow, which is an absolute universal, is the very yellow that we see with our eyes in this patch or that patch of yellow. "It will be apparent," he says (*NJ*, 183), "how much this theory has in common with Kant's theory of perception. It differs chiefly in substituting for sensations, as the data of knowledge, concepts; and in refusing to regard the relations in which they stand as, in some obscure sense, the work of the mind." In fact, Moore not only maintains that the very same objects we see with our eyes are concepts or universals, but he also maintains that we see propositions, which are complexes of concepts: "It now appears that perception is to be regarded philosophically as the cognition of an existential proposition" (*NJ*, 183).[2] Whether this is or is not the extreme "Platonism" of William of Champeaux I am not competent to say; but it most assuredly is that very form of extreme realism that Hochberg contends is "not at all . . . involved, even implicitly, in his [Moore's] discussion."

If one takes what Moore *says* in "The Nature of Judgment," and if one does not mix it up with what one thinks he should have said, one might summarize the ontology of that paper as follows. There are two kinds of simple concepts or universals: *a priori* concepts (e.g., attribute, substance), which do not have any temporal duration, and which may be said (meaning no more than that) to be nonexistent; and empirical concepts (e.g., red, yellow), which do possess temporal duration and which do contingently exist—that is, get connected with the concept existence. All substantives or things, including minds, judgments, and propositions, are composed of simple or adjectival concepts. Existential or empirical propositions are those that contain empirical concepts in their compositions, e.g., "This body is heavy"; *a priori* propositions are those that contain only *a priori* concepts, e.g., "A substance has attributes." There *are* no absolute particulars; only relative particulars, i.e., particular combinations of universals. All that there is, all that we perceive or know, consists ultimately of simple concepts, which are completely independent of each other and of any substantive thing, like mind or judgment. In fact, minds and judgments are merely complexes of concepts.

Now this ontology may be absolutely absurd and wrong. It may be, as Hochberg says, that Moore is "fusing together" concepts and objects, and it may be that this is a very grave categorial error. But whatever Moore may be doing and however wrong it may be, it is obviously nothing resembling nominalism. If a name is to be applied to Moore's ontology of 1899, it might be termed "Absolute Reductive Realism," for whereas nominalists would say that all that there are in the last analysis are particulars, Moore is saying that all that there are in the last analysis are simple concepts, or adjectival universals.

It may be profitable here to return to the charge Hochberg makes that Moore is fusing concepts with objects or particulars. This charge, I believe, is essentially correct. Where Hochberg goes wrong—probably due to nominalistic leanings of his own—is in interpreting this fusion to mean that Moore reduces concepts or universals to particulars. But the case is just the other way around: Moore, if he is reducing anything to anything else, is reducing particulars to universals.

The ontology of *Principia Ethica* does, as Hochberg maintains, seem to be very similar to that propounded in "The Nature of Judgment." But for that very reason, the difference between natural and nonnatural properties cannot, as Hochberg thinks, be explained as a difference between particulars and universals. It will have to be explained as a difference between two sorts of universals—empirical and *a priori* universals. Moreover, only on this assumption is it possible to account for the fact that there is, in Moore's mind (but not in Hochberg's), no difference in "structure" between the fallacy of defining good (adjectival) in terms of a natural object and that of defining it in terms of a metaphysical or nonnatural object. Says Moore on page 39 of *Principia Ethica*, "It should be observed that the fallacy, by reference to which I define 'Metaphysical Ethics' [i.e., the fallacy of defining good, adjectival, in terms of some nonnatural object] is the same in kind [i.e., as defining it in terms of a natural object]; and I give it but one name, the Naturalistic Fallacy."

Argument D. Since Moore plainly maintains in "The Nature of Judgment" that universals exist, the present argument has really no application to that paper. However, it may seem to have some application to Moore's subsequent philosophizing, for there he does sometimes—as in the lectures of 1910-11[3]—assert that universals do not exist. Moreover, he subsequently gives up the view that the world is composed solely of concepts or universals. By the time of the 1910-11 lectures, for instance, he explicitly maintains that there are at least three sorts of absolute particulars: sense-data (e.g., *patches* of yellow), acts of consciousness (e.g., the act of knowing as opposed to the object known), and material things. And this would appear to remain his view until his very last published writing, "Visual Sense-Data" (1957). Finally, whereas Moore is inclined in these subsequent writings to assert that universals do not exist, he does maintain that sense-data, acts of consciousness, and material things do exist. It may appear, therefore, that Moore was essentially a nominalist in his philosophizing subsequent to "The Nature of Judgment." This, however, would be a complete misconception.

What this misconception rests upon primarily is the nominalistic assumption that the major ontological division is between existence and nonexistence. But this simply is not Moore's view. For Moore, the major ontological division is between being and nonbeing. Moore is, in fact, not even very sure that there is any real or significant difference between existence and being. If there is, it only amounts to the possession of temporal duration, or (in the lectures of 1910-11) particularity. Thus, even if truths or facts and universals do not exist—that is to say, even if they possess no temporal duration and therefore are not parts of Nature—this does not mean that they are not significant constituents of the Universe. On the contrary, Moore always maintains that they are significant constituents of the Universe. He commends metaphysicians for recognizing that they are (*Principia Ethica*, p. 110). And in his lectures of 1910-11 he reiterates the point, contending that the important thing is not that universals, facts, etc., exist or do not exist, but that they *are*, as opposed to chimeras which *are not*. I quote from the last two pages of *Some Main Problems of Philosophy*:

> I have distinguished three different kinds of constituents of the Universe, namely (1) particulars, (2) truths or facts, and (3) universals. And there does seem a certain amount of reason for saying that, of these three kinds of things, it is only particulars

which "exist"; that truths and universals do not exist, but *only* have *being* or *are*. It is certainly more natural to say of a particular thing that it "exists" than to say this of the truth that twice two are four, or of the number two itself; though the usage is certainly not fixed. If, therefore, anybody chooses to say that universals don't exist, and in that sense are not "real," I don't want to deny that this may possibly be the case. There may, I think, possibly be some property, which is what we generally mean by "existence," which *does* belong to all particulars over and above *the* property in virtue of which we call them particulars, and which does not belong to truths or universals. I think it is doubtful whether this is the case; I think it is doubtful whether particulars have any kind of reality which truths and universals have not got: whether, in short, the only difference between them does not consist simply and solely in the fact that particulars *are* particulars, whereas truths and universals are not. But whether this be so or not—whether or not we ought to recognize a distinction between existence and being, *over and above* the distinction between particulars on the one hand and truth and universals on the other—what I want to insist on is that this distinction between existence and being is in any case not nearly so important as that between things which do have being and those which simply have not got it, are purely imaginary, and don't belong to the Universe at all. The property of being which certainly does belong to truths and universals *as well as* to particulars is ever so much more important than any which distinguishes them from one another.[4]

And having made these points clear, Moore goes on to attack those who degrade universals—patently, the nominalists:

The fundamental question for philosophy is to discover whether certain things do or do not belong to the Universe. And it is, I think, this fundamental distinction which is overlooked by those who talk as if universals . . . were . . . pure fictions and something negligible. Those who talk in this way do, I think, really mean to degrade universals to the levels of griffins and chimaeras. . . . If you fix clearly in your mind the sense in which there certainly are no such things as griffins and chimaeras, that seems to me to give the sense in which it is important to enquire whether there are such things as universals or not. And if you do fix this sense clearly, it seems to me quite plain that there *are* such things, that universals are not in any way to be classed with griffins and chimaeras; that, on the contrary, there is *the* most fundamental difference in the Universe between the two, a difference ever so much more important than that which separates universals from particulars.[5]

Now it is not my intention here to rewrite Hochberg's paper and to state what I think are the confusions in Moore's ontology and their sources. Nor is it my intention to explain just what Moore's final views are on the nature of universals, especially universals like shades of color. It will have to suffice to affirm dogmatically that Moore does maintain that a shade of color is not a particular, and that, though I see a patch of some shade of color when I see a yellow patch, the particular (or sense-datum) is the patch, not the shade of color of which it is a patch.[6] My one concern has been to correct what I feel to be certain very grave misrepresentations of Moore's ontology in Hochberg's article: in particular, those misrepresentations that tend to give Moore the appearance of a nominalist. Before concluding, however, I would like to make this further, though minor, correction. Hochberg, in a footnote (p. 125), tells us that "the ontological status of mind is not discussed by Moore in this paper [i.e., "The Nature of Judgment"]." For Mr. Hochberg's information, I quote the last four sentences of that paper:

> For we must, if we are to be consistent, describe what appears to be most substantive as no more than a collection of such supposed adjectives: and thus, in the end, the concept turns out to be the only substantive or subject, and no one concept either more or less an adjective than any other. From our description of a judgment, there must, then, disappear all reference either to our mind or to the world. Neither of these can furnish "ground" for anything, save in so far as they are complex judgments. The nature of the judgment is more ultimate than either, and less ultimate only than the nature of its constituents—the nature of the concept or logical idea.

Notes

1. G. E. Moore, "The Nature of Judgment," *Mind*, XXX (April, 1889), 191. References to this article will henceforth be made by the abbreviation NJ.
2. How seriously Moore took this view, even some time after the publication of *Principia*, is suggested by J. M. Keynes in his *Two Memoirs* (London, 1949), where he recounts that "Moore had a nightmare once in which he

could not distinguish propositions from tables" (p. 94). Keynes adds, percep-
tively, "But even when he was awake, he could not distinguish love and
beauty and truth from the furniture. They took on the same definition of
outline, the same stable, solid, objective qualities and common-sense reality."
This is hardly the perspective of a nominalist!

3. Hochberg seems to date those lectures, now comprising the contents
of *Some Main Problems of Philosophy* (London: Allen & Unwin, 1953), as
belonging to the year 1913. Moore, in the preface of *Some Main Problems
of Philosophy*, describes them as having been delivered in 1910-11. The same
date, 1910-11, is suggested also in his autobiographical note in Paul A.
Schilpp (ed.), *The Philosophy of G. E. Moore* (Evanston: Northwestern
University Press, 1942), p. 27.

4. *Some Main Problems of Philosophy*, pp. 372-73.

5. *Loc. cit.*

6. See *Some Main Problems of Philosophy* (London: Allen & Unwin, 1953),
p. 30, footnote 2; also appendix, pp. 374-78. See also *Philosophical Papers*,
"Are the Characteristics of Particular Things Universal or Particular" (London: Allen & Unwin, 1959), p. 26: "For I maintain that the same indivisible
quality [Moore is speaking of specific colors] can really *be* locally or temporally separate; maintaining that all this means is that it can really belong
to both of two concrete things or events which are, in the fundamental sense
appropriate to concrete things or events, locally or temporally separate."

Eight

SOME REFLECTIONS ON MR. NELSON'S CORRECTIONS

Herbert Hochberg

MR. NELSON SETS OUT by stating that I *suggest* that Moore is *essentially* a nominalist. His assertion, depending on quite vague uses of the two terms 'suggest' and 'essentially,' is overly simple and decidedly false. I spoke, throughout my paper, of the nominalistic and realistic strains in Moore's thought. In this vein I said such things as: (1) "Moore thus explicitly recognizes two sorts of entities—existents and nonexistents. Within the first category we have . . . particulars. In the second there are properties . . . " (p. 373). (2) ". . . for his nominalism is tempered by the addition of universals, as nonexistent entities, to his ontology" (p. 373). (3) "Like the realist, Moore retains the exemplification relation and atemporality of universals; but, identifying, like the nominalist, *existing* with *being in time*. . . . " (p. 373). (4) "For once one has confused simple objects with universal concepts, what one says may be interpreted as indicating both realism and nominalism" (p. 384). (5) "Moore might be thought to have nominalistic leanings in that (*a*) he has simple objects; (*b*) concepts are nonexistents; and, most important, (*c*) he confuses concepts with simple objects" (p. 393). (6) "For his simple objects . . . are *composed* of concepts, which are clearly not mind-*dependent* but are the ultimate *independent* entities. In this sense Moore is, of course, far from being a nominalist" (p. 394).[1]

Reading the above quotations should make it clear why Mr. Nelson uses 'suggest' and 'essentially' instead of citing any quotation from my paper. However, my abundant use of the term 'nominalism' may have been misleading. Let me, then, briefly restate what is involved. Moore asserts in *Principia* (1903) that nonnatural properties do not exist and that natural properties are existent, substantial parts of particular objects. These claims are made in connection with, and are a crucial part of, his distinction between natural and nonnatural properties. I have argued that, when he speaks of properties existing in time in *Principia*, he is talking of what some call perfect particulars, others quality instances, or, in my essay, simple objects. The paper, "Identity," of 1901 is quite explicit on the subject of such quality instances. Moore argues there that such things exist and are parts of ordinary particular objects. He there deliberately and explicitly separates such entities from Platonic universals.[2] Consequently, in 1903 we have Moore adhering to the two themes that nonnatural properties do not exist and that natural properties do exist, after explicitly, in 1901, holding that particular quality instances do exist. Moreover, in 1901 such quality instances are held to stand in a fundamental asymmetrical relation (exemplification?) to some universal. But there is a problem, for in 1903 he speaks of two kinds of properties, natural and nonnatural, whereas, in 1901, he spoke of quality instances and universals. What is the difference? A fundamental difference, which fits Moore's characterization of 1903, is, I suggest, that nonnatural properties are construed as universals, while natural properties are existent, particular, substantial quality instances. But then, what has happened to the universals, like red, of 1901 and the universal concepts of 1899? The answer is that Moore, in 1903, has fused such universals with their quality instances. This explains both the distinction between natural and nonnatural properties and why it is made the way it is in 1903. If we then go back to the 1899 paper, we can see the origin of the view and the confusion that dominates *Principia*. All of this was involved in my speaking of Moore's nominalism, as I hoped would be clear from my paper. To put it succinctly, what was "essentially" involved in my "suggestion" that there were nominalistic strains in Moore's thought was twofold: first, there is his distinction between substantive existent quality instances and the merely adjectival, nonexistent universals; second, there is his apparent abandoning, in *Prin-*

cipia, of universals like yellow in favor of instances of yellow. That is, when he speaks of *the property yellow* in *Principia* he is talking of *a quality instance,* but when he speaks of *the property good* he is speaking about *the nonexistent universal.* This, and only this, is what I essentially meant by speaking of Moore's nominalism.

Mr. Nelson proceeds to give three apparent arguments for three claims that he believes must be involved in Moore's 1899 paper, if my analysis of it is correct. First, Moore must maintain that every existential assertion is either necessarily and self-evidently true or false. Mr. Nelson does not bother to clarify, for us, his use of terms like 'necessary' and 'self-evident.' But that is not crucial, as his argument is inept in any reasonable sense of those problematic terms. He considers the assertion that there exists a spider in the house next door. He believes that, on my analysis of Moore, we refer either to the concept (of the spider next door) or to the spider. If the former, the judgment is (necessarily?) false, since concepts do not inhabit houses; if the latter, it must be true since existence is part of the composite which is the spider. As Mr. Nelson offers no argument to support his belief, it is not clear what particular error is responsible for it, for there are several possibilities. He could, for example, simply have confused the object, which the phrase 'the spider next door' would designate, if there were such a thing, with the concept which the phrase "means" or "expresses," whether there is a spider or not. If we do not confuse these entities, it is clear that the description would not refer to the concept. But then, it is also clear that there is a possibility that it does not refer at all, even if there is a concept it expresses or means. Along this line, Mr. Nelson might think that since the concept existence is part of the combination of concepts which is the spider, on my analysis of Moore, when we speak of the spider *we mean* "the combination of concepts . . . including existence." Hence, the sentence 'the spider exists' would be true by virtue of its meaning and, in that sense, necessarily true. In part, such a line of thought would mix meaning (a concept) with reference (an object). The phrase 'the spider next door' may refer to, and *in that sense mean,* the spider, if there is one, but the concept existence is not part of the meaning of the phrase 'the spider next door' for it is not part of *the concept of the spider next door.* Mr. Nelson would have made a more relevant objection if he took the case of 'Paul is yellow.' Here, the concept yellow is part of the concept of Paul. Hence one may, as I mentioned in my paper, face the problem of turning such sentences into analytic truths, on a suitable notion of *analytic*. But even here, it is not necessary that one hold such propositions to be analytic. For one can hold, as Russell did in *An Inquiry into Meaning and Truth* and as I have argued elsewhere,[3] that the term 'Paul' simply functions as a designating label in such sentences. Even on a reference theory of meaning, we could distinguish between the referent as the meaning of a simple label and the sense in which a sentence like 'All bachelors are unmarried' is held to be true in virtue of *the meaning* of its terms, since one is involved in the definition of the other. The proper name 'Paul,' being a primitive or undefined term, does not have yellow as part of its meaning in the sense in which either *being unmarried* may be said to be part of the meaning of the term 'bachelor' or being white may be said to be part of the meaning of the phrase 'the white winged horse.' We must not be misled by thinking that the two claims that (1) the object is the referent (or even the meaning) of the term 'Paul' and (2) that the object is composed of concepts, including yellow, imply that yellow is part of the meaning of the term 'Paul,' and, hence, that 'Paul is yellow' is analytic or true by the meanings involved. To analyze the object as a composite of concepts is not to say that the proper name of the object is defined in terms of the predicates referring to the concepts involved. In short, the sentence 'Paul is yellow' is not to be confused with a sentence like 'A complex of concepts containing yellow contains yellow.' Moore's view complicates matters, since we must deal with the complex concept of Paul, which, apparently, provides the meaning for the term 'Paul' instead of the referent doing so. But one can attempt to make a similar point in such a context, and there are indications Moore would do so in that the sentence is true if certain concepts do in fact combine, on his view. Moreover, his treatment of the term 'this' fits such a pattern. Hence, I "suggest" that one may keep the basic features of Moore's ontology, as I have outlined it, without turning sentences like 'Paul is yellow' into tautologies. Alternatively, one may hold that the label 'Paul' merely functions as an abbreviation for 'the yellow . . . ' and argue that, properly understood, the sentence 'Paul is yellow' is analytic or necessary or redundant. But, no matter which way one tries to deal with statements like 'Paul is yellow,' the existential statements do not turn out to be necessary on my analysis of Moore.

Mr. Nelson's choice of terminology reveals his difficulty in comprehending the questions involved. Thus, he says that I implicitly ascribe to Moore the view that "every existential proposition is necessarily true because particulars contain existence as part of their essence." If the notion of "essence" has any relevance here, it would serve to indicate those parts of the object which are also parts of the concept of it, i.e., those concepts which are constituents of the spider as well as of the concept of the spider. These concepts could be any whatsoever *except for that of existence* (perhaps the temporal, spatial, and relational ones also). I had, in fact, mentioned that Moore's view is reminiscent of earlier philosophers who took the object to be a composite of essence *and* existence. It seems obvious what Mr. Nelson has done. He uses the term 'essence' so that any constituent concept of an object is held to be part of the latter's essence, since the object is taken as a composite of such concepts. He then seeks to use the term 'essence' to attack my analysis. Now, it is perfectly proper to introduce terminology. But having done so, one should not make use of other, and older, connotations of a term. Thus, Mr. Nelson proceeds to argue that, on my analysis, things *necessarily* exist since *existence is part of their essence.* In so doing, he cavalierly makes use of the traditional connection between the notions of 'essential' and 'necessary,' and hence becomes entangled in his own terminology. Moreover, Mr. Nelson proceeds to compound his mistake. For, even if he were correct in claiming that, on my analysis, those things which exist do so necessarily, it would still not follow that all existential propositions used to assert that a particular exists (as opposed to a concept) are necessarily true. Mr. Nelson has committed what is known as a "howler." From the way he puts matters, there may be three further errors responsible for his claim. First, he sets up a dichotomy so that we must be referring to either the concept of the spider or the spider in the sentence in question. He then holds that in the former case the proposition is false, in the latter it is true. He does not seem to recognize that we might not be referring to anything at all. This could be due to his taking 'referring' in an ambiguous sense that covers both referring and, as some put it, purporting to refer. Mixing these two could lead one to ignore the possibility of my purporting to refer to the spider but actually referring to neither such a thing nor the concept of it. Thus one could come to believe that if he is not referring to the concept of the spider, he must be referring to an object, the spider. In short, if one believes that he is always referring to something in existential statements, either a concept or an object, and if he also believes that reference to a concept is precluded in certain cases, he will conclude that we must refer to an object in those cases. But surely, he would only come to believe that he is always referring to something if he mixes referring with purporting to refer. A second mistake that might be involved is the possibility that Mr. Nelson identifies an existential statement's being false with its being about concepts rather than particulars. That is, he could have unwittingly transposed the clauses of his claim that if the statement is about concepts it is false. This simple error could also lead him to hold that if it is not about concepts, but particulars, then it is true. Thus, just being "about" a particular, in the sense of purporting to refer to one, would suffice to make an existential statement true. Finally, he could have confused a conditional statement with the assertion that the spider exists. For, *if there is a spider*, then, *given my analysis*, it is necessary that there is a combination of concepts including existence. This no more implies that the combination (the spider) necessarily exists than 'if p then necessarily p' implies 'p is necessarily true.'[4]

Moore, says Mr. Nelson in stating his second complaint, "explicitly maintains that some concepts exist in parts of time" and, therefore, I was mistaken when I held that a concept, for Moore, does not exist in time since only particulars, and not universals, exist in time. Moore does say, in this instance, what Mr. Nelson quotes him as saying. I, too, quoted such passages. The problem arises if we ponder, rather than merely parrot, the statements. In this vein let us consider the particular patch, Paul, and the property yellow that we may truly attribute to it. There is clearly a sense in which I may say that Paul existed before another yellow patch, say Peter. Yet we would not wish to hold that yellow existed before yellow. All we would mean, if we did assert such a thing, would be that a yellow thing existed before a different yellow thing. Moore, like any philosopher who thinks about the issues of particulars and universals, recognizes such a trivial point. This means that the phrase 'exists in time' is ambiguous. For, while I can say of Peter, Paul, and the universal yellow that they all exist in time, I do not mean the same thing in the case of the universal and in that of the particulars. This is particularly so on Moore's view, since he does explicitly hold that objects are (1) complexes of concepts and (2) existential propositions. Peter and Paul are composites, for Moore. Moreover, they are composites of concepts. They are existent objects, on his view, since certain concepts (yellow, square, etc.) combine with the concept existence and temporal concepts. One may then say that they are temporal objects in that *they contain* a temporal concept, *not* in that *they com-*

bine with a temporal concept. For what combines with a temporal concept and the concept of existence must be another concept or set of such that is itself a concept. *In this sense,* the concept yellow cannot be coherently said to be *in time.* The concept yellow can be said to be in time in the sense that it combines with temporal concepts (in a yellow object like Paul). But this I certainly did not deny. In fact, it is a crucial part of my analysis of Moore. Thus, to quote Moore as saying that some concepts exist in time in that they combine with temporal concepts and existence neither resolves nor clarifies anything but merely introduces the problem. To get back to the problem, let us return to the case of Paul.

There is a difference between the *object* and the *concept* of it. When I assert 'Paul exists' that statement is true if there is a certain combination of concepts connected with existence and each other.

> When I say "This paper exists," . . . if it is true, it means only that the concepts, which are combined in specific relations in the concept of this paper, are also combined in a specific manner with the concept of existence.[5]

What then exists is Paul; but what is connected with existence are the constituent concepts of the object (some of which are also "in" the concept of it). Consider, next, the simple concept yellow. Suppose it combines with existence and a temporal concept. The composite of yellow, existence, and the temporal concept cannot be identified with the *simple* concept yellow. This is a mere tautology. But two alternatives are possible. One could hold that what goes for complex concepts like that of Paul does not go for simple ones like yellow. Hence, in the present case, there is not a composite entity which is the simple particular (or existential proposition). Alternatively, one could hold that what goes for complex concepts also holds for simple ones. Then, there is an existential proposition or object which is the composite of yellow, existence, and a temporal concept. There is an inherent ambiguity, which I noted in my paper, that creates a problem for the unwary reader. When we say 'Paul exists' or 'Paul is yellow' it appears as if we are connecting the subject and predicate, but what we are asserting, on Moore's pattern, is that certain combinations of concepts are entities or, to put it in another way, that certain concepts combine with each other. Thus, when we say 'red exists' or 'yellow exists,' we are likewise asserting that there is a certain combination, if we treat the existential statements uniformly. Moreover, there are fairly clear indications that

Moore tended to think that what applies to complex concepts applies to simple ones as well:

> The opposition of concepts to existents disappears, since an existent is seen to be nothing but a concept or complex of concepts standing in a unique relation to the concept of existence. Even the description of an existent as a proposition (a true existential proposition) seems to lose its strangeness, when it is remembered that a proposition is here to be understood, not as anything subjective—an assertion or affirmation of something—but as the combination of concepts which is affirmed.[6]

The pattern is clear: existents are combinations of concepts including existence, i.e., true existential propositions. Thus, in spite of the ambiguity invited by speaking of the existent as a composite of concepts standing in a relation to existence as well as speaking of it as a composite of concepts which are related to each other and to existence, it is clear that what exists in the case of Paul is the object, but what stands in relation to existence is a concept or set of such and not the object. Applying this pattern to simple concepts introduces the simple objects. It is also clear that if one then insists that a simple concept like red exists, he cannot mean the same thing that is meant by saying Paul exists. Hence, one must either hold that composites are ultimately composed of nonexistent concepts (but entities nevertheless), or consider the constituents to be other than simple concepts, or hold that the simple concepts exist in some other sense. By 1901, Moore takes the first step at resolution; the constituents of the existent objects are explicitly taken as existent simple objects. The pattern of 1899, I have argued, dictates the solution of 1901 or, at least, sets the stage for it. That the solution is announced in 1901 and exploited in 1903 in *Principia* is the external evidence for the interpretation of the 1899 paper. That it is the only way of reconciling, coherently, the statements of 1899 is the internal evidence. But let me spell it out a bit further.

Mr. Nelson would have it that the objects, like Paul and the spider, do not contain but are related to existence, and likewise for the simple concept red. But, as we saw, Moore clearly identifies existent objects with existential propositions. On this ground alone simple concepts cannot be existents! He also tells us that propositions are composites of concepts. Existential propositions, moreover, contain the concept existence: they are not related to existence. As Moore puts it:

> A proposition is a synthesis of concepts. . . . A proposition is constituted by any number of concepts, together with a specific relation between them; . . . Existence is itself a concept; it is something which we mean; and the great body of propositions, *in which* existence is joined to other concepts or syntheses of concepts. . . .[7]

It immediately follows that existent objects contain existence, rather than stand in relation to it. Furthermore, Moore explicitly states "All that exists is thus composed of concepts necessarily related to one another in specific manners, and likewise to the concept of existence."[8] It is clear that what is related to the concept existence is not the composite existent but the other constituent concepts of the object. Aside from such statements, we might ask, if Paul is related to existence and does not contain it, what distinguishes the object from the concept of it on Moore's view? It will not do to say that one stands in a relation to existence that the other does not, if both are composed of the same constituents. Moore would probably hold that this presupposes that they are already different entities.[9] If it is held that they are distinguished in that the constituent concepts stand in one relation in the object and in another relation in the concept of it, then we distinguish the object from the concept of it, not in that the object stands in a relation to the concept of existence, but in that it contains a distinguishing combinatorial relation. Even if Moore intends to distinguish the relations that combine the constituent concepts into the concept of Paul and the object Paul (the R_1 and R_2 of my present paper), it is, as he makes explicit, the fact that a relation holds *among existence and the other constituent concepts* that is the basis for there being an object. One cannot then maintain that the object Paul is related to existence in a different way from that in which the object is related to its color, i.e., containing it. We might also note that one could not say, about the concept existence itself, that it exists in that it combines with itself. Or, perhaps more modestly, I for one would not know what that means.[10] Yet existence is the crucial concept in the analysis of existents. If one is forced to take it as a nonexistent simple building block of the universe, one should not worry about taking universals like red as such also. Be that as it may, suppose, for the moment, that one takes the universal concept red to be an existent, since it combines with existence and a temporal concept on occasion. There would still be the composites of the concept red, existence, and a temporal concept. Such composites are, for Moore, existential propositions and, moreover, entities which contain existence and time. Moreover, there could be several of them containing red, since that concept may combine with existence at several times. There are, after all, several different red things. These relatively simple composites would still differ from the universal red and are clearly the prototypes of the quality instances of 1901. To see that they may also be the prototypes of the natural properties of 1903, we need only recall that a natural property, for Moore, is capable of existing "*by itself* in *time* and not merely as a property of some natural objects." Thus, in the case of a natural property, we have, in the language of 1899, the combination of a concept, existence, and time. This is precisely the composite of the 1899 paper. Perhaps I have not demonstrated that the natural properties are such composites.[11] We should still note that Moore speaks of objects in *Principia*, as he does in 1899, as *composites* of properties (concepts in 1899). Further, I have at least demonstrated that there are simple objects for Moore in 1899; the composites like that of red, existence, and a temporal concept. There are no such composites for concepts like good in 1903. Hence, even if Moore was talking about the *universal* red as a natural property in 1903, there would still be the fundamental difference that natural properties have corresponding simple objects while nonnatural ones do not. But, if we now recall the 1901 paper, the matter seems fairly clear. For there, Moore explicitly declares the constituent property of an object like a red square is not the universal red but a quality instance that exemplifies it. It is that quality instance which is in space and time. But, if I am mistaken and the doctrine of 1903 harks back to that of 1899, rather than to that of 1901, in that the constituents of objects are universal properties, there still remains the second fundamental distinction between natural and nonnatural properties. The latter are exemplified by objects, while the former combine with other natural properties to constitute the object. Hence, natural properties are not exemplified, but contained. The 1899 paper would thus still be the ontological basis of the distinction between natural and nonnatural properties in 1903.

Mr. Nelson's third complaint is that on my analysis Moore will have to maintain that existence "arises out of nonexistence" and "temporal particulars out of nontemporal universals." If 'arises out of' merely is a more "dynamic" sounding synonym for 'is analyzed in terms of,' then all Mr. Nelson does here is to repeat, in different words, that I have said that existent particulars are analyzed in terms of nonexistent universals. Thus he repeats his earlier complaints. If 'arises out of' means something else, I must confess its meaning escapes me.

Mr. Nelson proceeds to "analyze" four arguments of mine, which he labels A, B, C, D. A involves the question of the existence of simple concepts, which we have covered in detail. But in his discussion he makes much of the distinction between substantives and adjectives in *Principia* and identifies adjectives with properties and qualities. What he overlooks is that Moore tells us in *Principia* that natural properties are substantives, not adjectives. Hence his identification of property with adjective is a bit off. For the rest, he devotes a number of words to arguing that Moore holds that concepts can combine with existence: of course.

His discussion of B opens by stating that I hold that there is a distinction between a concept and what the concept is of. Surely: Moore clearly makes the distinction, and I do not think we would want to identify the concept of the spider with the spider. As Mr. Nelson noted earlier, spiders live in houses, concepts of them do not. But Nelson takes this innocent distinction as evidence that I believe that when there is a concept then there is something that it is of. This does not follow nor did I assert it. He next says that I mention that concepts are of particulars for Moore. I do not find such a statement. What I said was that concepts like the concept red were not to be confused with concepts like Paul, for the concept red was not the concept *of* red. Whether there could be further concepts *of* universals like red, as distinct from the concept red, was something I did not discuss, though I did discuss the concept truth which applies to propositions. Mr. Nelson then says that I hold that Moore's ontology of 1899 contains "absolute particulars— that is, particulars that contain no universals in their composition." He then cites Moore on this matter. He does not cite my paper on this, and that is understandable. For I held no such thing about the 1899 paper. The simple particulars of which I spoke in connection with the 1899 paper were clearly composed of universals, as I explicitly said. Need one do more than recall the distinction between C and C*? Mr. Nelson obviously overlooked the way I used the term 'simple object.' The simple particulars of which I spoke, like yellow$_1$, were explicitly stated to be simple, relative to complex particulars like Paul; but (see quote [6] on pages 141-42 above) they, in turn, were construed as complexes of universal concepts.

In argument C Mr. Nelson reveals what is most charitably described as excessive carelessness. He writes, quoting me,

> How else does he pass from the antecedent, "if one holds that there is only one simple object which is contained in all yellow patches," to the consequent, "one would then have not only a universal concept, but also a universal particular"? Hochberg passes to this consequent on the assumption that "the simple object which is contained in all yellow patches" is something different from the concept yellow. Here he may again be thinking in psychological terms. But Moore is not.[12]

If one compares his quotation with the text of my paper one discovers that a single word has been omitted by Mr. Nelson. Between the words 'one' and 'simple,' in the second line of the above quotation, my article contains the word 'such.' The term 'such' would make it apparent that the quoted statement depends on a preceding discussion. The preceding discussion, in turn, reveals that I pass from the antecedent to the consequent quite easily. For the "one *such* simple object" I am talking about is, as I am using my terms, by definition a particular. It is a simple object, in my sense, that is held to be common to several different ordinary objects. In short, it is a particular that functions like a universal. This, I suggested, could be one way of taking a certain medieval gambit of extreme realism. Mr. Nelson says he is not competent to talk about William of Champeaux. This I will grant him, but I find it ironic that after such a declaration of lack of competence, he asserts that it is precisely that form of realism (William of Champeaux's) that is involved in Moore's view. One would think, or at least hope, that the one declaration would prevent the other. In any case, what Mr. Nelson has obviously done is take the realism involved to be that which holds we must acknowledge universals. This, to be tedious, Moore of course does, but it is not relevant to my remark about extreme realism.

Mr. Nelson closes his paper by saying that "It will have to suffice to affirm dogmatically that Moore does maintain that a shade of color is not a particular." I can understand his need to be dogmatic, but it will not suffice. For, again, he oversimplifies things. To be sure the patch, say Paul, is distinct from the property yellow. But, for Moore, to speak of the property yellow clearly involves, in 1901, two quite distinct entities: the particular property in Paul and the universal exemplified by it, i.e., by the particular property. Hence, the color yellow is a universal, but the color in Paul is not.

There is one point on which Mr. Nelson is correct. I did mistakenly give 1913 as the date for the lectures of *Some Main Problems of Philosophy*. He is correct in noting that they were given in 1910-11.

Notes

1. As my paper in the present volume is a rewritten version of the original, all quotations shall be from the original and page references will be to *The Review of Metaphysics*, XV (March, 1962). None of the changes is relevant to Mr. Nelson's arguments, except for a less abundant use of the term 'nominalism' in the present version. This does not at all affect how I characterized Moore's view, but merely, I hope, clarifies the characterization.

2. I shall not quote from that paper as one of the key quotations already occurs in my essay, and this volume contains a lengthy analysis of the paper "Identity" in my "Moore and Russell on Particulars, Relations, and Identity."

3. See the last two chapters of the *Inquiry* (London: Allen & Unwin, 1940), and my "Things and Qualities," in Daniel Merrill and William Capitan (eds.), *Metaphysics and Explanation* (Pittsburgh: University of Pittsburgh Press, 1966).

4. Mr. Nelson's discussion of Moore on necessity is quite inadequate and based largely on piecemeal quotation. Without getting involved in a lengthy discussion, one can see how far off he is when one notes that what Moore is after, and ends with, is the necessity of the simple existential judgment 'Red exists now.' Moreover, what he means by necessity, here, is simply that a true proposition is true for all time, if true at all. In fact, Moore comes to hold: "Our result then is as follows: That a judgment is universally a necessary combination of concepts, equally necessary whether it be true or false." G. E. Moore, "The Nature of Judgment," *Mind*, XXX (April, 1899), p. 192. The key point is that Moore is seeking to have the ground of the proposition's truth be the proposition itself, and not, in Bradley's fashion, the relation of concepts to reality. This is behind the identification of existents with existential propositions. But it also creates difficulties for the identification of objects with existential propositions.

5. *Ibid.*, pp. 180-81.

6. *Ibid.*, pp. 182-83. This quotation lies behind the major change in my paper. I had earlier misunderstood Moore to be holding that existential propositions were among the existents rather than, as he explicitly says, that existents are existential propositions. This enables one to simplify the treatment of the relations connecting concepts into complexes.

7. *Ibid.*, p. 180. Italics added.

8. *Ibid.*, p. 181.

9. This is exactly the argument pattern Moore uses in his paper "Identity" (*Proceedings of the Aristotelian Society*, I [1901]) to argue against qualitative

individuation (an apparent change from the 1899 paper) and which Russell much later adopts in "On the Relations of Universals and Particulars." This is not to say that I hold his argument in "Identity" to be correct (see my analysis of it in this volume). For here the question is not to distinguish two ordinary objects that are composites of the same universals in terms of relational properties, but to distinguish two different types of objects. In any case the question is whether Moore would be likely to accept such a line of thought.

10. One could say that the concept existence is an existent in the sense that it combines with other concepts to constitute existents. Thus, by saying it exists one merely means that there are existents. This is, I believe, a strand of Moore's thought, in 1899. To say 'Red exists' sometimes seems to mean no more than that there are red things. This is suggested, as is Moore's tendency to fuse the simple concept with a combination containing it, by the following passage: "It is at first sight tempting to say that the truth of a proposition depends on its relation to reality; that any proposition is true which consists of a combination of concepts that is actually found among existents. . . . But if this constituted the truth of a proposition, concepts too might in themselves be true. Red would be a true concept, because there actually are red things; and conversely a chimera would be a false concept, because no such combination either has been, is, or will be (so far as we know) among existent things" ("Nature of Judgment," p. 180). What is peculiar about the passage is that he would not have to conclude that red is a true concept since there are red things, as red is not a "combination of concepts." One can raise the problem Moore does here only if he tends to fuse simple concepts with combinations involving them. Also, note that red would be called "true," not if the *universal* red existed but *if red things existed*; this is how the concept would be related to reality. It is quite suggestive that the simple concept red is contrasted with the *nonexistent combination* of the chimera. This clearly involves pairing the concept red and red things as the concept of Paul and Paul are paired.

11. However, if any arguments against taking simple concepts as existents are cogent and if the statements of 1903, to the effect that natural properties exist in time by themselves, are taken as later versions of earlier statements like 'Red exists now,' then the point has been demonstrated.

12. J. O. Nelson, "Mr. Hochberg on Moore: Some Corrections," p. 135 above.

Nine

MOORE AND RUSSELL ON PARTICULARS, RELATIONS, AND IDENTITY

Herbert Hochberg

IN HIS ESSAY "On the Relations of Universals and Particulars"[1] Russell stated that his view was "closely similar to that of Mr. Moore's paper 'Identity.'" The view he purported to establish was that *particulars*—instances of universals—exist as well as universals. In this paper I wish to examine the arguments of Moore and Russell for the existence of particulars. In so doing, we shall see that in a sense Moore and Russell did not share the same view as to what particulars are and that neither proved that particulars, as they considered them, exist. But they did prove the existence of "particulars" in some sense of that term. First we shall consider Moore's argument.

I. Moore on Difference and Particulars

Before stating Moore's argument I will provide a setting for it by discussing something that is crucially, though only implicitly, involved.

This paper was presented to seminars at Queen's College, Edinburgh, the University of St. Andrews, the University of Sussex, and Göteborg University during 1965-66.

Moore argues for particulars by arguing against the view that an ordinary object, e.g., a colored square, is a composite of universal properties. He seeks to refute this and establish the existence of particulars by arguing against the denial of numerical difference. To deny numerical difference is to assert that for two objects, say two white squares, to differ they must differ conceptually, i.e., in a property or "predicate." He thus implicitly equates three claims:

(A) There are no particulars;

(B) There is only conceptual difference; and

(C) Objects are composed of universal properties (concepts, qualities).

One can understand why he equates (A), (B), and C. Suppose one holds (D) *that two complex entities to be two must differ in a constituent*. If one also held that objects were composites of their universal properties, he would hold that two such composites must differ in at least one constitutent property. Thus, if there are two, they differ conceptually. Likewise, if one object had a property that "another" did not, there would clearly be two objects and not one; otherwise, one and the same object both would and would not have a certain property. Hence there will be two objects if and only if they differ conceptually. On the other hand, if two objects can only differ conceptually, then one is led to take them as composites of qualities. For, if they were not, they would contain something other than a quality to ground their difference. But this would give rise to the possibility of the objects' differing without differing in a quality. Implicitly assuming (D) can thus lead one to equate (B) and (C). To hold that objects are composed only of universal properties and hence (assuming [D]) that if objects differ they differ in a concept, or conceptually, is to deny that there are constituents of the different objects which are *not* universals and which *just differ* from each other and from every other similar sort of thing in any other object. Such things, if there are any, would be *particular* to each object, as opposed to universals which are *common* to different objects, and hence they would be, simply, *particulars*. They are particulars not only in that they are particular to different objects, but in that they *just differ* from each other. They are *just* particular, or different, as opposed to *differing in a way*, or property. Different concepts or universals, like whiteness and squareness, may be held to just differ also, but they are different concepts and may be held to differ conceptually or "in a way." (This makes use of an ambiguity in the notion of conceptual difference, which is another factor in Moore's argument that we shall

have to consider later.) In this way the proponent of (C) denies particulars and asserts (A). Since (C) is equated with (B), to assert (B)
is also to assert (A). But (B) also *directly* fits with (A), since, if there
were particulars, two objects could, by (D), differ in that their constituent particulars differed, and hence the objects need not differ in
a universal property or "conceptually." Likewise, two particulars, being
such things, would *just differ* and not differ *in a property*. The phrase
'in a property' requires comment. Holding that particulars are constituents of ordinary objects, one holds that they are related to the other
constituents, the properties, of the objects. In a sense, then, one speaks
of both the object and the special constituent of the object, the particular, as "having" properties—just as, in one sense, for Aristotle, the
combination of form and matter *has* the form and, in another sense, the
matter *has* it, or is related to it. Thus, two objects, having different
particulars, could differ in a constituent, but not in a property; and
their particulars would also not differ *in a property* in that they would
be related to exactly the same properties. The existence of particulars
is thus equated with the recognition of numerical difference as opposed
to conceptual difference. Two objects, differing only in constituent
particulars, would differ numerically, and the two particulars would
also differ numerically. Hence denying (A) is equivalent to denying (B).

These points will be taken up again as we examine Moore's argument.
For the moment let them serve as a background for his argument, which
runs as follows:

> Let us suppose that there is no such thing as numerical differ-
> ence. In that case, when two things have the same predicate, the
> only difference between them consists in the difference between two
> different predicates, one of which belongs to one and the other
> to the other. But what are the things to which these different
> predicates belong? We predicate of the things both a common
> predicate, and a different predicate of each. Either then we must
> say that the things are the different predicates, and that it is
> to those that the common predicate belongs; or else we must say
> that the things are another pair of different predicates, to each
> of which one of the first pair and to both of which the common
> predicate belongs. But in either case the common predicate belongs
> to or is predicated of that which is different in each of the things.[2]

As Moore sees it, to hold that there is no such thing as numerical
difference is to hold that two things with the same *predicate* must
differ in another predicate. Moreover, the difference of predicate or

property will be the only difference between the objects. If we ask what are the things of which we predicate both the common and different predicates, we must conclude that we predicate the common predicate of the different predicate. For, since the two things are analyzed into (1) a point of difference, (2) a relation of predication, and (3) a common point, and since the latter two are identical in each of the two things, he concludes that the things "turn out to *be* merely their points of difference." One cannot even say that the "groups" consisting of the common predicate, the differentiating predicate, and the relation of predication are different, since only the different predicates in each are different, and nothing can be true of the groups except that they are three.

> Accordingly our two must be analyzed into: (1) point of difference; (2) relation of predication; (3) common point; of which (2) and (3) are absolutely identical in each. But, if this is so, the things turn out to *be* merely their points of difference. Of the group (1) (2) (3), which is what we originally supposed to constitute a thing, nothing can be true except that they are three. We cannot say of (a) (2) (3), which is what we originally called the one thing, that *it* is different from the other (b) (2) (3). It is only (a) and (b) which differ from one another and are two. In fact our original supposition was that (3) could only be predicated of (a) and (b), not of anything else. And if this supposition holds it is plain that anything else which we might try to predicate of the group, as such, would turn out to be predicated only of (a) and (b). We can never by any possibility get a number of predicates to combine in forming a new thing, of which, as a whole, anything can be predicated. We must start, on this theory, with two points of difference—two simple predicates having conceptual difference from one another; this is essential to there being two things at all. And then we may try to form new things, also differing from one another, by finding predicates of these points of difference. But whatever we find and however we may add, we still leave the points of difference as they were—the only things of which duality can really be predicated. For anything we predicate of them, and the relation of predication itself, may always both belong to some other point of difference, so that every property by which we may try to distinguish our new thing from the old, will merely identify part of the new thing with something else, without producing any whole, which, as a whole, differs from everything else in the world, in the way in which our original points of difference differ from one another.[3]

Moore concludes that the view that there is only conceptual difference, and hence that things may be analyzed solely into predicates and the relation of predication, is false. His argument may be put in the following way. Consider four things: a white square, a white circle, a black square, a black circle. Assume, for simplicity, they have no other non-relational properties. Call them Peter, Paul, Mary, and Joan. To say that Peter is white, on the view Moore wishes to refute, is to say that the predicate white is related by predication to the predicate square, the latter being the point of difference with the white circle, Paul. Moreover, Peter is identified with the predicate square. But to say that Mary is black is to say that black is related to square, by predication, and to identify Mary with the predicate square, since that is the point of difference with the black circle, Joan. We thus identify Peter with Mary. Moreover, they cannot be differentiated, even by introducing relations, since it will always be the same *universal* square that is involved in any relation to anything else.

> We can never say, "This red differs from that red, in virtue of having a different position"; or "in virtue of having a different spatial relation to this other thing"; or "as being the one I think of now, whereas that was the one I thought of then." The positions differ, the spatial relations differ, my thinking now differs from my thinking then; but it is always the same red which is at both positions, and is thought of at both times.[4]

Thus Moore feels that he has reduced the opposing view—the view expressed by (A), (B) and (C)—to an absurdity.

Moore's argument depends on his holding that the view which he is refuting implies that:

1) predicates cannot combine in forming a new thing, of which, as a whole, anything can be predicated;
2) the different predicates "in" the things are the only things that really differ;
3) the things are identified with such distinguishing predicates—with their points of difference; and
4) predication is then a relation between predicates.

To examine his argument we must consider why he attributes these four propositions to his opponent.

We may start by noting an inherent ambiguity in the dichotomy of conceptual and numerical difference. Conceptual difference has to do with concepts or universals (properties, predicates, qualities). But when one holds that two things differ conceptually, is he holding that they differ in a property but that they need not be properties, or is he asserting that only properties (concepts) differ conceptually? Even if one does not insist that only concepts differ conceptually, we have two senses of conceptual difference, and the two senses may then be confused. If one thinks of conceptual difference in the sense in which concepts are said to differ conceptually, he can come to hold that a philosopher who asserts that there is only conceptual difference also asserts that only concepts (predicates) may differ. This would immediately explain why one would attribute (1), (2), (3), and (4) to a philosopher who claims that there is no such thing as numerical difference. For if only universals can differ, then universals cannot combine into things other than universals which, in turn, would differ. Since predication is a relation between two different things, it then must hold between universals or concepts as the only things capable of differing. One could not then predicate of something which was a combination of concepts but not itself a concept. This could lead one to hold that the properties combined into something, the colored patch, which was itself a property. This would be grotesque since, first, we would confuse the property white-square with *a* white square; second, one would not predicate white of the property white-square; third, the properties white and square do not combine into the complex property white-square by means of the predication or exemplification relation.[5]

That the sense of conceptual difference whereby concepts differ conceptually is involved in Moore's argument seems to be indicated by his saying, "We must start, on this theory, with two points of difference—two simple predicates having conceptual difference from one another; this is essential to there being two things at all." Properties, or "predicates" as Moore says, thus conceptually differ from each other, and this does not seem to have anything to do with their differing in that one *has* a second level property that the other does not have. They just differ; but that is considered, in the beginning of the paper, to be conceptual difference. Later, after numerical difference has been introduced, Moore will hold that two concepts differ both numerically and conceptually. But the distinction between the two senses of difference, as applied to properties, will not be explained. Perhaps what is involved is this: When we say that two properties differ conceptually *we mean* that they are *different* properties, but when we say that they differ numerically *we mean only* that they are *different things*. There is thus a difference between the idea of two predicates' differing conceptually and the idea of their just differing. When we think about it, we just "see" the difference between what is meant by "conceptual difference" and "numerical difference" as applied to predicates. Moore's use of this sort of appeal to our just seeing or realizing that concepts or ideas are different (that the concept of *conceptual difference* is different from the concept of *numerical difference,* for example) is, I believe, crucial to his notion of philosophical analysis. It is one of the key themes in his rejection of the "naturalistic fallacy," and it stems ultimately from his early view that the world is composed of concepts (Platonic universals) which the mind grasps in some way.[6] Thus one just sees that two concepts are different as one ordinarily sees that a table is not a chair— simply and directly. All this aside, the point is that stressing the sense of conceptual difference, whereby two simple concepts are said to differ conceptually, may lead one to think that the opponent of numerical difference really holds that only concepts differ conceptually. This suggestion may be made more plausible by putting it a bit differently. Moore thinks that, according to the opponent of numerical difference, two things, like Peter and Paul, differ *only* in a concept or predicate. Differing only in a concept they differ in *no other way.* Hence, their difference *reduces* to the difference of different concepts. The assertion that things differ *only in* a concept may then be taken to mean that *only concepts really differ.* This clearly fuses the two senses of conceptual difference.[7]

The reduction of the assertion that Peter and Paul differ conceptually to the assertion that a constituent concept of the one differs from a constituent concept of the other could thus lead one to hold that predication, on the view Moore wishes to refute, relates concepts and not a "thing" and a concept. Moore could also be led to this conclusion by another sense of 'reduction.' He could hold that to analyze a thing into other things forces one to acknowledge that what is really there are the elements which, on the analysis, make up the object. Hence, to predicate something of the original object is really to predicate of a constituent of it, for only the constituents are really "there." In short, the object is reduced to its constituent elements. To hold that the original object is analyzable into its predicates, in the special relation of predication, is then to hold that to predicate one of the properties of the "thing" is to predicate it of some other quality of the thing. For one could not predicate a property of itself or of the relation of predication. To predicate white of Peter is then to predicate the property white of the property square. In this connection it is highly relevant to note that, after Moore introduces his special kind of particulars, instances of universals (this whiteness, this redness), which are constituents of ordinary objects like Peter, the predication relation is taken to hold between such particular predicates and universal predicates. The relation between ordinary objects and *particular* predicates becomes that of whole to part—or, to put it another way, the ordinary object "dissolves" into its component particular predicates.

Just as the notion of reduction may provide one key to Moore's argument, his concept of 'group' may provide another. He holds that "nothing can be true of the group (a), (2), (3) except that they are three." Thus the group cannot be considered as an individual or particular to which properties may be attributed—particularly not the properties that are constituents of it. Moore may be thinking of a group as a class. This would explain his insistence that one cannot predicate properties like white, square, etc., of the group. For one does not predicate a member of a class of the class. Even if one includes the relation of predication in the class this would not help, since the group is still thought of as a class, as opposed, say, to being considered as a complex entity composed of members of the class in a special relation. On this latter alternative such a composite individual would then be the subject of predicative ascription. As this is really the most cogent version of Bradley, one wonders why Moore does not explicitly consider it, especially as he himself had advanced a similar view only a short time earlier. But more about this shortly. Moore also does not consider the possibility of expressing 'Peter is white' as a statement of class membership, with Peter as a class of qualities. One reason for this may be that he takes a class to be a universal as opposed to a particular. Hence a class of qualities could not be a *particular having* those qualities. Thus, at one place, Moore states that "A class-concept, on the other hand, does imply at least one *member* conceptually different from it. . . . It is, moreover, always also a universal, but may have no particulars."[8] But there is another reason why class membership would not be considered by Moore, and this brings us to the core of his argument.

We start from the statement 'Peter is white,' where 'Peter' refers to an individual and 'white' to a quality or universal. Thus, the sentence is taken by Moore to assert a relation between the individual and the quality. This relation is indicated by the predicative 'is.' If one then analyzes the individual into a set of qualities in a relation, this linguistic "picture" of things will no longer do. For, whether Peter is taken to be a complex of qualities in a special relation or a set whose members are the qualities and the relation of predication, what was a relation between an individual and a quality is transformed into a relation among a collection of qualities. Thus, a critic of such a view might hold that, since what corresponds to predication in language is a relation among a group of qualities, to predicate in a statement is to assert a relation among such qualities. Predication in language is thus fundamentally altered from what it appears to be in the original expression. One may suggest that, upon such an analysis, ascriptions of predication are replaced either by ascriptions of class membership or by the relation of part to whole. Thus, if the group of qualities is taken as a class, then the statement 'Peter is white' becomes transcribed as 'White is a member of Peter'; and, if Peter is taken as some sort of complex of qualities (but not a class) in some structural relation, then the sentence is transcribed as 'White is a part of Peter' or 'Peter contains white.' Yet, on either alternative, the linguistic expression ('contains,' 'part of,' 'member of') does not stand for a relation between the referents of the signs the expression connects. The relation connects the qualities which constitute Peter.[9] Taking the original sentence to assert a relation between an individual and a quality can then lead one to hold, first, that only an analysis which leads to the assertion of a relation between an individual and a quality will capture the sense of the original expression; and, second, that if it is claimed on the analysis in question that a relation holds between qualities, then one must assert just that. Hence, if the relation holding among the qualities is the predication relation, one is forced to predicate white of another quality. Thus, Moore believes that on the view he is attacking one is forced to claim that white is predicated of another quality and not of the individual which is white. It also seems as if Moore is relying on a primitive picture theory of language, requiring one's metaphysical analysis to correlate entities to the elements of the ordinary sentence we start with and literally to retain predication. Starting from a sentence with a subject, predicate, and predication relation, we must end up with an individual connected by a relation, i.e., the referent of the predicative 'is,' to the referent of the predicate. The alternative he is attacking does not provide an analysis of the object that mirrors the original sentence in this way. Forcing the proponent of this view to identify the relation that connects the qualities with predication (exemplification), Moore reduces the view to absurdity, since the various qualities of an object must then exemplify each other.

That one must ultimately predicate qualities of qualities on the view he wishes to refute is integral to the way Moore states his argument. As he states it, it is also a variant of the argument that qualities cannot differentiate objects, since we can have two different things alike in all qualities. But Moore also has another argument, which does not rely on the absurdity of attributing different qualities of objects to each other. He is arguing that a quality cannot distinguish an object, since it *may* belong to any other object and hence will be a common rather than a distinguishing feature. Since this is so for all qualities, it follows that it holds for any set of predicates, since one may consider a set of properties as a complex property and hence something which could belong to two things. Likewise, it holds for the property taken as the point of difference.

Three arguments are operating here. First, if predication is assumed to be of some predicate, the point of difference is a universal. As no universal, by itself, necessarily distinguishes an object, the universal taken as a point of difference need not. Second, if we take a complex of predicates as individuating ones, we may ask "What is the object of the predication?" If we say "a predicate," the first argument reappears. If one says something else, he abandons the view Moore is purporting to refute. As Moore sees it, no other alternative is open, since he refuses, as we saw, to take a complex of qualities as an object, in some sense, of predication. Third, no complex predicate need individuate, since it may belong to more than one object. This third argument can be stated independently of Moore's forcing his opponent to predicate of a quality as the subject and point of difference. What Moore is insisting upon is that a set of qualities, to individuate, must necessarily do so, but cannot by the very fact that they are universals. What he has in mind is, I take it, something like the following. Take two white, bright squares. Assume that they have no more properties. A list of the properties involved would not indicate how many things there were. Even if one included a spatial coordinate or a pair of spatial coordinates, it would still be possible for there to be one thing at two places or two things at one place. But suppose, instead of listing universal properties, one considered particularized properties; this white, that white, etc. Since particular properties are individuals, this white is just numerically different from that white. They are not sharable, not being universals.

Nor would it make sense to hold that one ordinary object that is white contains two particular whitenesses. Thus, given that two whitenesses are involved, it follows that we are dealing with two white objects and not one. Moore thus implicitly requires that from a metaphysical analysis we must be able to derive ordinary facts. It does not suffice to say that properties (universals) may individuate, since no two objects have all in common. What individuates must be such that it is not possible for two objects to have "it" in common. This requires something introduced for that purpose, and which hence necessarily individuates, particular properties. We shall return to the details of this argument. For the present we may note that Moore argues in this way against conceptual individuation to suggest that the concepts we have of *differing* and *differing in a quality* are just not the same. The purpose of his arguments is to get us to see this conceptual difference.

Can *two objects* have all properties in common? The answer one gives may be taken to reflect one's notions of 'object' and of 'difference.' Moore is arguing that from the notion of a *universal* property and of the analysis of an object, as a group of such properties, it follows that it is not possible. To claim it is possible is to claim there is another notion of difference besides conceptual difference. We saw earlier that the claim that there is only conceptual difference is equivalent to the claim that an object is a group of qualities. Hence, to show that this latter is mistaken is to argue for the *possibility* of *two objects* having all properties in common and, consequently, for the *existence* of *numerical difference* as distinct from conceptual difference. Thus, Moore takes the argument we considered to establish the possibility that two objects have all properties in common. One aspect of his argument seems to rely on this being assumed to be the case. For universals may not individuate, since, being universal, they *may* be common to more than one object. However, Moore is not begging the question. He is arguing that no listing of universals can guarantee or necessitate individuation. As we noted above, if we list the nonrelational universals of our two white squares (white, square), it will not follow from the list of properties that there are two individuals, i.e., that some object is different from some other object. If we add the relational universal left-of this will not help, since it is logically possible for a thing to be to the left of itself. Hence, it does not follow that there are two objects from the list of universals: white, square, left-of. This part of Moore's argument is obscured by his holding that relations cannot individuate, since the relation would have to be "predicated of" a universal, say, white, which would be the *same universal* in both objects. Thus, he makes use of his contention that one must predicate *of* universals (on the view he is criticizing) to argue that relations do not help. But leaving that aspect aside, we can see that he is also claiming that if universals are to individuate they must necessarily do so. Yet, being universals, they cannot. Even if one were to contend that it is logically impossible for two objects to share all properties (including relations), by the very notion of object, this would not touch Moore's argument, for this latter claim would hold that from the fact that there are two objects it follows that they differ in a relation. Moore is implicitly arguing that from no list of universals would it follow that there were two objects rather than one. But he goes further and takes this to show that it is possible for two objects to have all properties in common. Holding (I) that a set of properties does not necessarily determine whether one or two objects exemplify members of the set, one holds it is possible to have one set of properties and two objects. This is easily confused with (II), the possibility of there being two objects *each* of which exemplifies *all* the properties in the set. Thus Moore, in "establishing" (I), takes it that (II) is established. Then the view against which he is arguing is refuted, for that view is equated with the denial of (II). One must then distinguish three main aspects of Moore's argument. First, there is the aspect which relies on the absurdity of predicating of predicates. This is weak, for his opponent need not hold, as Moore does hold, that one is forbidden to predicate of groups. Yet Moore has shown something. His opponent cannot take the 'is' of predication in 'Peter is white' to reflect the tie of exemplification between the referents of the subject and predicate terms. Thus, one who analyzes objects as complexes of universals does not have a neat picturing of "facts" by sentences. Second, there is the argument which confuses (I) with (II), and is thus mistaken. Third, there is an argument that is based on (I) alone. For one may argue that the view Moore wishes to refute is refuted in that it does not guarantee individuation in view of (I). These latter aspects call for further comment.

Since (I) is fused with (II), Moore does not seem to have established, by arguing for (I), that it is possible for two objects to share all properties. It may be that in a way it is just obvious to Moore that it is possible—that there is just a *conceptual difference* between the concept of numerical difference and that of conceptual difference. At various points in his writings Moore makes use of the idea that one notes, on examination, that two concepts just differ. In this vein he would not be offering an argument, but either proposing an explication of his notions of "thing" and "difference" or simply reporting a sort of intuitive insight about the "concepts" of difference. This latter would somehow be based on not "seeing" any contradiction in there being two objects which share all properties. In the former case one may look upon Moore's analysis as clarifying his notion of "thing." For example, adhering to the possibility of two things' sharing all non-relational properties, one would deny that a thing could be taken as a class of properties, since, as the term 'class' is commonly understood, we could not have two classes with all members in common. Likewise, in view of such a possibility, one could not hold a thing to be a complex of properties and also hold that the only sense of difference was "conceptual difference." Moore's analysis can thus be taken to point to internal inconsistencies in certain conceptions of 'thing' and 'difference.' But there is a clear sense in which Moore can be said to provide an argument for the distinction between conceptual and numerical difference. Even though (I) and (II) are not identical claims, one may argue that (I) implies (II). For, given that universals cannot provide a ground for individuation or difference, one may be led to hold that something other than a property must provide such a ground. Two different objects will then differ in virtue of their containing (or being connected with) such "individuators." But then we have a further sense of difference: differing with respect to such individuators as distinct from differing in a property. Thus we have a concept of difference distinct from conceptual difference. Or, to put it another way, given that something other than a universal property is the ground of individuation, it becomes a logical possibility for two objects to share all properties but differ only in respect of their individuators. Arguing for numerical difference in such a way, one argues that two things need not differ in a property. As we noted earlier, this can be taken as equivalent to arguing against things as being complexes of universal properties. As we also noted, another crucial assumption in all this is that complexes must differ in a part or constituent. This assumption leads one to hold that something other than a property must be a part of two complex things which are "conceptually identical." But one could deny the assumption that to differ complexes must differ in a part. This shows that holding things to be composites of properties is not equivalent to holding that there is only conceptual difference. Alternatively, if one equates these two claims, as we have seen that Moore does, then if one also holds that there is numerical difference as distinct from conceptual difference, he will naturally come to equate numerical difference holding between two objects with there being a special kind of entity—particulars. Thus, he introduces numerical difference together with his particulars, particular properties, or property instances. We shall consider such things later. First, we shall take up the crucial question of relational properties and individuation. For while it may well seem unproblematic that, via the notion of numerical difference, it is logically possible for two objects to have all nonrelational properties in common, it might seem quite problematic when we explicitly note that conceptual difference includes relational difference. That is, it appears to be a consequence of the distinction between conceptual difference and numerical difference that it becomes logically possible for two objects to share all relational properties and yet be different.

II. Relations and Individuation

Moore's argument against individuation by relations is the last step in his refutation of the view of things as complexes of qualities which differ only conceptually. As he states it, his argument depends on his holding that predication, on the view he seeks to refute, reduces to predication of one quality of another. Hence, since qualities are the only subjects, any relations between the complexes of qualities (objects) would really have to hold between (constituent) qualities of the objects. Thus he argues:

> We can never say, "This red differs from that red, in virtue of having a different position," or "in virtue of having a different spatial relation to this other thing" or "as being the one I think of now, whereas that was the one I thought of then." The positions differ, the spatial relations differ, my thinking now differs from my thinking then; but it is always the same red which is at both positions, and is thought of at both times. And whenever we attempt to say anything of the red at this position, as, for instance, that it was surrounded by yellow, or that it led me to think of a soldier's coat, exactly the same must be true of the red at that position, which was surrounded by blue or led me to think of a house on fire. We are unable to distinguish the two except by

their relation to other things, and by whatever relations we attempt so to distinguish them we always find we have not succeeded. We can never say, "The red I mean is the one surrounded by yellow, and not the one surrounded by blue." For the one surrounded by yellow is also surrounded by blue: they are not two but one, and whatever is true of that which is surrounded by yellow is also true of that which is surrounded by blue.

All this I regard as a *reductio ad absurdum* of the theory that there is no difference but conceptual difference. If any one can avoid assuming that something may be true of a quality at another position, then he will be entitled to assert that all difference is conceptual difference. But this will at all events not be possible for those who hold that things conceptually the same may be distinguished by their relations to other things.[10]

As Moore states it the argument is cogent. If one holds that, when two red spots are such that one is to the left-of the other, he must express this by holding that the quality red is to the left of the quality red, then the spatial relation cannot serve to enable us to describe the one spot in a way which will not also describe the other. But the cogency of the argument is based on the insistence that a universal is the term of the relation. Let us consider a more general version of the argument that relations cannot be used to differentiate objects. The spatial relation cannot be what serves to differentiate the objects, since we must presuppose them to be different to begin with. Otherwise, it *could be* one and the same object which stands in the spatial relation "being to the left of" to itself. Thus, one assumes that there are two, or, what comes to the same thing, that the spatial relation is asymmetrical. Since it is logically possible for an object to be to the left of itself, we must hold that the two are different independently of their standing in the relation. In short, a spatial relation cannot differentiate, since it is not logically necessary that it hold between two different things. So stated, the argument explicitly incorporates the demand that the existence of the purported basis of individuation, or difference, logically imply that there are two things rather than one. This is the requirement Moore implicitly uses against qualitative individuation.

Just as it is held to be possible for two objects to have all nonrelational properties in common, this argument holds that the relational property need not distinguish, since it could be a further common quality. Thus the exemplification of the relation would not provide a ground for there being two objects; i.e., from the fact that the relation was exemplified, it would not follow that there were two objects rather than one.

To get at the argument, let us ignore relations for the moment. Suppose one were to argue as follows: Consider two colored patches, one black, one white. On the view that there is only conceptual difference, such a difference in color could serve to differentiate the objects. But this will not do, for it could be one and the same object which is both black and white. Hence we must assume that there are two different objects. Thus the difference in quality will not serve to ground the difference between the objects—i.e., that there are two rather than one. The one object that possibly is both black and white would contain both qualities. There would not be two sets of qualities, one containing black and one containing white, that would correspond to two distinct objects.

This argument reveals that one supposed argument against relations' individuating has nothing *essentially* to do with relations. It is an implicit argument against qualitative individuation. Hence, the supposition or, if you will, fact that two objects have all nonrelational qualities in common is irrelevant. More important, however, is the fact that the opponent of individuation by qualitative difference does not really grant that qualities would serve to individuate if it were impossible to have two things that shared all qualities, for the same argument he uses against relational individuation could still be raised against individuation by nonrelational qualities. But this fact, in turn, reveals the weakness of this argument against relational individuation. Consider the case of the black patch and the white patch in a more extreme way. Suppose one holds that he observes, of the black spot, that it is not white. He also observes that the white one is white. Hence, to say that there is only one spot is to say that it is both white and not white. Here one cannot play on its not being a matter of pure logic that something cannot be both black and white. Recognizing that such a theme is involved, we may feel justified in rejecting the claim that one spot could be both black and white. This, in turn, could lead us to reject the implicit criterion that we must logically derive the existence of two objects from the facts that something is black and something is white or, alternatively, from the fact that something is to the left of something else, in order to hold that qualities and relations are sufficient to individuate. But, that aside for the moment, we have a way of putting the case so that to say that there is only one object is to say that it is both white and not white. Clearly something has gone wrong. Given that something is white and something is not white we must, to avoid contradiction, conclude that there are two objects. But exactly the same point can be made in the case of relations. We observe a white spot to the right of a white spot. We then may be said to observe, of *a spot,* that *it has* a white spot to its right, and observe of *a spot* that it *does not have* a white spot to its right. Consider the property indicated by the predicate 'WR' where

WR $(x) =$ df. $(\exists y)(Wy \, \& \, R \, (y, x)$

where 'W' stands for 'white' and 'R' for 'right of.' To say there is only one spot is then to say that '$(\exists x)$ (WRx $\& \sim$ WRx)'. Thus, just as in the nonrelational case, one contradicts one's self.

The point is that the argument against using relational properties to individuate. is also an argument against using nonrelational properties for that purpose. Moreover, the argument can be stated quite simply. The (universal) quality white cannot be what distinguishes Peter from Paul, since there must be something which has the quality and something which does not. Those "things" or "subjects" must already differ, and hence the quality does not distinguish them. This holds for any quality or set of qualities; hence the difference between Peter and Paul must be accounted for by something other than qualities. Being other than qualities, or concepts, such individuators need not differ conceptually but only "numerically." Their numerical difference will, in turn, account for the difference between Peter and Paul—i.e., that there are two rather than one. Putting the matter as I just did leads to another variant of the argument against relations' individuating. For one may argue that a relation cannot distinguish relata, since the exemplification of the relation presupposes distinct relata. Hence, to attempt to ground the difference between Peter and Paul in a relation in which they stand would involve us in a vicious circle. To find what is involved, let us consider the case of a nonrelational quality and the claim that predicating such a quality presupposes a subject distinct from it. There is one obvious sense in which we may take this claim. To predicate is to attribute a quality to something other than the quality—or, perhaps better, to hold that a quality is exemplified is to presuppose that there is something other than the quality. Hence the act of predicating and the relation of exemplification presuppose two things, a quality and a subject. Thus, if we predicate white of Peter, and thus assert that Peter exemplifies the color, we presuppose that Peter is not identical with the color white. This seems an obvious enough consequence of what is involved in the notions of predicating and exemplifying. But one may also hold that, if Peter is considered to be a composite or collection of qualities including white, then, first, the patch is not really distinct from the quality, and, second, predicating one term of another would not then reflect, in language, a relation between two things. One may believe so, thinking that if white is part of Peter then a sentence like 'Peter is white' becomes tautological, since the predicate is contained in the subject. For, as these phrases are used, since the predicate is contained in the subject, the subject is not distinct from it in that the subject cannot be conceived of apart from the predicate. Thus, the belief that sentences like 'Peter is white' become tautologically empty if the patch is viewed as a composite of qualities can lead to the further belief that, on such a view, the subject-predicate distinction in language no longer reflects a relation between two "distinct" things. What is required, in part, is an analysis of what does happen to statements like 'Peter is white' if the patch is held to be a composite of qualities. Nevertheless, the position cannot be ruled out simply by insisting that something completely distinct or independent must be related to the quality by exemplification. This would, in effect, be to require, as we have seen that Moore implicitly does, that since the subject and predicate terms are distinct, in that one is not defined in terms of the other, they must refer to objects that are not parts of each other. To require this is to use the subject-predicate distinction and the demonstrative function of names to derive an ontology.[11]

We start from an object and a quality which we can distinguish. This does not determine a metaphysical position, except in so far as any position will have to reflect this distinction. However, that does not preclude the view that the relation between the object and the quality is a whole-part relation. A similar point holds in the case of relational properties. We start from two things in a relation. That there are two objects is a fact from which we begin. But it is argued that a relational property cannot distinguish two things alike in all nonrelational properties, in that the exemplification of the relation presupposes that there are two. This suggests that, just as the subject is held to be necessarily independent of its quality in the nonrelational case, the two objects must be independent of the relation they exemplify. Thus one comes to hold they must be two, whether or not they exemplify any relation. But it is not clear what "presuppose" means in such a line of thought. It is clear that a two-term relation's being instanced or exemplified presupposes two things simply in that what one means by a two-term relation's being exemplified is that two subjects stand in the relation. (Forget, for the moment, the ambiguity of the word 'term' whereby a reflexive relation is a two-term relation.) The exemplification of a relation requires subjects, just as the exemplification of a nonrelational quality requires a subject. However, the fact that a quality is exemplified by a subject, and hence presupposes such a subject, need not be taken to establish that such a quality cannot be held to distinguish the subject, for there is an ambiguity in the notion of a quality's being exemplified by a subject. On the one hand, we can take that in a neutral sense as another way of expressing that an object has a quality. This would then be susceptible to alternative analyses, one of which could be that the object is a composite of qualities containing the particular quality in question. On the other hand, one could have a particular analysis in mind, to the effect that an exemplification relation holds between a quality and a subject that is independent of it, i.e., not containing it as a part, and whose difference from any other subject and from the quality does not depend on any quality. We have seen how one can be led to believe that a quality cannot individuate if one implicitly holds that the subject and quality must be independent for the meaningful ascription of a predicate to a subject.

We also saw that, for Moore, another aspect of the issue was the contention that a universal quality could not individuate an object, since it could belong to more than one object, whereas what individuates *must necessarily* individuate. Something "necessarily individuates" when it is logically impossible for two objects to "have it." In this vein the possibility that two things share all qualities is equivalent to the impossibility of qualities' being the basis of individuation. Recalling these points helps clarify the problem of relational individuation, since they bring us to some further fundamental and distinct senses of 'presuppose.' To take a relation as the ground of individuation might be held to imply that the exemplification of the relation must necessarily individuate. Thus if a has R to b and the two are held to be distinguished by the relation, then it is held that '$a \neq b$' must follow from 'Rab.' But '$a \neq b$' only follows from 'Rab' *and* the assertion that R is either irreflexive or asymmetrical, given the standard definition of '$=$.' However, to assume that R is irreflexive or asymmetrical is held to beg the question. On this line of thought what is assumed is that one must prove '$a \neq b$', i.e., that there are two things, on the ground that the relation R is exemplified. Nonrelational qualities are held not to be a ground of individuation, since it is logically possible for two things to have any set of these: relational qualities, like R, are held not to individuate since it is not logically necessary for two things, rather than one, to exemplify the relation. If, by the claim that 'relations cannot distinguish or individuate objects since they presuppose distinct terms,' one means that from 'Rxy' we cannot infer '$x \neq y$,' then what one says is trivially true.

However, suppose one maintains, in connection with an earlier point, that one sees that a is to the right of b and that b is not to the right of b. The opponent of relational difference might balk at the latter claim, since the denial that relations individuate stems, in part, from the argument that we cannot hold that b is not to the right of b unless we presuppose b is different from a. That is, we must assign the names 'a' and 'b' to different objects to start with. Yet everyone would acknowledge that there are two objects from the outset. This cannot be the point of the argument against relational individuation. One may argue that holding '$\sim Rbb$,' with 'R' for 'right of' is to presuppose that $b \neq a$, since one holds 'Rab' to be true. But 'presuppose' is a problematic term here. Assume the Russell-Leibniz definition[12] of '$=$,' 'Rab,' and '$\sim Rbb$.' It follows that $a \neq b$. This gives one sense of 'presuppose': one proposition, Q_1, presupposes another, Q_2, if Q_1 implies Q_2. Here, it is paradoxical. On the one hand, the argument against using relations to individuate insists that from a relation's holding of a and b it must follow that $a \neq b$; on the other hand, if '$a \neq b$' follows from a set of statements, the assertion of such statements presupposes that $a \neq b$. In part, the paradox stems from the acknowledgement that there are two objects to start with together with the implicit demand that one prove that there are two. In part, it stems from another sense of 'presuppose' that is involved. We shall take up the former point later. We can investigate the latter by starting, once again, with nonrelational qualities.

Consider our two objects, a and b. Let two sets, A_1 and B_1, of non-relational properties be coordinated to them, A_1 to a, B_1 to b. It is understood that each member of the set associated with an object is ascribable to that object. We can uniquely indicate the objects by reference to the sets so long as the latter differ in one member. Having the representative sets differ can then be taken as the basis for asserting that the objects differ. We may even identify the objects with the sets. To have a member of A_1 not be a member of B_1 is logically to imply '$A_1 \neq B_1$.' By the very "notion" of set, if one has a member that the second does not, they are two and not one. We may then feel we have not "presupposed" that there are two objects by identifying a with A_1 and b with B_1 and proving '$A_1 \neq B_1$.' Suppose that the same set is coordinated with both objects, since they have all nonrelational properties in common. Is it in principle possible to alter the picture by the use of relational properties so that two distinct sets are coordinated to the two objects? Let it be the case that the object a is to the right of the object b. Let $\{ F_1, \ldots, F_n \}$ be the set of nonrelational properties both share. Can we then form two sets $\{ F_1, \ldots, F_n \}$ and $\{ F_1, \ldots, F_n, R \}$ to coordinate to the two objects? One may say "no" for two reasons. First, R is not a quality of either object; it is a quality holding *of* or *between both*. One notion in the original program was that every member of the set could be ascribed to the associated object. R cannot be so ascribed. This brings us to another fundamental sense in which relations are held to "presuppose" objects and hence to be unable to differentiate them. If one identified the members of the associated set as the parts of the object, one would be led to hold that a relation cannot be a part of an object. Not being a part, as each nonrelational quality is, the relation must be exemplified by the object as a whole (together with another object). Thus, as it is not capable of being a part, the relation's being exemplified presupposes the differentiated object in a way a nonrelational property's being exemplified does not. In short, a constituent does not presuppose the object of which it is a part as a property of the whole presupposes a subject to exemplify it. This is one way of asserting that, if objects are held to be composites of qualities, then they must *exemplify* relations, whereas they *contain* nonrelational properties. The point involved also ties in with Moore's forcing his opponent to predicate one quality of another. For the object, considered as a composite of qualities, could not be said to exemplify one of its parts. Thus, one either abandons the exemplification relation or takes something other than the composite object as the subject of it. To speak of a nonrelational property's being exemplified by the object, on such a view, is thus to speak elliptically. A second objection to the use of the set $\{ F_1, \ldots, F_n, R \}$ would be that we could not determine with which object to coordinate it except by fiat.

Suppose we alter the picture by bringing in relational properties as opposed to relations. Let 'R^b' be defined by 'R^{b}x = df. Rxb' and the set $\{ F_1, \ldots, F_n, R^b \}$ be associated with a. The new set removes both *prima facie* objections, since every member of it can be ascribed to a and it is clear with which of the two objects the set is to be associated.

However, one can raise some new objections, as well as again raising the point about presupposing the existence of the differentiated object rather than "accounting" for it. With respect to this latter point, a critic may point out that a's exemplifying R^b "presupposes," by the definition of 'R^b,' that a has R to b, which, in turn, presupposes the existence of a and b to exemplify the relation. Here we must separate *three* senses of 'presuppose.' We have already distinguished between the sense of 'presuppose,' where Q_1 is said to presuppose Q_2 if Q_1 implies Q_2, and the sense where a relation or quality which is exemplified by, but not a part of, an object is said to presuppose the object. A third sense would be that in which R^b or 'R^{b}a' is said to presuppose R or 'Rab,' respectively. This is not the same as the notion of 'presuppose' based on logical implication. For, given the definition of 'R^b,' 'R^{b}a' and 'Rab' imply each other—but only one is said to presuppose the other. Hence, a defined predicate's being ascribed to something may be said to presuppose that the predicates defining it are ascribed, or a property indicated by the defined predicate may be said to presuppose the properties indicated by the defining predicates. One may also point out that there is a sense in which R^b presupposes R that is not symmetrical. Given that R^b is exemplified, it follows that R is; but, given that R is exemplified, it does not follow that R^b is. Hence, R^b may be said to presuppose R in a sense that R does not presuppose R^b. In spite of this, the crucial sense in which R^b is said to presuppose R reduces to the fact that 'R^b' is a defined predicate. The issue is then whether the property indicated by such a defined predicate may be said to be part of the object a. There are three questions here. First there is the question of whether or not properties indicated by defined predicates are to be taken as existents in one's ontology. Second, there is the question of whether or not such properties, if acknowledged as existents, may be taken as parts of objects. Third, there is the question of whether properties indicated by predicates like 'R^b,' in whose definition relational predicates occur, may be taken as parts of objects, since the relations themselves are not such parts. If one who seeks to

account for individuation by relational properties is assumed to acknowledge (1) that he must account for difference in terms of an entity
in his ontology, and (2) that such an entity must be a part of the
object, he will have to hold that defined predicates indicate entities
which may be parts of objects.

In thus answering the first two questions, he can meet the objection
posed by the third by holding that the sense of presupposition involved
in one predicate's being defined in terms of another is not crucial for
this issue. It appears so only if we take it to reflect some sort of
ontological or temporal ordering so that it appears as if a's having R^b
requires a's having R to b as a condition, but not vice versa. But given
the definition, this is misleading, or, at least, it says no more than that
'R^b' is defined by means of 'R' and 'b.' One may also be bothered by the
fact that by definition 'R^ba' and 'Rab' say the same thing. For if one
statement involves exemplification of a relation by two composites, how
can the other involve a property's being a part of an object? With this
question we arrive at the issue of internal relations. On one side we
have the insistence that since 'R^b' is defined by reference to a relation,
which admittedly is not part of an object, it cannot refer to a property
that is such a part. On the other side, one may insist that the exemplification of R by a and b if and only if a has R^b reflects the fact that,
when a relation is exemplified, objects have correlated relational properties as parts. He may then suggest that the definitions of relational
predicates like 'R^b' in terms of corresponding relations differ from
definitions like that of 'WS' as 'being white and square.' In the
first place, only one predicate, a relational one, is involved in the definition of 'R^b,' and, in the second place, what is achieved is not an
abbreviation but a means of expressing something we could not express
before: that an object has a relational property. Thus, in the context
of the philosophical issues and positions involved, to say 'R^ba' is not
to say exactly the same thing as 'Rab,' though '$R^ba \equiv Rab$' is analytic.
Here, in a way, we have come to a dead end. To insist that 'R^b' cannot
be cogently employed in the issues we are discussing is to insist that it
cannot be treated like other one-term predicates applicable to a, because
'R^ba' is equivalent to 'Rab.' To insist that 'R^b' can be employed is to
hold that the definitional equivalence between the statements does not
force us to treat the property R^b as an external property. In a way,
one philosopher holds that, as relations are external, in that they are

exemplified by composite objects, so are relational properties. The
other holds that, since relational properties may be taken as internal,
there is a sense in which relations are internal to objects.

Other objections arise to the use of 'R^b.' The definition is peculiar
in that the property indicated is not, as WS might be taken to be, a
complex of other properties. The name 'b' occurs in the definition and
hence the use of such a predicate may be said to "presuppose" differentiated objects in yet another sense. Also one might object that, since
the name 'b' occurs in the definition of 'R^b,' the property, in some sense,
contains the object b as a part just as WS might be said to contain
white and square as parts. Thus, a, containing R^b, is no longer a
complex of properties only. Finally, one may object that to use 'R^b' in
the list of members of the set associated with a is to abandon the use
of it as a defined predicate, for it cannot be replaced, on the list, by
its definition. In part, one here plays with the phrase 'defined predicate.'
'R^b' functions like any other contextually defined predicate in that it
is replaceable in statements in which it occurs as a predicate. To use
it on the list is not to use it in a statement as a primitive predicate; it
is merely to make use of it as a one-term predicate. If, instead of predicates, we used propositional functions on the list, we could use 'Rxb'
in place of 'R^b.' As for the object b's being a part of the property R^b,
we clearly have a different sense of the term 'part.' If one considers the
referents of terms occurring in a definition to be "parts" of the referent
of the defined predicate, then, in this sense, b is part of R^b. But
R^b is held to be a part of a in a different sense. If one is more impressed
by the similarity of term and by the transitivity of 'part of' (as a spatial
relation, for example), he may come to insist that on such a view b is
part of a and all things are parts of all other things. But as long as
we are clear about how such slogans arise, no harm is done. It is only
when one begins to conclude, on the basis of an ambiguous use of
expressions like 'part of' or 'internal to,' that 'a is part of b,' or 'everything is everything else,' or 'all is one,' that problems may arise.

The claim that the use of the name 'b,' in the definition of 'R^b,'
presupposes the difference of a and b, raises more interesting aspects
of the issue. What one apparently has in mind here is that the terms
'a' and 'b' must be coordinated to the two objects via reference to the
sets A_1 and B_1. In short, to individuate by properties and/or relations is
taken to involve providing definite descriptions for the two objects.
Thus we cannot employ purely indicative terms, like names, for the

objects, in order to construct predicates to use in such definite descriptions. Assume that one agrees to this condition. In our case, one might then suggest the use of 'R¹' defined as

$$R^1x = df. (\exists y)(F_1y \ \& \ F_2y \ \& \ Rxy)$$

and reminiscent of 'WR' used earlier. With 'F₁,' and 'F₂' for 'white' and 'square,' 'R¹' expresses 'having a white square to the right.' A question arises about a description that uses 'R¹' instead of 'Rᵇ' to refer, uniquely, to *a*. Whereas one may claim that he sees that *b* is not to the right of itself, he may admit the possibility that *b* has another white square to its right. Hence 'R¹' would, or could, apply to both *a* and *b* whereas 'Rᵇ' would apply only to *a*. Hence 'R¹' need not enable us to construct an individuating description. Here we return again to the idea that, to hold that a property individuates, one must hold that it necessarily does so. An ambiguity arises from the fact that, if a property set does individuate, then it is necessarily the case that two things cannot have all the members of the set. This is not to say that a property set that in fact is an individuating set is necessarily one. That a set of properties like $\{ F_1 \ldots F_n, R^1 \}$ can serve to individuate, i.e., uniquely describe, *a*, is a matter of fact, not logic. The point is that its being a matter of fact does not weigh against relations' being used to individuate. It will only appear to do so if one holds that, for a set of properties to individuate, it must logically follow that only one thing has the properties belonging to the set. But this is an extreme requirement. In a way we have a corollary of the requirement we discussed earlier: a relation can be the ground of difference of two objects only if it logically follows, from the fact that the relation is exemplified, that there are two objects. Here it is suggested that a set of properties, including relational ones, *can individuate* if and only if it logically follows that only one object can have them all. In fact, this does seem to be involved in Moore's argument that universal properties cannot individuate, since, being universals, any one or any set can be had by two objects. However, to employ this notion as a criterion is to require that the statement that if something has the set only one thing has the set be a logical truth. This is far too strong. All that can reasonably be required is that, given a situation, like our domain of two white squares, we can construct descriptions that are in fact individuating ones, or, better yet, that there are no reasons which in principle prevent us from doing so. But the raising of the question of the necessity of

a set of properties individuating enables us to see a difference between
a property like R^1 and a property like W. If we have two squares
where one is white and the other black, then, holding that something
cannot be both white and black, I must hold that there are two
objects. I can immediately construct descriptions based on the one
being white and the other being black or not white. But if I see, in
the case of two white squares, that one has R^1, I *may hold* it to be
possible that the other does also, even though I do not see that it does.
In this sense I can see, in the former case, that the objects differ in
a color quality in a way that I cannot see, in the latter case, that the
objects differ with respect to R^1. What is involved here is not really
a difference between nonrelational and relational properties, but one
between the use of existential clauses and the use of names. We can
see that this is the relevant factor when we note that 'R^b,' unlike
'R^1,' does not involve a similar problem; for R^b cannot be a property of
both *a* and *b*, just as white cannot be a property of the black square.
The use of the demonstrative term '*b*,' in the definition of 'R^b,' is thus
the basis of the difference between 'R^b' and 'R^1.' But this difference is
not crucial if we do not require that purported descriptions necessarily
individuate. Another factor involved is the contrast between definite
descriptions and names. Descriptions contain universally quantified
clauses; hence to ascribe a property via a definite description is to
make an implicit claim about everything. In this way, an element of
corrigibility is involved in the use of definite descriptions that is
apparently not involved in the use of names. This feature of descriptions
reveals another facet of the issue. As we have considered matters thus
far, the proponent of relational individuation accepts the condition that
he must refer to objects by definite descriptions employing relational
predicates. His critic may now argue that by so doing he distorts
a simple fact of experience. When one is seeing and asserting that
there are two squares there is, in the first place, no doubt that there
are two and, in the second place, no implicit claim about anything else,
much less about everything else. To use descriptions to assert that there
are two or that one is to the right of the other is to lose these two
features of the situation. Hence, the proponent of relational individuation
must distort what is involved in seeing, and asserting, that one square
is to the right of the other. By contrast, the use of proper names, under
the rule of one name for one thing, preserves these features. The first

is preserved in that to use two names reflects that there are two objects; the second is preserved in that statements such as '*Rab*' are atomic sentences. To use only descriptions to refer to individuals precludes there being atomic sentences about individuals. We have thus apparently come to another implicit criterion imposed by the opponent of individuation by relations. But it really amounts to a restatement of the idea that when one says '*a* differs from *b*' he may mean that they simply or numerically differ and not mean that they differ in a property. What is captured by the use of names, as opposed to descriptions, is that *a* and *b* "just differ." What is relevant here, however, is not that we might mean that two things just differ without intending to claim that they differ in a property, but whether or not two things may be two without differing in any way whatsoever. It is one thing to assert that when I say 'p $\vee$ q' I don't intend or mean to say '$\sim$ ($\sim$ p & $\sim$ q)': it is another thing to claim that ' $\vee$ ' cannot be defined in terms of '$\sim$' and '&' because of this. Similarly, that one can think or notice that *a* differs from *b* without thinking or noting that they differ in a property does not mean that the claim that two things to differ must differ in a property is mistaken. What the imagined antagonist of relational individuation seems to be suggesting here is that he has the idea or experience of two things' just differing, and this is distinct from, and irreducible to, the notion of things' differing in a property. But there is an ambiguity in this. It is one thing to suggest that one has a thought involving the notion of disjunction without considering a definition of it; it is another thing to insist that one has a thought of disjunction as distinct in meaning from any purported definition in terms of negation and conjunction. The former is irrelevant; the latter begs the question. For, in effect, in the latter case what is being claimed that is relevant to the issue under discussion is not merely that we notice two things without noting how they differ, but that two things can differ without differing in a quality. The proponent of relational difference is then being asked how he can account for that possibility. Of course he cannot, but the question is whether that is a possibility. We may recall here Wittgenstein's cryptic "refutation" of the claim that to differ was to differ in a quality. The claim is false, he contended, since it was logically possible for two things to share all properties. To settle the issue by having an idea of "numerical difference" as distinct from "conceptual difference" is not adequate[13]—especially as one consequence is the possibility of two objects' sharing all relational properties, and a second is the invention of special entities to account for objects' "numerically differing."

Throughout the discussion of relations and individuation two issues have been left dangling. One concerns the assumption that properties or relations, to individuate, must be "parts" of objects. The second concerns the assumption that the proponent of relational individuation may not use proper names of objects in a perspicuous language but must construct descriptions for them.

The use of the phrase 'part of' lends a specious plausibility to the argument against relational individuation in that one implicitly uses the idea that colors, and shapes, being located in space "where" the object is, may be spoken of as parts, while a relation, and hence a relational property, cannot be said to be "where" any one object is. This makes use of an analogy between 'part' in a spatial sense and 'part' in what we may call a "metaphysical" sense. However, once we forget about misleading analogies, we recognize that to say white is a part of a is to speak in a very special and esoteric sense. It has been tied up with the theme that to think or conceive of the object is to think in terms of qualities of it. Thinking in terms of qualities of the object, we reduce, in thought, the object to such qualities. But what is involved here can be captured without using the phrase 'part of.' We can consider the object to be coordinated to a set of qualities or consider the name of the object coordinated to a list of properties. This can also be taken to express the idea that what is really involved is having, in principle, unique descriptions. What is then wrong with including 'R^1' on such a list? Supposedly its use "presupposes" the existence of two distinct objects. But there is a completely innocent sense of 'presuppose' involved in that we start out, without dispute, with two objects. But the opponent of relational individuation falls back on another, and not so innocent, sense of 'presuppose' that we have considered. As we have seen, what he requests is not that we start from two objects and coordinate two sets of qualities to them, but that, from inspection of the members of the sets alone, we demonstrate that there are two objects. And this can be achieved only if, on the list of all elements of both sets, there occur two unique elements so that it logically follows from the existence of such elements that there are two objects. Such a logical guarantee is furnished by such elements' being just the kinds of entities they are, i.e., particulars or individuators. To be a particular is to be particular to, or capable of belonging to, one and only one subject. In short, the requirements of individuation are so set up that only special things called individuators can individuate. We can see how empty the line is if we consider a defect of Moore's view. For Moore, our two white squares would each be composed of a set of particularized properties, say W_1, S_1 for one, and W_2, S_2 for the other. From a list of the ingredients 'W_1, W_2, S_1, S_2,' it would follow that there was more than one thing, since we build into the idea of, or role of, a particularized property that two of the same kind cannot belong to one object. After all, it would be absurdly redundant to hold that an object has two colors that are exactly alike. But suppose we consider a case where we have a white square and a black circle with no other properties. For Moore one is composed of W_1, S_1, and the other of B_1, C_1. But, from the list "W_1, B_1, C_1, S_1,' we cannot conclude that there are two objects, *without the assumption that one object cannot have two colors and shapes.* But this is exactly the same assumption required of the proponent of differentiation by universal properties; only the type of case is different. *Paradoxically, by his own implicit criterion, Moore cannot ground the difference of two objects which differ in all properties on the same ground that his opponent,* supposedly, *cannot differentiate two objects that share all nonrelational properties!* But we can avoid this problem. All we need do is introduce into each set a unique element, say X_1 and X_2. These elements are such that each can belong to one and only one object. Now, from a list of the ingredients of the sets, we can determine exactly how many objects there are. But such individuating entities only perform their task if we implicitly rule that to each object we coordinate one individuator. That this is the very idea of an individuator is just another, more innocent-sounding, way of putting the matter. But once the coordination feature enters the picture, the proponent of individuators presupposes as much as the proponent of qualitative individuation. Both make use of the fact that there are two objects to start with, and both coordinate sets of elements to them. In one sense, then, all alternatives presuppose that there are two objects. This is crucial, since the opponent of relational individuation argues, in effect, that one cannot hold that two things differ relationally without mentioning or referring to, and hence presupposing, the existence of the two things. But this involves a shift in the sense of 'presuppose.' Supposedly, the proponent of pure individuators can hold that there are two things, ordinary objects, without covertly referring to them, since he need refer only to the individuators. But the individuators do the job they do only under the implicit rule that no two are to be coordinated to one object. What the issue comes down to then is this. Assume one coordination of the two sets $\{F_1, \ldots, F_n, R^1\}$ and $\{F_1, \ldots, F_n\}$ to the two objects a and b and another of the two sets $\{F_1, \ldots, F_n, X_1\}$ and $\{F_1, \ldots, F_n, X_2\}$ to the same two objects. Consider only the first pair of sets and not the objects. It is *not* logically necessary, by our coordinating procedure, that one must coordinate the sets to two objects, since it is logically possible that all the members of the set $\{F_1, \ldots F_n, R^1\}$ are predicable of both objects. This is obviously another way of saying that from the assertion that all the members of $\{F_1, \ldots Fn, R^1\}$ are exemplified it does not follow that there are two objects. By contrast, the sets $\{F_1, \ldots, F_n, X_1\}$ and $\{F_1, \ldots, F_n, X_2\}$ *must be* coordinated to two objects, since we have a rule that no two X_i can be coordinated to the same object, and each X_i must be coordinated to a different object. Or, to put it another way, from the list '$F_1, \ldots, F_n, X_1, X_2$' it follows that we must coordinate the members to two objects. Thus we are back to the basic implicit criterion that from a list of the members of the coordinate sets, and the coordination procedure, it must logically follow that there are two objects. This points up why the opponent of relational individuation feels that to individuate by relational properties "presupposes" that there are two objects in a way that individuating by special "individuators" does not. To hold that relational properties suffice, one *must* speak of coordinating the sets and, hence, group their members, according to which object, a or b, has which properties. We then have two sets, by virtue of our forming or grouping them, one for each object. The proponent of pure individuators reflects how many objects there are *without* forming the sets, since for each X_i there is one object. Once again we reach a dead end, for all that is reflected is the logical possibility, in the same sense of that phrase that allows one square to be "possibly" black and white all over, of R^1's being exemplified in a domain of one object. By contrast, each X_i is just that sort of entity that is not possibly "in" or "associated with" two objects. The argument that qualitative individuation "presupposes" what individuation by particulars does not, thus amounts to the requirement that a ground of individuation must be such that it is logically impossible for two objects to share "it." Pure individuators, or "bare particulars," are precisely those entities invented to fill this requirement.

There is a specious argument which may tempt one to accept the requirement of a logical guarantee that the pure individuators satisfy. Consider the case of universals. Briefly one holds that a universal "in," or associated with, each object is the ground of a true predicative ascription in the case of a predicate like "white." But then, given that the ground exists, it logically follows that the object is white. Is it not then reasonable to have a similar requirement for the solution of the problem of individuation? This argument derives its plausibility from an ambiguity. What provides the ground for the truth of the predicative ascription is the *universal's being a part of* (or associated with) *the particular object*. It is not the presence of the predicate on a list of entities or the fact that the universal is exemplified by *something*. In a similar way, *the presence of a relational property in* or associated with *one object, and not another, does logically guarantee* that *they are different*. This must not be confused with the fact that a relational property's being exemplified does not logically guarantee that there are two objects. If one confuses these two very different conditions, he may be led to require entities from whose existence alone we can logically derive that there are two objects rather than one—to pure individuators or particulars.

To use a property like R^1 instead of R^b to differentiate *a* from *b* is to acknowledge that one may not use proper names, but must construct descriptions, if one holds that relational properties may individuate objects. One motive for acknowledging such a restriction may be thought to be involved in the very idea of an ontological analysis. To give such an analysis may be taken to be tantamount to providing a list of entities one takes to be constituents of the objects being analyzed. In effect, one maps such a list onto an object. But we could not then include the name of the object on such a list. Here we are in danger of being entranced by the notion of mapping such a list. It is one thing to agree that the name of the object cannot occur on a list of constituents of the object; it is another thing to hold that, in a perspicuous language, the name of the object must not occur. One thing involved we have already discussed: the apprehension that, if the name of an object occurs in a definition of a predicate like 'R^b,' then to hold that R^b is "part" of *a* is to hold that *b* is "part" of *a*. But as we saw, one need not hold that *b* is a part of *a* if one holds that R^b is a part of *a*. There is another point involved. We need not think in terms of mapping lists of ingredients, but rather in terms of true statements of a perspicuous or ideal language. Why could one not then use the names 'a' and 'b' to assert '$\text{R}ab$' instead of constructing descriptions? It would appear that the only reason would be a principle to the effect that the use of such names, as primitive terms, commits one to simple entities corresponding to them. The view that the objects a and b are complexes of qualities acknowledges that the objects have constituents, and, hence, are not simple. Thus, in a perspicuous language, names must not occur for them. But the above stated "picturing" principle is not sacrosanct. We may look at the issue in the following way. We start out with two objects and coordinate to them the names 'a' and 'b.' This, indeed, presupposes that there are two objects, but only in that innocent sense in which any account of individuation presupposes that there are two—as a fact from which we start. Having the names 'a' and 'b,' we can then say, in a perspicuous language, '$\text{R}ab$' and define 'R^b.' All this has nothing to do with the analysis of either a or b. One need not require that the perspicuous language show or picture the ontological analysis of the objects, in that the signs which refer to them reveal that they are complexes and of what they are composed. Such an analysis is stated explicitly by one's comments about both the perspicuous language and the object. To use the signs 'a' and 'b' is not to presuppose that there are particulars, in the sense of either Moore's particulars or pure individuators, unless one adopts a picturing principle as a necessary requirement for a language's being used as a tool in ontological analysis. Perhaps one adopts such a principle in the belief that one then avoids making metaphysical statements which reflect one's ontological analysis. For, with such a principle, one may believe his metaphysical analysis "shows itself." Such a Wittgensteinian motive is understandable, if one fears that metaphysical assertions cannot be meaningfully made and believes he can avoid making them by employing such a principle. But both these claims are certainly arguable, and the latter is, perhaps, silly. If we separate the question of the ontological analysis of an object from the use of a purely demonstrative or indicating sign to refer to it, we avoid another motive for the introduction of pure individuators, since such entities may be taken as hypostatizations of the simple indicating function of proper names.

One last point emerges in connection with the previous discussion of R^b, or R^1, being a "part" of the object a. One could hold that only non-relational properties were parts of objects, but that objects exemplified relational properties as well as relations. That is, one would not include, in the ontological analysis of the object, any relational properties. Thus, two objects could have the same ontological analysis in the sense of the same constituents, i.e., the same nonrelational simple properties. They would be two in virtue of *exemplifying* different relational properties. The immediate objection to this would be the old one, that we already presuppose that they are two. But again it is the innocent sense of 'presuppose.' Coordinating two names to the two objects clearly presupposes that there are two, but no more than coordinating two pure individuators to the two objects "presupposes" that there are two. If one then asks what accounts for there being two, since every part of one is now held to be a part of the other, the reply would be that the fact that one exemplifies R^b, and the other does not, accounts for there being two. In this sense, the property R^b can be held to be a ground, but need not be held to be a part or constituent. In short, to say that there are two objects is equivalent to saying that one has a property the other does not have. But "having a property" covers the two cases of constituent nonrelational properties and nonconstituent relational properties. Or, to put it another way, the problem of individuation need not be thought of as a quest for unique ingredients of objects. Rather, we can consider it as specifying conditions that will hold if and only if there are two objects. One proposal is that one object have a property that the other does not have. It is clear that if a has F and b does not, a must differ from b. They differ in a property and hence are different. That is, if '$(\exists x) (\exists y) (Fx \& \sim Fy)$' then '$x$ is not identical with y,' on any reasonable use of 'identical.' Hence, given that some object has F and some object does not, we may conclude there are two objects. The critical question is whether the implication holds in reverse, for there is the idea that to give an analysis of "difference" or a solution to the problem of individuation, the equivalence between 'there are two objects, a and b' and 'a has a property b does not have' must be analytic. But whether it is will clearly depend on how one takes the notions of *object* and *difference*. If one claims that an object contains a pure individuator which is the ground of difference, the implication does not hold. If one takes the "identity of indiscernibles" to be involved in the notion of object, then the implication trivially holds. It is pointless to argue whether the claim that indiscernibles are identical, as such, is an analytic truth. Russell recognized this when he "proved" the identity of indiscernibles to be analytic by taking objects to be classes of properties. To hold to the above stated equivalence is then to state, in part, what one takes an object to be, i.e., what one means by 'object.' In a way one then *makes* the identity of indiscernibles analytic, *given this notion of object.* Considering the matter this way, however, precludes attempting to "prove" that the identity of indiscernibles holds for objects. In this discussion I have not attempted to prove such a thing; I have argued that attempted refutations of qualitative individuation, and hence claims that there are particulars, either "bare" or quality instances, are not cogent. Ultimately one who argues against relational individuation or qualitative individuation, either by requiring the logical guarantee we discussed earlier or by merely insisting on a special notion of 'numerical difference,' may be said to have another conception of an object. Thus, again, we reach a point where argument ceases.

III. Russell on Particulars

Having argued that particulars exist, Moore proceeds to characterize them. As we have noted, his particulars are neither objects like colored squares nor substrata. Thus he speaks of a particular's being related to *its* universal and also "When it is asserted of one of them that it is black and woolen, this is not to be understood as an assertion that one individual has two predicates, but that two individuals have a certain relation."[14] Particulars are thus particularized properties or quality instances. *The whiteness* of a white square object a is a particular which is a constituent of a and numerically different from *the whiteness* of another object b, though both whitenesses are related to one and only one universal, whiteness. Both the whiteness *of* a and that of b are conceptually identical with all other whitenesses, and with each other, but all are numerically different. All such conceptually identical particulars stand in a fundamental asymmetrical relation to the universal whiteness, which is also conceptually identical with, but numerically distinct from, each such particular.[15] An ordinary object like a is then taken as a composite of such quality instances, a color, a shape, etc. In this way Moore has two kinds of individuals, as opposed to universals. One kind, the quality instances, are simple, while the other, ordinary objects, are complex.

Russell also argues for particulars. His arguments essentially reproduce Moore's and, because of our lengthy discussion of Moore, require only brief comment. It is clear from the way Russell characterizes the view that he is refuting—the view which denies that there are particulars—that he insists the proponent of such a view must hold universals to be the terms of spatial relations.

> The theory of sensible qualities which dispense with particulars will say, if the same shade of colour is found in two different places, that what exists is the shade of colour itself, and that what exists in the one place is identical with what exists in the other.[16]

Since the universal whiteness would be one and the same in both patches, nothing can distinguish the two patches:

> It will become impossible to distinguish the two patches as two, unless each, instead of being the universal whiteness, is an *instance*. It might be thought that the two might be distinguished by means of other qualities in the same place as the one but not in the same place as the other. This, however, presupposes that the two patches are already distinguished as numerically diverse, since otherwise what is in the same place as the one must be in the same place as the other.[17]

In short, the term of the spatial relation cannot be the universal whiteness, since we will then have one, and not two, objects when white is to the left of white. We could not then account for the difference of the two objects. Nor can the terms be collections of universals, since it is logically possible for the two objects not to differ in nonrelational properties:

> They may or may not have intrinsic differences—of shape, or size, or brightness, or any other quality—but whether they have or not they are two, and it is obviously logically possible that they should have no intrinsic differences whatever. It follows from this that the terms of spatial relations cannot be universals or collections of universals. . . . Moreover, however many qualities we add, it remains possible that the other subject may also have them; hence qualities cannot be what constitutes the diversity of the subjects.[18]

This tendency to treat a collection or bundle of universal qualities as a complex universal quality is revealed again when he claims:

> But these subjects cannot be mere bundles of general qualities. Suppose one of our men is characterized by benevolence, stupidity, and love of puns. It would not be correct to say: 'Benevolence, stupidity, and love of puns believe that two and two are four'. Nor would this become correct by the addition of a larger number of general qualities.[19]

Moreover, it also seems that Russell is insisting that the predication relation between a subject term and a predicate must be preserved from common usage. For he seems to be suggesting that a quality of an individual cannot be predicated of a collection of qualities and hence the individual cannot be construed as such a collection. If he is not suggesting this, it would appear that he is rejecting a metaphysical view on the ground that it involves odd or incorrect locutions.

In addition to the above arguments, Russell also contends that the logical possibility of one thing's having the two relational properties of being surrounded by red and being surrounded by black (simultaneously) shows, first, that such relational difference cannot ground the diversity of the two patches, and, second, that we presuppose the numerical diversity of two patches if we hold that nothing can have both relational properties.[20] All the above arguments we have considered earlier. However, Russell's central argument may appear to be a new argument. He takes his main argument to be based on the twofold claim that spatial relations like "right of" *imply* diversity of their relata and that it is an evident fact of experience that spatial relations are exemplified. In short, from '*a* is to the right of *b*' it follows, because of synthetic but self-evident characteristics of "right of," that *a* is different from *b*. Given that *a* is to the right of *b*, we may conclude that *a* is different from *b*. Hence *a* and *b* are neither universals nor collections of such. If they were universals they would not need to be diverse, since whiteness could be to the right of whiteness; and if they were collections of universals, the same possibility would arise, since the collection of whiteness, a shape, a size, etc., could be to the left of such a collection. This latter claim obviously depends on taking a collection of universals to be a complex universal. It should then be apparent that Russell's argument that particulars exist, since spatial relations imply diversity, is new only in that he explicitly insists that a bundle of universals is a universal. For the argument involves the claims: (1) two collections of nonrelational universals could not be two if they had all constituents in common; (2) relational properties cannot differentiate objects, since, first, relations are not intrinsic constituents, and, second, an irreflexive relation holding between *a* and *b* implies that *a* is different from *b* and, hence, presupposes their difference rather than grounding it;[21] and (3) a collection of universal qualities is itself a universal rather than a particular, since the collection at two places would be one and the same collection. Perhaps (1) and (3) can be taken as different ways of putting the same claim. That aside, Russell's argument for particulars from the assumption that *a* is to the right of *b* is really a compact way of putting together the various other arguments we have considered.

It is clear that Russell is right when he holds that, if '*a* is to the right of *b*' implies '*a* is different from *b*,' than *a* and *b* cannot be universals if a universal, simple or complex, is taken to be something that can be at two places at the same time.[22] Thus, whether one considers the universal whiteness or the complex universal white-square, neither could be the term of a spatial relation. But it is not at all clear that a particular cannot be a complex of universals, i.e., it is not clear that a complex of universals need itself be a universal. One may claim that a complex of universals, *a*, is one particular, while there may be a different particular, *b*, which is a complex of exactly the same universals. In short, one may deny both that a complex of universals is itself a universal and that two complex objects to be two must differ in a constituent. Even if one rejects only the claim that a complex of universals is itself a universal, one can still maintain that Russell has not shown that one needs particulars other than as complexes of universal properties. For one may still hold that a relational property like R^b or R^1 could be a constituent of *a*. This returns us to our earlier discussion of relational individuation. But we might note that to reject R^b as a ground of individuation, on the basis of its being a universal and hence possibly holding of both *a* and *b*, would be awkward for Russell. On the one hand he would hold that it is self-evident that *a* is not *b* if *a* is to the right of *b*, while on the other hand he would admit that *b* could be to the right of itself.[23]

Even if Russell and Moore have successfully argued that there are particulars, they have not shown that a particular cannot be a complex of universals. At most they have shown that a view which holds that there are only universals cannot account for two objects, alike in all non-relational qualities, exemplifying spatial relations, and, hence, admittedly being different. Simply put, Russell's argument for particulars amounts to the claim that an object cannot be a universal, since if it were it could be here and there. While this is true of universals, it is not true of either ordinary spatial objects or particulars. Hence such objects *must be*, or contain, *particulars* and not be complexes of universals which are, in turn, universals. But this does not involve their being, or containing, particulars in the sense of either quality instances or substrata. For they may be complexes of universals, which are not universals.

Moore's particulars are quality instances. Russell's particulars may also be quality instances. But there are things Russell says that indicate he is arguing for substrata or bare particulars. While he does speak of instances of whiteness he also holds that such an instance has other qualities, i.e., shape and brightness:

> What exists here is something of which whiteness is a predicate—not, as for common sense, the thing with many other qualities, but an instance of whiteness, a particular of which whiteness is the only predicate except shape and brightness and whatever else is necessarily connected with whiteness.[24]

Perhaps the common sense object would be the composite of the particular and the qualities whiteness, the shape, and brightness. In any case, Russell does distinguish the particular from the several qualities it has. We can then distinguish this kind of view from one which would hold that a quality instance has only one quality. On this latter view, the common sense object, the white patch, would be construed to consist of an instance of whiteness, an instance of a shape, and an instance of a degree of brightness. These three quality instances would be different particulars and not qualities of a bare particular or substratum. The former view would seem to involve a substratum exemplifying various universals, whereas the latter avoids a substratum by holding *each* quality of the patch to be a *particular* constituent of it. I am suggesting that Russell's view is the former and Moore's is the latter. If this is so, then even though both have argued for particulars, they have not argued for the same kind of entity. Moreover, if the argument of this paper is correct, neither established what he purported to prove, though they perhaps did establish that particulars exist in that objects cannot be taken *to be* universals.

Notes

1. Bertrand Russell, "On the Relations of Universals and Particulars," reprinted in R. C. Marsh (ed.), *Logic and Knowledge* (London: George Allen & Unwin, 1956).

2. G. E. Moore, "Identity," *Proceedings of the Aristotelian Society*, I (1900-1), 108.

3. *Ibid.*, pp. 108-109. Moore uses 'predicate' and 'property' synonymously. As this will cause no confusion I shall follow his use.

4. *Ibid.*, p. 109.

5. Moore implicitly forces his opponent to hold that a complex of universal qualities is itself a universal quality. Russell, as we shall see, explicitly uses the claim as a key point in his argument. This is one obvious idea that lies behind the claim that there cannot be two complexes of the same universals, *for* it would be *one* universal thing and not two particular things. Moreover, there is some justification for Moore and Russell to argue this way. Bradley is clearly one opponent Moore has in mind, and Bradley did hold that the seeming judgment "*a* is white" is really to be construed as a predicate attributed to Reality as the subject. Without getting involved in an analysis of Bradley, we may note that one thing he had in mind was that we must consider the object *a* in terms of a set of qualities, say F_1, F_2, . . . , F_n, and what we do in judgment is to assert that the combination of qualities, F_1, F_2, . . . , F_n plus white, exists. In speaking of this as attributing a predicate to reality, he explicitly confuses a combination of qualities which could be a quality, like the complex property red-square, with a particular construed as a combination of qualities.

6. G. E. Moore, "The Nature of Judgment," *Mind*, XXX (1899). Also see my "Moore's Ontology and Nonnatural Properties," Essay 6 above.

7. Without considering in any detail the problems surrounding the notions of identity and difference, we may note the following different senses of "conceptual" and "numerical" that are relevant to Moore's discussion:

a) Two objects, like Peter and Paul, numerically differ in that they contain constituents which just differ.

b) Two objects, like Peter and Paul, numerically differ in that to consider them as different is not to consider them as differing in a concept.

c) Two entities, like the constituents of Peter and Paul which are not universals, just differ numerically.

d) Two concepts, like white and square, are just different and hence differ numerically.

e) Two concepts, like white and square, are different concepts and hence conceptually differ.

f) Two objects, like Peter and Paul, are conceptually different in that they contain different concepts.

g) Two concepts, like white and square, are different in that one is a color and the other is a shape, and they hence are different sorts of concepts.

8. "Identity," p. 117. Moore speaks of a "class-concept" here and not of a class. But as he also speaks of members of "it" that does not seem crucial.

9. Moore takes the group to contain the predication (exemplification) relation. Hence, if the group were a class, the predication relation would be a member of the class. It would not hold between the class and a member of it and hence would not be indicated by the sign for membership. If the group were not a class, but the complex of qualities in a relation EX, then EX would hold among the qualities and not between the complex, as a whole, and the constituent qualities. Thus the relation EX would not be indicated by the phrase 'is a part of' or 'contains.' One could suggest taking the group to be a class with only the qualities as members, but then one would face the problem of what makes some classes of qualities objects and some not. (For a detailed discussion of this question see my "Things and Descriptions," *American Philosophical Quarterly*, III, [1966], and "Universals, Particulars, and Predication," *Review of Metaphysics*, XIX [1965].) In any case, to

take the group as a class is to give up predication, which Moore assumes we cannot do, and to make the group a universal, which we also cannot do.

10. "Identity," pp. 109-10.

11. See my "Things and Qualities" in Merrill and Capitan (eds.), *Metaphysics and Explanation* (Pittsburgh: University of Pittsburgh Press, 1966).

12. The definition is 'x $=$ y $=$ df. $(F)(Fx \equiv Fy)$'.

13. As I mentioned above, such a theme may be part of Moore's argument. That this line of thought fits Moore's "style" of argument is apparent when we recall his refutations of idealism and naturalism.

14. "Identity," p. 127.

15. The fundamental asymmetric relation is not the basis of conceptual identity, since Moore holds that the universal is conceptually identical with each instance of it.

16. Russell, *op. cit.*, p. 110.

17. *Ibid.*, p. 113.

18. *Ibid.*, pp. 118, 120. Russell also seems to be suggesting that, in so far as we see that the two patches are two irrespective of whether they differ in a property, we cannot ground their difference in universals. This "phenomenological" argument has been touched on in Section II above and is discussed in my "On Being and Being Presented," *Philosophy of Science,* XXXII (No. 2, 1965).

19. Russell, *op. cit.*, p. 120.

20. *Ibid.*, p. 117.

21. (2) is involved in so far as Russell recognizes that if relations can individuate he has not proved that particulars, as he construes them, exist. Hence he must, as he does, argue the points in (2). His arguments do not differ from those discussed in Section II of this essay.

22. One may propose that the object could be construed either as a complex universal, which contains a spatial property, or as a universal of a higher type, which is exemplified by all the ordinary qualities of the object including an individuating spatial property. The spatial property will supposedly take care of the problem of individuation. Structurally, such a gambit resembles what Russell later did in *An Inquiry into Meaning and Truth*, though he there took the object to be a class of the second level. Some problems of this view are discussed in "Things and Descriptions." Here, we need note only that such "universals" violate the claim, implicit in Russell's present argument, that a universal is what can be at two places or, at least, common to two objects.

23. Of course Russell would reply that the very use of R^b begs the question. But that is another point and returns us to the discussion of relational individuation.

24. Russell, *op. cit.*, p. 111. There is a problem of interpretation caused by an ambiguity in Russell's use of 'particular' and 'instance.' Not only does he speak, like Moore, of a particular as an instance of a quality and suggest that quality instances, not universals, are constituents of ordinary objects; he sometimes speaks of a particular as if it were the composite of a bare particular and the qualities it exemplifies. In spite of this, I think the existence of bare particulars or substrata is what he is arguing for.

PART THREE

METHODOLOGY AND
EPISTEMOLOGY

Introduction

AMONG THE ISSUES of greatest importance under the heading of Moore's methodology and epistemology are perhaps the following: Moore's defense of common sense and his views regarding the role of common sense in philosophy; his comments regarding ordinary language; his emphasis upon the importance of analysis as a philosophical method or activity; his proof of an external world; and his various efforts to solve the problem of perception. The first four of these topics are discussed in various essays in this section.

In his widely known essay, "A Defence of Common Sense," Moore claimed to *know* with *certainty* a large number of propositions, such as 'There exists at present a human body, which is *my* body,' 'This body was born at a certain time in the past, and has existed continuously ever since,' 'The earth had existed also for many years before my body was born,' etc. In addition to these "truisms," Moore also claimed to know with certainty that many other human beings have known other propositions similar to Moore's truisms about themselves. And, further, Moore claimed that all these and similar truisms are *wholly* true and that he was using expressions such as 'The Earth had existed for many years past,' etc., in their ordinary sense.[1] Moore, then, has no doubt as to the truth or the understanding of his truisms. We may know them to be true and know what they mean in the ordinary sense; but what we may not always know is their correct *analysis*.[2]

In "Defending Common Sense" (Essay 10 in this volume), Norman Malcolm maintains that, in his "Defence," Moore was not defending common sense at all when he uttered assertions such as 'I know with certainty' that 'there exists at present a living human body which is *my* body,' etc. According to Malcolm, these statements were made in situations where there was no question as to whether Moore had a body, etc., and Moore's assertions do not belong to common sense—i.e., to ordinary language—at all. What Moore wanted to do (says Malcolm) was to attack all philosophers who held views from which it would follow that no one could know that propositions like 'Here's a hand' are true. According to Malcolm, Moore saw that statements such as 'I don't know that this is a hand' are *misuses* of language; but he did not see that his statements, 'I know this is a hand,' etc., are misuses too. In "On Speaking with the Vulgar" (Essay 11 in this volume), Max Black argues that Malcolm's accusation is mistaken, and he claims that Moore was using ordinary language and not talking nonsense by misusing it.

The remaining essays in this part deal with the nature and role of analysis in Moore's philosophy. In "Moore and Philosophical Analysis" (Essay 12 in this volume), Morris Lazerowitz argues that Moore "has made prominent a method for obtaining results in philosophy"—the method of analysis or of analyzing concepts. Lazerowitz proposes to examine this technique in order to see "what it is and what it can accomplish."

In "The Paradox of Analysis" (Essay 13), M. S. Gram discusses a form of the paradox which was first stimulated by certain views of G. E. Moore on analysis. Gram argues that the paradox is generated by a faulty assumption regarding the nature of philosophical analysis, and attempts a solution of the paradox which *denies* the claim that the statement of an analysis must be an analytic identity statement and thereby trivially tautologous.

In "G. E. Moore's Proof of an External World" (Essay 14), I have raised questions such as: In what sense is Moore's "Proof" a proof? in what, precisely, does the proof consist? etc. And I have argued that the answer to such questions involves Moore's notion of analysis as *a* method in philosophy.

Notes

1. G. E. Moore, "A Defence of Common Sense," in *Philosophical Papers* (London: Allen & Unwin, 1959), pp. 32-36.
2. *Ibid.*, pp. 36, 53.

Ten

DEFENDING
COMMON SENSE

Norman Malcolm

Skeptizismus ist *nicht* unwiderleglich, sondern offenbar unsinnig, wenn er bezweifeln will, wo nicht gefragt werden kann.

Denn Zweifel kann nur bestehen, wo eine Frage besteht; eine Frage nur, wo eine Antwort besteht, und diese nur, wo etwas *gesagt* werden *kann.*—Wittgenstein, *Tractatus Logico-Philosophicus,* *6.51.

IN "A DEFENCE OF COMMON SENSE"[1] G. E. Moore wrote down a list of propositions which he called "truisms." The following are some of the propositions in that list: "There exists at present a living human body, which is *my* body"; "The earth had existed for many years before my body was born"; "Ever since it was born it has been either in contact with or not far from the surface of the earth"; "I am a human being"; "I have often perceived both my own body and other things which formed part of its environment, including other human bodies." Moore said that every one of the propositions in his list "I *know,* with certainty, to be true."[2]

In his "Proof of an External World"[3] Moore gave what he considered

Reprinted by permission of the author and the editor from *The Philosophical Review,* LVIII (1949), 201-20.

to be "a perfectly rigorous proof" of the existence of "things outside of us."[4] He said that he could prove that two human hands exist. "How? By holding up my two hands, and saying, as I make a certain gesture with the right hand, 'Here is one hand,' and adding, as I make a certain gesture with the left, 'and here is another.' "[5] He said that this would not have been a proof unless (among other things) "the premiss which I adduced was something which I *knew* to be the case, and not merely something which I believed but which was by no means certain, or something which, though in fact true, I did not know to be so." But, he continued,

> I certainly did at the moment *know* that which I expressed by the combination of certain gestures with saying the words, 'there is one hand and here is another.' I *knew* that there was one hand in the place indicated by combining a certain gesture with my first utterance of 'here' and that there was another in the different place indicated by combining a certain gesture with my second utterance of 'here.' How absurd it would be to suggest that I did not know it, but only believed it, and that perhaps it was not the case! You might as well suggest that I do not know that I am now standing up and talking—that perhaps after all I'm not, and that it's not quite certain that I am![6]

Again: "I *do* know that I held up two hands above this desk not very long ago. As a matter of fact in this case you all know it too. There's no doubt whatever that I did."[7] Again: "I have, no doubt, conclusive evidence for asserting that I am not now dreaming; I have conclusive evidence that I am awake. . . ."[8]

I wish to put forward the contention that there is something wrong with Moore's assertions. What I have to say, however, will not be in support of the philosophers who have argued that it is not certain that the earth has existed for many years, or that Moore did not know for certain that he was a human being, or that it is not perfectly certain that he held up a hand during his lecture to the British Academy.

What then is it which, according to me, is wrong with Moore's assertions? I believe that, in the two essays from which I quoted, Moore *misused* the expressions "I know," "I know with certainty," "It is certain," "I have conclusive evidence." I wish to show that Moore's use of those expressions, as illustrated in those essays, is contrary to their ordinary and correct use.

Moore said that he *knew* that the statement "Here's a hand," which he uttered as he held up his hand before the audience at his British Academy lecture, was true. That assertion implies that it would have been correct for him to have said, at a time when he and his audience had a clear view of his hand, "I know that here's a hand." At this moment I am holding a pen, there is a desk before me, I am seated in a chair, and through the window I see a near-by tree. Let us imagine that there is another person in this room who has a clear view of me seated in this chair, before this desk, with this pen in my hand, and who has an unobstructed view of that near-by tree. Moore's assertion implies that it would be correct for me to say to that person "I know that I am holding a pen," "I know with certainty that I am sitting in a chair and before a desk," "It's perfectly certain that that [pointing at the tree] is a tree." I contend that I should misuse language if I were to make any of these statements.

Consider the sentence "It's perfectly certain that that is a tree." If we are walking on a meadow in a heavy fog and a tall, indistinct object looms ahead, and one of us wonders whether it is a tree or a telephone pole, it would be a natural thing for one of us to say, "It's perfectly certain that that is a tree, because if you look carefully you will see the faint outline of the branches on either side." That is one example of circumstances in which the sentence "It's perfectly certain that that is a tree" would be correctly used, although it might not be *true* that that object was a tree. Whether or not it was a tree could be determined by walking closer to it. Consider another example: We are seated in the audience at an open-air theatre, the stage of which is bordered by trees. The stage scenery is painted to represent a woodland, and the painting is so skillfully executed that we are in doubt as to whether that which we see on one side of the stage is a real tree or a painted tree. Finally one of us exclaims "I know that that is a real tree, because just now I saw the leaves move in the breeze." This would be a natural use of language. If a doubt remained as to whether it was a real tree the matter could be finally settled by approaching nearer to the stage. Consider still another example: We are examining an elder plant and the question arises as to whether it is properly called a "tree" or a "shrub." One of us says, "I know that that's a tree because I heard a botany professor say that elders are 'trees' and not 'shrubs.'" Whether or not it is proper to call it a "tree" could be determined by consulting an authoritative book on plants.

Three cases have been described in which it would be a correct use of language, although it might be false, to say, "I know that that's a tree"; and innumerable other cases could be given. Let us notice some features common to these three cases: (1) There is in each case a question at issue and a doubt to be removed. (2) In each case the person who asserts "I know that that's a tree" is able to give a reason for his assertion. (3) In each case there is an investigation which, if it were carried out, would settle the question at issue. I wish to show that all of these features are missing when Moore says in a philosophical context "I know that that's a tree."

(1) Consider the circumstances in which, according to Moore, he would have spoken correctly if he had said, during his British Academy lecture, "I know that here is a hand." He and his audience had a clear view of his hand. If his hand had been concealed in a bag it is unlikely that he would have pointed at the bag and said to his audience "I know that here is a hand." Or if it had been rumored that Moore had an artificial hand which closely resembled a human hand, it is likely that he would have changed the example. Perhaps he would have pointed at his head and said, "It's certain that this is a head." The point is that he would have chosen to utter the sentence "I know that here is a hand" in circumstances where there was not even any *question* as to whether there was a hand where he pointed! This feature alone of his use of the sentence "I know that here is a hand" would mark it as not an ordinary use of that sentence. If Moore was having a discussion with someone who had produced an argument in favor of saying that it is never certain that any perceptual judgment is true, Moore would point at a tree which stood close by in plain view of both of them and declare "It's perfectly certain that that is a tree." He would not choose circumstances for uttering that sentence in which the outline of the tree was obscured by heavy fog; or in which there was any question as to whether the thing at which he pointed was a real tree and not a section of painted scenery, or a real tree and not a mirror image of a tree; or in which there was any question as to whether it was properly called a "tree" or a "shrub." He would pick circumstances for saying "It's perfectly certain that that's a tree" or "I *know* that that's a tree" in which there was no question at all as to whether the thing at which he pointed was a tree.

The first respect, therefore, in which Moore's usage of the expression "I know," in the philosophical contexts which we are considering,

departs from ordinary usage is that Moore says "I know that so and
so is true" in circumstances where no one doubts that so and so is true
and where there is not even any question as to whether so and so is
true. It will be objected: "His opponent has a philosophical doubt as
to whether so and so is true, and there is a philosophical question as
to whether so and so is true." That is indeed the case. What I am saying is that the philosophical doubt and the philosophical question are
raised in circumstances in which there isn't any *doubt* and isn't any
question as to whether so and so is true. Moore's opponent would not
raise a philosophical question as to whether it is certain that an object
before them is a tree if the object were largely obscured or too distant
to be easily seen. If he said "I wish to argue that it isn't certain that
that object is a tree" and Moore replied "I can't tell at this distance
whether it is a tree or a bush," then Moore's opponent would *change
the example*. He would not want to use as an example for his philosophical argument an object with regard to which there was some doubt
as to whether it was a tree. The use of an object as an example for
presenting his philosophical doubt is spoiled for him if there *is* any
doubt as to what the object is. It must be the case that there is no
doubt that the given object is a tree *before* he can even raise a philosophical question as to whether it is certain that it is a tree.

It will be objected, "Moore's opponent may truly doubt that the object is a tree in the respect that he may be in doubt as to whether he is
dreaming." It is indeed the case that one of the most powerful arguments for the view that the truth of no perceptual judgment is ever
certain is the argument used by Descartes for the purpose of proving
that one can never know for certain that one is not dreaming. Suppose
that we were watching Descartes through the window of his room
while he wrote down that argument which produced in him an astonishment "such that it is almost capable of persuading me that I now
dream." Suppose that we saw him facing the fire, sometimes placing a
fresh log on it, sometimes placing a kettle to boil, as he formulated the
considerations which aroused in him that "astonishment." Wouldn't it
be unnatural to say in such a case that Descartes was "in doubt" as
to whether there was a fire, even if we heard him exclaim, "Perhaps I
dream and there is no fire here"? Compare that situation with one in
which we are watching through the window a man seated in a room
whose view of the fire is cut off by a screen. Twice the fire has gone
out and he has started it again, and frequently now he lays down his

writing in order to peer over the screen. It would be natural to say in such a case that each time he rose to peer over the screen he was in doubt as to whether there was a fire. The sort of circumstances in which it would be unnatural to say of a man that he "doubts" that there is a fire are the very circumstances in which that man might express a philosophical doubt as to whether there is a fire!

Consider this case: A man awakes from sleep and sees a fire burning brightly in the grate. He is astonished because he has no recollection of having started a fire. He shakes his head as if to rouse himself, stares hard at the fire, says, "Perhaps I dream and there is no fire," dashes cold water in his face and looks at the fire again, walks to it with hand extended to feel its warmth, and, continuing to express astonishment, calls in his neighbor from the next apartment, to whom he addresses the question "Am I dreaming, or do I really see a fire?"

This man is in doubt as to whether he is dreaming or awake, in the ordinary sense of those words. His doubt is expressed in *actions* of doubting. When a man is entertaining a philosophical doubt as to whether he is dreaming or awake he does not perform actions of that sort. We must not understand this to mean merely that he does not, *in fact,* perform actions of that sort, although he *could* do so. The truth is that if he did perform actions of that sort then we should no longer say that he was entertaining a philosophical doubt. The very actions which would count in favor of saying that he was *in doubt* as to whether he was awake would count *against* saying that he was feeling a philosophical doubt.

It will be said that Moore's philosophical opponent may be in doubt as to whether he is seeing a real tree or is instead suffering from hallucination. Let us consider the sort of circumstances in which I (or any philosopher) should give utterance to a philosophical doubt as to whether I was having a hallucination. I should fix my eyes upon some object in plain view at close range, such as the chair in that corner. I should say or think "How do I know that I see a chair? Perhaps I am having a hallucination. Perhaps I am really looking at a dog and because of my hallucination it seems to me that I see a chair." I should turn over in my mind one or more of the several philosophical arguments which have been offered to prove that it is never absolutely certain that one is not having a hallucination. If as I looked at that chair it should suddenly turn into a dog, or seem to, then I should be enormously startled. I should think "Is this a hallucination? Is it a dog I see?" I should be apprehensive of the thing in the corner. I should look about me with anxiety to see whether anything else in the room presented an unusual appearance. I should have ceased my philosophical reflection. I should have been jarred out of my philosophical doubt! I should be *in doubt,* in the ordinary sense of the words, as to whether I was having a hallucination. If I said "Do I really see a dog or is this hallucination?" I should *not* now be expressing a philosophical doubt. If the thing in the corner continued to look and behave and sound like a dog, and if everything else around me looked entirely normal, then I should begin to feel confident that it was really a dog I saw. And if my wife, when I called her in, should express astonishment at there being a dog there, then it would be a natural thing for me to say "I thought for a moment that perhaps I was having a hallucination or was dreaming. Now I know that I'm not. It really is a dog!" Once I was perfectly reassured that I was not having a hallucination, then I could resume my philosophical reflection—that is, I could proceed again to entertain a philosophical doubt as to whether I was having a hallucination.

Let us compare the natural use of the sentence "I know that I'm not dreaming or having a hallucination," which we have just described, with Moore's philosophical use of it. One feature of the circumstances of its natural use was that something *extraordinary* had occurred. Another feature was that my anxiety as to whether I was suffering from hallucination or had actually seen a chair turn into a dog, expressed itself in such actions as rising from my chair in alarm, glancing apprehensively about me, scrutinizing closely the thing in the corner, calling in my wife. Another feature was that as a result of performing those actions my anxiety and doubt were removed. Now consider the circumstances in which Moore, in his British Academy lecture, said "I have, no doubt, conclusive reasons for asserting that I am not now dreaming; I have conclusive evidence that I am awake. . . ."[9] Nothing extraordinary had occurred. Neither Moore nor anyone present had any reason to think that he was dreaming. Neither he nor anyone present had any doubt about it. There was not even any *question* as to whether he was dreaming. Yet in those circumstances Moore uttered the sentence "I have conclusive evidence that I am awake." Ordinarily a statement like that would be made only if there was some reason to think that he was dreaming, and only if he or someone else felt a doubt about it, and only if he had done something to remove the doubt.

None of these things are true of the circumstances in which Moore made his statement. His use of the sentence "I have conclusive evidence that I am awake" was an enormous departure from ordinary usage.

With respect to the objection, therefore, that Moore's philosophical opponent does have a doubt as to whether he really sees a tree or is, instead, dreaming or having a hallucination, it should be answered: Moore's opponent has a *philosophical* doubt as to whether he is dreaming, but this does not imply that he is *in doubt* as to whether he is dreaming. To call a philosophical doubt a *doubt* is as misleading as to call a rhetorical question a *question*. We should not say that a man was feeling a philosophical doubt as to whether he was having an hallucination if he was, *in the ordinary sense of the words,* in doubt as to whether he was having a hallucination. Nor should we say that he was raising a philosophical question as to whether he might not be dreaming if the circumstances were such that there *was* some question as to whether he was dreaming.

(2) The second thing that we noticed about the natural use of the sentence "I know that that is a tree" is that the person who utters it is able to support his assertion with a *reason.* Suppose that we were on the top of a high hill and were curious as to whether something which we saw in the valley below was a tree or a shrub. If one of us said "I know that it is a tree," it would be natural to ask "How do you know?" This question is a request for a reason, for proof, for evidence. Many different reasons might be given, e.g., "I was down at that place yesterday and remember seeing a tree there"; or "If you will compare the height of it with that of the barn nearby you will see that it must be a tree." If the person answered our question with "I have no reason" or "I have a reason but I don't know what it is," we should think it rather queer. We should think that he should not have said, "I know that that is a tree" but should have said instead, "I am inclined to believe that that is a tree but I have no reason for it." We should feel that the use of the word "know," unaccompanied by a reason, was inappropriate.

Now a striking thing about Moore's utterance, in a philosophical context, of a statement like "I know that that is a tree," is that he cannot offer any reason in support of his statement. In his British Academy lecture he said: "How am I to prove now that 'Here's one hand, and here's another'? I do not believe I can do it. In order to do it, I should need to prove for one thing, as Descartes pointed out, that

I am not now dreaming. But how can I prove that I am not? I have,
no doubt, conclusive reasons for asserting that I am not now dreaming; I have conclusive evidence that I am awake: but that is a very
different thing from being able to prove it. I could not tell you what all
my evidence is; and I should require to do this at least, in order to
give you a proof."[10] He insisted, however, that "I can know things,
which I cannot prove. . . ."[11] In "A Defence of Common Sense" he
said, "But do I really *know* all the propositions in (1) to be true?
["(1)" is the list of propositions such as "there exists at present a
living human body, which is *my* body," "the earth had existed for
many years before my body was born," "I am a human being," etc.]
Isn't it possible that I merely believe them? or know them to be highly probable? In answer to this question, I think I have nothing better
to say than that it seems to me that I do know them, with certainty. . . . We are all, I think, in this strange position that we do *know*
many things, with regard to which we *know* further that we must have
had evidence for them, and yet we do not know *how* we know, i.e.,
we do not know what the evidence was."[12]

Moore's remark, "I can know things which I cannot prove," possesses on the surface of it a certain plausibility. In ordinary life circumstances do occur in which we should say that someone knew that
so and so was true although he could not prove it. I might know, for
example, that Mr. R. entered the apartment house on the night of the
crime. If the district attorney asked, "How do you know?" I might reply, "I saw him." If the district attorney asked, "How do you know
that it was Mr. R. you saw?" I might reply, "Because I had a clear,
close view of his face." If my testimony was doubted, I might prove
that Mr. R. did enter the apartment house that night by producing
several reliable witnesses to testify that they too saw him enter it. If,
however, I was not able to produce those other witnesses, because they
were all dead, I would not be able to prove it, although I knew it. In
this case there was something which the district attorney would have
called proof *if* I could have produced it.

The philosophical context in which Moore would say "I know that
that is a tree" is very dissimilar. Although Moore's opponent asks
"How do you know that that is a tree?" there is nothing which he
would *call* a proof that it is a tree. There is not even anything which
he would call a *reason* for saying that it is a tree. It would be pointless
for Moore to say to him, "I know that it is a tree because I see that

it is a tree"; or to say "I know that it is a tree because I have a clear, close view of it." In the philosophical context these remarks would be utterly irrelevant. If Moore were to say, "I know that I do see a tree and am not suffering from hallucination, because just now I saw my wife point at the place I am looking and heard her say 'I must trim that tree,'" the philosophical reply would be, "That is no reason, because it may be part of your hallucination that you saw and heard your wife." There is nothing at all which Moore could offer in defense of his statement "I know that that is a tree." There is nothing which in that context would be called "proof" or "reason" or "evidence" for that statement. It follows from this that Moore's use of "know" in that context is a departure from its ordinary use. In ordinary discourse we are reluctant to say that someone *knows* that so and so is true if he cannot give some reason or some evidence for saying that so and so is true. If he can offer no reason or evidence at all then we are inclined to say that he should not have said that he *knew* that so and so is true. Moore's philosophical usage of "know" breaks this connection between the ordinary use of the word "know" and the being able to give a *reason*.

It also breaks the connection between the ordinary use of the word "know" and the being able to give a *proof*. Let me make this clearer. As was noted before, we do permit it to be said, in some circumstances, that a person knows something which he cannot prove. He *may* know that that thing at the base of the cliff is a tree, and not a bush, because he says that he was down there a month ago; but he cannot *prove* that it is a tree because the recent landslide prevents those who doubt his word from climbing to the bottom and seeing for themselves whether it is a tree. We all understand perfectly well, however, that there is something which we should call a proof. If by some extraordinary feat we *were* able to descend, then his assertion would be proved or disproved, because then we should have a close view of the thing. His claim would have been proved true or false, depending on the outcome.

In the philosophical context the difficulty in the way of proving that the thing at which we are looking is a tree is not that none of the procedures of proof appropriate to normal contexts of doubt can, in fact, be carried out. The difficulty is that there is no procedure whatever which, even if it *were* carried out, would be called a "proof" that the thing we see is a tree. In this context there is not, therefore, a *concept* of proof. In ordinary discourse the statement, "I know it, although I cannot prove it," is made in circumstances where there is a concept of proof, but where a proof cannot, *as a matter of fact,* be obtained. In the philosophical context anyone who says "I know it is a tree, although I cannot prove it" is trying to fit the concept of *knowledge* into a context in which there is no concept of *proof.* To try to divorce in this way the concept of knowledge from the concept of proof is a radical violation of the logic of ordinary language.

(3) These last remarks pertain to the third feature of the ordinary use of "I know that so and so"—namely, that in any particular context in which it is used there is an investigation which would settle whether "So and so" is true. Let us take as an example the sentence "I know that I see a hand." It will be helpful to consider some of the different contexts in which the words "Is that a hand I see?" might be uttered:

(a) I see a man standing a thousand yards from me. Some object is thrust above his head. I cannot tell whether it is one of his hands or is some other object. "Is that a hand I see?"

(b) I see a man seated twenty feet away. One of his hands is in plain view. I know that sometimes he wears gloves which are the color of flesh. Perhaps I see the surface of a glove and not the surface of a hand. "Is that a hand I see?"

(c) I am sitting half asleep before the fire. Suddenly I seem to see a hand thrust through the window curtains ten feet away. Am I dreaming? Am I "seeing things"? "Is that a hand I see?"

(d) I know that the man sitting across the table from me has an artificial hand, but I don't remember whether it is his left or his right. One hand of his rests on the table. I am not sure whether it is a hand of flesh and blood or an artificial hand. "Is that a hand I see?"

In each of these cases it would be natural to use the same sentence "Is that a hand I see?" But in each case there is a *different question* at issue. To each of these different questions a *different investigation* is appropriate. In (a) I should close the distance to a hundred yards and look again. In (b) I should approach to within three feet and look closely for seams, or lightly pass my finger over part of the surface. In (c) I should rouse myself with a shake of my body, open my eyes wider, look more sharply, change slightly the posture of my head in order to obtain a different angle of vision. In (d) I should reach across and press the hand firmly with my fingers. The actions of investigation, "the ways of finding out," which were suitable in one case would not be suitable in the other cases.

Let us suppose that in each of these cases there is another person to whom I direct the interrogatory sentence, "Is that a hand I see?" and who replies with the declarative sentence "I know that it *is* a hand." Just as the interrogatory sentence might be said to express in each case a different *question,* so in each case the declarative sentence might be said to *mean* something different—to make a different *assertion.* The sentence "I know that it is a hand" refers to the same question which the interrogatory sentence expresses in *that* context, and it refers to the investigation which would answer *that* question. In each context in which the sentence is uttered it refers only to the question and the investigation which belong to *that* context. In every ordinary context the assertion "I know that it is a hand" implies that there is an appropriate investigation which would, if it were carried out, decide that particular question at issue.

A surprising thing about the philosophical context in which Moore would say "I know that that is a hand" is that his sentence is not connected with *any investigation.* Moore himself indicated this when he discussed, before the British Academy audience, the difficulty about proving his premises.

> Of course, in some cases what might be called a proof of propositions which seem like these can be got. If one of you suspected that one of my hands was artificial he might be said to get a proof of my proposition 'Here's one hand, and here's another' by coming up and examining the suspected hand close up, perhaps touching and pressing it, and so establishing that it really was a human hand. But I do not believe that any proof is possible in nearly all cases. How am I to prove now that 'Here's one hand, and here's another'? I do not believe I can do it.[13]

Indeed he cannot do it. The reason he cannot is that there is no investigation to be undertaken. If someone in Moore's audience had stood up and said, "Let me feel it; then I shall know whether it is a hand," he would have shown that he did not *understand* what was going on. His remark would have shown that he did not understand that the question whether anyone knows that it is a hand is a *philosophical* question. It would be the same if he had proposed any other investigation. He would understand the philosophical nature of the question only if he saw that there was no investigation to be undertaken.

It is inaccurate, therefore, to say, as I said in the preceding paragraph, that Moore "cannot" prove that it is a hand he is holding up.

The accurate thing to say is that it does not make sense to ask for a proof in those circumstances. A proof is the result of an investigation. If the context does not allow for an investigation it does not allow for a proof.

I believe that Moore thought that it did make sense to ask for a proof of "Here's a hand" as he stood before his audience, and that he was troubled at not being able to give one. That he thought so is shown from the fact that he was willing to assert, "I *know* that here's a hand." The ordinary uses of "know" and "proof" are joined in such a way that if it makes sense to assert "I *know* that so and so is true," it also makes sense to ask for a *proof* that so and so is true. Thinking that a request for a proof that "Here's a hand" was in that situation a legitimate request, but one he could not satisfy, Moore was led to contend that he knew something which he could not prove. His contention gives aid and comfort to his opponents, the very skeptics whom he wishes to overthrow. For they are inclined to say, "If you cannot prove it then you don't know it." This retort of theirs would be justified if the request for a proof were legitimate. But it isn't. To say "Prove that here's a hand," in circumstances like those in which Moore said that he could not prove that "Here's a hand," is to utter nonsense. There the hand is, right before everyone's eyes; what would it mean to "prove" that it is a hand? The sentence "Prove that here's a hand" has the grammatical form of a request, but in those circumstances it does not *function* as a request. If the philosopher who says, "Try to prove that here's a hand; you can't do it," doesn't want any of the actions of investigation carried out which are normally carried out in order to satisfy a request for a proof that something we see is a hand, then it is very misleading, if not downright wrong, to say that he is "requesting a proof."

It may be objected: "The philosophical question 'How do I know that this is a hand?' is a request for a *philosophical* investigation, and since it does refer to an investigation the request for a proof is not senseless." It is true that when the question "How do I know that this is a hand?" is asked philosophically it is appropriate to undertake a philosophical investigation. But this investigation is not of a kind which could result in a proof that "Here's a hand." "Investigation" here means something quite different. There are a number of philosophical arguments which seem to prove that it cannot ever be known with absolute certainty, "beyond the possibility of doubt," that any statement like

"Here's a hand" is true. The examination of these arguments is a philosophical investigation, and it is a labor of great difficulty and importance. But even if one were to succeed in refuting all of these arguments one would not have proved that "Here's a hand" is true. What we mean by proving that something that we see is a hand is not a philosophical activity. It would be a philosophical activity to show that none of the reasons offered by various philosophers for saying that no one *can* know such a thing as "Here's a hand" are good reasons. One would not have proved thereby that in any particular case when one said, "That's a hand" one was right. Proving the latter would not be doing philosophy at all.

When Moore said, "I cannot prove that 'Here's a hand'" his statement made it seem as if none of the methods of proving such a thing could, as a matter of fact, be carried out. The truth of the case was not, however, that none of the actions and procedures which, in various circumstances, are regarded as methods of proving that a thing we see is a hand, could, as a matter of fact, be carried out. The truth of the case was that all of those actions and procedures were *irrelevant* to that context! Instead of saying, "I cannot prove that 'Here's a hand,'" it would have been more exact to have said, "This is a situation in which the word 'proof' does not have a correct use." In such circumstances it is neither correct to say, "I cannot prove that that's a hand" nor to say, "I can prove it." Likewise, it is not correct to say, "I know that that's a hand," and not correct to say, "I don't know that that's a hand." It is an essential part of the usage of "know," as well as of "prove," that it is joined to an *inquiry*. The statement "I know that that's a hand," in its ordinary meaning, implies that there is a mode of inquiry, an activity of finding out, a procedure of investigation, which, if it were carried out would result in a proof that "That's a hand." Moore's assertion "I know that 'Here's a hand'" was extraordinary because it did not have that implication. Moore was well aware that it would have been completely pointless for anyone to have brought the hand closer to his eyes or to have pressed it, or to have performed *any* of the actions of investigation which would be customarily joined to that assertion. In such a case to declare, "I know that 'Here's a hand'" is as eccentric as to labor at turning the crank of an automobile which one knows to be without an engine. If you take away from that sentence its connection with actions of investigation you turn it into an empty utterance.

I am contending that if Moore and I were sitting within a few feet of an apple tree which was in plain view of both of us, it would be a misuse of ordinary language for either of us to point at it and say, "I know that that's a tree." Someone might be inclined to reply, "It would be queer, undoubtedly, for either of you to utter that sentence in such a case; but what would make it queer is that *it is so obvious to both of you that it is a tree* that there is no need to say it! To utter that sentence in those circumstances would be an odd use but not a misuse."

This reply contains a mistake. The mistake lies in the assumption that in those circumstances it would be correct to say "It is obvious that it is a tree." Consider this example: We are looking at something a mile away on the side of a hill and because of the distance and angle of view we cannot make out whether it is a tree or a bush. As we approach it, it more and more distinctly assumes the shape of a tree, until, at a point several hundred yards from it, one of us says "It's perfectly obvious now that it is a tree." This is an ordinary use of those words. In the first place, a doubt existed. The use of those words was to remove the doubt. They were like saying, "You need not have that doubt any longer." In the second place, further investigation would not be unreasonable. If one of us had weak vision and still doubted that it was a tree he could walk closer. There would come a point, still at a considerable distance from the tree, at which he too would say, "Yes, it obviously is a tree."

Suppose now that we should walk right up to the tree and begin to pick apples from it. If one of us should then say, "It's obvious that this is a tree," that would be a *mis*use of those words and would raise a laugh. In the first place, no one has any doubt on the matter and the utterance of those words is not fulfilling its normal purpose, which is to remove doubt. In the second place, there is no further investigation which would "back up" those words. Should we pick more apples? Should we take photographs? Should we strip the bark? None of those things would be called "making certain" or "further verifying" or "trying to find out" whether it is a tree. There is nothing which, in those circumstances, we should call "trying to find out whether it is a tree." This means that, in those circumstances, we don't attach any sense to the question "Is it a tree?" We don't know what to *do* with it. In those circumstances the sentence "It's obvious that it's a tree" is a *misfit*. It doesn't *belong* there. It is a set of idle words. It has no function. It has a function only in those contexts where we attach sense to the question "Is it a tree?"

To the argument of this paper the following objection may be made:

> You said that a philosophical question as to whether it is certain that a thing before us is a tree, can be expressed only in circumstances where there isn't any doubt and isn't any question about its being a tree, and that in a philosophical discussion Moore would say, 'I know that that's a tree,' in circumstances where there was no question that the thing at which he pointed was a tree. Now in ordinary language, 'There's no doubt that it is a tree,' or 'There's no question about its being a tree,' are *equivalent* to 'I know that it's a tree' or 'It's certain that it's a tree.' It follows from your own argument that Moore speaks both correctly and truly when he says, in such a context, 'It's certain that that's a tree,' and that he does not misuse language in the least.

This objection rests on a misunderstanding of a matter which I am anxious to clarify, and which, I fear, my previous remarks have not sufficiently clarified.

I declared that a man who is entertaining a philosophical doubt as to whether what he sees is a tree does not have any doubt that it is a tree. This statement may easily mislead, because it makes the case appear to be this—that when a man has a philosophical doubt he does not, *in fact*, have any doubt, although of course he *could* have a doubt. The truth is that, in the sort of circumstances in which a man expresses a philosophical doubt (and it must be expressed in circumstances of that sort—otherwise we should not call it a philosophical doubt) as to whether, for example, there is really a fire in the grate before him, it is *nonsense* to say "He doubts that there is a fire." It isn't that, *in fact*, he doesn't doubt. It is, rather, that it would be a misuse of language to say "He doubts," and, therefore, a misuse of language to say "He doesn't doubt."

My statement, "A man who is expressing a philosophical doubt as to whether there is a fire before him isn't in doubt as to whether there is a fire," is analogous to the statement, "An automobile isn't intelligent." The latter statement doesn't mean that, in fact, automobiles are not intelligent at the present time, although next year's models may be. What it means is expressed more accurately by the statement "To say that 'this automobile is intelligent' or that 'this automobile isn't intelligent' doesn't make sense. It is a misuse of words to say of an automo-

bile that it 'is intelligent' or 'isn't intelligent.' " My statement about
the man expressing a philosophical doubt is put more accurately by
the statement, "In the circumstances in which a man expresses a philosophical doubt as to whether there is a fire before him it would be a
misuse of words to say either 'He doubts' or 'He doesn't doubt' that
there is a fire."

If a man who is preparing to cook his dinner on a coal stove touches
the stove and finds it hot, puts potatoes in the oven and sits down to
wait for them to bake, but doesn't look in the fire compartment to find
out whether there is still a fire—then we could say that he "doesn't
doubt" or "assumes" or "takes for granted" that there is a fire. If he
begins to show concern that the potatoes take so long to bake and tries
to open the door to the fire compartment to look inside but can't get
it open, then we could say that he "doubts" that there is a fire. It is a
feature *common* to both cases, i.e., the case in which we could say
that he "doesn't doubt" and the case in which we could say that he
"doubts," that he *doesn't see* the interior of the fire compartment
because of the closed door. But if the door was open and he watched
the flames as he waited, while occasionally stirring the fire, then it
would be as grotesque to say that he "doesn't doubt" or that he "assumes" or "takes for granted" or "believes" that there is a fire, as to
say that he "doubts" that there is a fire. In this case neither "doubts"
nor "doesn't doubt" makes sense.

The objection which opened this section may be answered as follows: When I say that a philosophical doubt as to whether, for example, an object before our eyes is a hand, is expressed in circumstances
where there is no doubt that it's a hand, the words "There is no doubt
that it's a hand" are not to be understood in the sense in which they
are equivalent to "It's certain that it's a hand." What is meant is that
in those circumstances a *doubt* is senseless. Instead of saying, "A
philosophical doubt as to whether this thing before me is a hand is
expressed in circumstances where there's no doubt that it's a hand,"
it is more accurate to say "A philosophical doubt as to whether this
is a hand is expressed in circumstances where it would be a misuse
of language to say *either* 'There's some doubt that this is a hand' *or*
'There's no doubt that this is a hand.' " Similarly, instead of saying,
"The question 'Is it certain that this is a hand?' is not a philosophical
question unless it is asked in circumstances where there's *no* question

that it's a hand," it is more accurate to say "The question 'Is it certain that this is a hand?' is not a philosophical question unless it is asked in circumstances where the question 'Is this a hand?' as ordinarily understood, would be without sense."

I am contending that Moore's philosophical assertions, such as "I know that here's a hand" or "I know that I am a human being," are made in circumstances where it is a misuse of words to say either "I know that here's a hand" or "I don't know that here's a hand," or to say either "I know that I'm a human being" or "I don't know that I'm a human being." To this the following objection will be made: "Either I know that I am a human being or I don't know it. One or the other *must* be the case."

If my contention sounds to you like an absurd paradox and this reply seems irrefutable, it is because you have before your mind the normal usage of "I know" and "I don't know." If I see something moving on the top of a distant hill it is true that either I know that it is a human being or I don't know it. In those circumstances we attach sense to the question "Is it a human being?" There is something which we should call "investigating" and "finding out" whether it is or it isn't. This is one of the contexts of the normal usage of "know" and "don't know." In these contexts "I know" is opposed to "I don't know." "Either I know or I don't know" is a rule which applies to these expressions when they occur in their normal contexts. But when these expressions occur in unnatural contexts this rule no longer applies. Consider the sentence, "My desk is good-natured." There is no paradox involved in saying that my desk neither is good-natured nor isn't good-natured. It would be fantastic to insist that either my desk is good-natured or it isn't and that it must be one or the other. We don't attach sense to the words, "Is it a good-natured desk?" There is nothing which we should recognize as an "investigation" into whether it is or it isn't.

Just as "good-natured" does not belong to certain contexts, so "I know" does not belong to certain contexts. If I should come up to you and ask with earnest countenance "Am I a human being?" you would be taken quite aback. It would not be clear to you what my words mean. You would not understand to what investigation they referred. You would not know what *sort* of thing an "answer" would be. You would be equally perplexed if I should solemnly declare to you, "I *know* that I'm a human being." My statement would seem to you as strange and outlandish as "My desk isn't good-natured."

There could be circumstances in which "Am I a human being?" would be a question with sense. Suppose that I have fallen from a height and have been knocked unconscious. Gradually I return to consciousness. I am dazed and confused. There is utter darkness, and I cannot feel my body. I dimly recall the fall and wonder if I am now "dead." Am I a spirit? Am I without a body? Or "Am I still a human being?" If I should then begin to feel my body and to sort out my limbs, I might exclaim, "I know that I am still a human being." Here is a usage of "Am I a human being?" and "I know that I am a human being" which has sense. The circumstances in which Moore said "I know that I am a human being" were quite unlike this. In his case there was no "question," no "doubt," and no "investigation." When I maintain that in the circumstances in which he uttered those words, neither "I know that I'm a human being" nor "I don't know that I'm a human being" was correct language, I do not contend against a law of logic.

I hold, therefore, that Moore was not defending "common sense" at all when he declared "I know with certainty" that "There exists at present a living human body which is *my* body," that "The earth had existed many years before this body was born," that "For many of these years large numbers of human bodies had, at every moment, been alive upon it," that "I am a human being." His assertions were made in circumstances where there was no question, and it wouldn't have made sense to raise a question, as to whether Moore had a body and was a human being, or as to whether the earth had existed before he was born, or as to whether there were other human beings living on it. Moore's assertions do not belong to "common sense," i.e., to ordinary language, at all. They involve a use of "know" which is a radical departure from ordinary usage.

Moore wished to attack all those philosophers who hold views from which it follows that no human being knows that he is a human being and that no human being knows any proposition like "Here's a hand" to be true. Moore, to his everlasting credit, saw that it would be a misuse of language for him to say (when writing in his study), "I don't know that I'm a human being," or to say (when holding up his hand in plain view before him), "I don't know that this is a hand."[14] Therefore, he stoutly affirmed, "I *know* that I'm a human being," "I *know* that this is a hand." He did not see that these statements too are a misuse of language.

Notes

1. In J. H. Muirhead (ed.), *Contemporary British Philosophy* (New York: Macmillan, 1925), 2d ser.
2. *Ibid.*, p. 224.
3. In *Proceedings of the British Academy*, XXV (1939).
4. *Ibid.*, p. 295.
5. *Ibid.*
6. *Ibid.*, p. 296.
7. *Ibid.*, p. 298.
8. *Ibid.*, p. 300.
9. *Ibid.*, p. 380.
10. *Ibid.*, pp. 299-300.
11. *Ibid.*, p. 300.
12. "A Defence of Common Sense," p. 206.
13. "Proof of an External World," p. 299.
14. Let me warn, if it is necessary, that what Moore "saw" is a controversial matter. Moore might deny that he then saw or that he now sees any such thing.

Eleven

ON SPEAKING
WITH THE VULGAR

Max Black

IN A RECENT ARTICLE,[1] Norman Malcolm has maintained that Moore
"*misused* the expressions 'I know,' 'I know with certainty,' 'It is certain,'
'I have conclusive evidence.' "[2] Malcolm refers especially to the use of
these expressions in Moore's two essays, "A Defense of Common Sense,"[3]
and "Proof of an External World";[4] but they have, of course, often been
used by Moore in the same way in other discussions. This use, says
Malcolm, is "contrary to their ordinary and correct use."[5] There is a
pleasant irony in finding this charge of violating ordinary language
brought against a philosopher whose "great historical rôle," it has been
said, "consists in the fact that he has been perhaps the first philosopher
consistently to defend ordinary language against its philosophical viola-
tors."[6] I think Moore was never defending ordinary *language*, but it is
quite certain he was trying to use it. If Malcolm's recent criticism is
sound, Moore was not even using "ordinary language"; whenever Moore
used the expression "I know" to refer to something about which there

Reprinted by permission of the author and the editor from *The Philosophical Review*, LVIII (1949), 616-21. Page references have been changed to
conform with Mr. Malcolm's article as reprinted in this volume.

was no question of doubt at all (as when he said "I know this is a hand" while looking at his own hand) he was speaking incorrectly or, not to put a fine point on it, talking nonsense.

That this is indeed the accusation might easily be overlooked. Malcolm says "Moore's use of those expressions . . . is contrary to their ordinary and correct use," which suggests these expression *had* a use in Moore's essays, though not the *ordinary* use. But the imputed fault did not consist in using *the wrong expression* as a man might who applied the term "knowledge" to a case of "opinion." Malcolm's accusation is more drastic: When Moore looks at his own hand, held up in clear sight before him, there is *nothing* about that hand he can "correctly" say: "It is not correct to say 'I know that that's a hand,' and not correct to say, 'I don't know that's a hand' ";[7] and each of these sentences, if spoken, would be "an empty utterance."[8] The circumstances were such as to make it nonsensical to say what Moore was trying to say: the sentences he used were empty; the audience who supposed they understood were deluded.

In order to show that this accusation is mistaken, I shall first examine some implications of the principles used in Malcolm's essay.

Let us suppose that on a fine summer's day we see in the distance a friend stretched out comfortably on the grass. We notice to our surprise that, though he stays at rest, a dog seems to be licking his foot. It is natural to ask: "Does Jones know that there is a dog licking his foot? Perhaps he's dozing, or in a philosophical brown study?" The first question is, on Malcolm's principles, expressed "correctly": We are really in doubt whether Jones knows about the dog; and we know what steps to take to settle the question.[9] So we come close enough to see that Jones's eyes are open and that he is following the movements of his pet Airedale with a tolerant smile. And *now* we say, "Yes, Jones does know there is a dog before him." This, too, on Malcolm's principles, is a perfectly "correct" way for *us* to speak; for there had been a doubt, removed by an investigation; and this supplied us with a reason for the assertion.

From the correctness of our assertion, "Jones knows there is a dog before him," it follows that the assertion is *true*. So, in the situation I have imagined, it was a fact that Jones knew the dog to be before him— a fact which we discovered by coming closer; he really *did* know the dog was there. Yet if *he* said so, he would have been making an "empty utterance"! For the dog was in his plain sight, and *he* never had any doubt about the matter.

The first paradoxical conclusion I draw from Malcolm's principles is this: There may be cases where somebody may in fact know *p*, and others may know that he knows it and say that he knows it, but he himself would be talking nonsense if *he* said that he knew it.

Following this line of thought, I might be in a position to prove that Moore, when he held up his hand at the Academy lecture, really *did know* that there was a hand before him. All I need do is first create a real doubt about the matter in somebody's mind and then dispel that doubt by suitable evidence. I could say, for instance, to somebody who had neither attended the lecture nor read the printed report: "When Professor Moore lectured to the British Academy, he held his hand in the air, almost as if he were giving a Hitler salute!" And the reply might be: "What an extraordinary thing! *Did he know there was a hand before him?* Could he have been unconscious of what he was doing?" Then I read aloud the relevant section of the published lecture, which shows that Moore was looking at his hand and talking about it—and the doubt is immediately dispelled. The innocent bystander could now correctly say: "Yes, I see now Professor Moore *did* know that there was a hand before him." From which it follows, as I claimed at the beginning of this section, that Moore really *did know* that there was a hand before him. His mistake consisted in trying to say what really was the case and what another man could say for him. John Doe could say it, but if Moore or Malcolm or I were to say it we would be abusing ordinary language—for none of us ever had any doubt about the matter. Now is it necessary for me to find some John Doe and put the doubt in his mind? Is it not sufficient that I *could* do it? I think it *is* sufficient; and that I have said enough to prove that Moore *did* know he had a hand before him.

Let us return to Jones and his dog. I said that *if* we had approached him in the manner described, it would follow that *we* could correctly say "Jones knew there was a dog before him," from which in turn would follow that Jones really *did* know there was a dog before him. Let *a* be the proposition, "Somebody first doubted whether Jones knew about the dog and then dispelled the doubt by coming closer"; and *b* the proposition, "Jones knew there was a dog before him." I have shown that *a* entails *b*, so that if *a were* true, *b would* be true. What would the situation be if *a* were false, e.g., if nobody ever did in fact see Jones

as he was lying there on the lawn, or have any doubt about the matter?
Should we say that *b* would then be false? Surely not. Nothing has
changed in Jones's relation to his dog—the dog is still licking his foot
and is still being watched. Nobody sees, nobody wonders whether what
seems to be happening really is happening; but after all, *b* is about
Jones and the dog, not about any third party. Surely we must say that
if nothing had changed except the presence of an observer, *b* would
continue to be true.

The second paradoxical conclusion I draw from Malcolm's principles
is: There may be cases where somebody in fact knows *p*, but *anybody*
who says so talks nonsense.

As we approach Jones and his dog, we call out, "Do you know there
is a dog licking your foot?" And he replies, "Yes, I know there is a dog
there." This must be "correct usage," for it gives *us* information. So it
is correct for Jones to say, "I know there is a dog there," *if we ask him*,
though nonsensical otherwise. Similarly, if someone had called from the
gallery, "Professor Moore, are you still looking at your hand, do you
know that it's still there in front of you? We're too far off to tell," it
would have been correct for Moore to say, "Yes, I know there's a hand
before me."

The third paradoxical conclusion is this: It may be correct for somebody to utter a sentence in reply to a question, but the same sentence
would have been nonsensical if he had uttered it without having been
asked.

Suppose, just before Moore pronounced the words in dispute, a member of the audience had said to himself, "I wonder if Moore knows that
he is holding his hand up in that curious way! I wonder if he knows
there is a hand before him?" This is a legitimate question, expressed in
correct language, since it expresses a genuine doubt which could be
dispelled by a process of investigation—for instance, by *asking* Moore.
And when Moore says, "I know there is a hand before me," the man
who was wondering need wonder no longer, he will not doubt that
Moore *knew*.

The fourth paradoxical conclusion is this: A nonsensical utterance
may be *understood* by a hearer.

Since *I* never had any doubt about Moore's actions, it would be non-
sensical for *me* to say, "Moore knew that there was a hand before him."
Let "*c*" be an abbreviation for the sentence to which I have just referred.
Let "*d*" be an abbreviation for the sentence, "Somebody first doubted

whether c and then had his doubt dispelled." I have asserted, previously:
"If d then c," i.e., "If somebody first doubted whether Moore knew that
there was a hand before him and then had his doubt dispelled, Moore
did know there was a hand before him." Let us call this conditional
sentence "e" (so that e is "If d then c"). Now in asserting e I seem to
have been speaking "correctly," for I had a real doubt whether e was
true and took steps to remove that doubt. But the consequent of e, viz.
"c," was an "empty utterance" in my mouth.

The fifth paradoxical conclusion is this: A nonsensical sentence may
be used[10] in a complex sentence, the whole of which is not nonsensical.

I think these paradoxical consequences indicate that there is something wrong with Malcolm's contention that Moore's use of the expression "I know" was improper. For Malcolm is himself using such expressions as "incorrect" and "contrary to ordinary usage" in a very unusual
way, as I have tried to make plain. But before I try to explain what
led him into the mistake, I want to show how Moore, by accepting
Malcolm's conditions for "correct usage," could so modify his procedure
as to be in any case beyond the reach of this kind of criticism.

The objection to Moore's saying, "I know that is a hand," is that
there is "no question of doubt" about the matter. Very well. Let Moore
arrange with one of his students *before* the lecture to come out from
the wings at a prearranged symbol and show *some* object to the audience
and to Moore himself. Moore is not to know what the object is until he
sees it, nor is his audience. "Now," says Moore at the right moment in
his discourse, "my student, Watson, is concealed in the wings. I have
told him to come out when I call and show some object to you and to
me. I haven't the faintest idea of what he will choose as the object. All
right, come out, Watson! Here he comes. Can you see what he is showing? *I* can't quite see yet. Is he *carrying* anything? It *looks* as if he's
going to show his hand. Ah, he is. That is a hand!" And from this point
Moore could proceed as in the printed lecture.[11] The preliminary ar-
rangements would be important to him only insofar as it allowed him
to say *at last*, "That is a hand," and, "I now know that is a hand." And
if he *were* allowed to say it, the rest of his argument would be undam-
aged.

Malcolm is committed to these consequences by taking too narrow
a view of the purposes served by "ordinary" or "correct" language. The
only use of "correct language" which he considers is that in which a
sentence is used to convey information or dispel a doubt. But there are

many *other* purposes served by indicative sentences: I may say "It is raining," *even when there is no doubt about it*, simply to record the fact (as a sea captain may record the weather in the ship's log), or to prove that I am awake, or to teach somebody how to speak English, or to remind somebody that I am a good weather forecaster. So the absence of the necessary criteria of ordinary or nonphilosophical doubt is no proof that a sentence is being used incorrectly.

I suspect that Malcolm is tempted to regard Moore's utterance ("I know that is a hand") as senseless because he can see no *ordinary* "point" or "purpose" to it. (If somebody were to say, out of the blue, "That's a hand," we might say "What on earth do you mean?" i.e., "What is the point of saying anything like that?") But Moore's utterance is not pointless—he uses it, in its ordinary sense, for an unusual philosophical purpose. He thinks that the truth of "That is a hand" is incompatible with the truth of the philosophical assertion, "There are no external things." His purpose is to use the common-sense assertion to *prove* that the philosophical thesis is false. And if we understand this, we can see the point of what he is doing. I think Moore's attempt to confute philosophical assertions by using common-sense premises is unsuccessful. But it is one thing to say he does not refute his philosophical opponents; it is a very different thing to say he is misusing ordinary language or talking nonsense.

Notes

1. "Defending Common Sense," *Philosophical Review,* LVIII (May, 1949), 201-20. Reprinted above, pp. 200-19.
2. *Ibid.*
3. In J. H. Muirhead (ed.), *Contemporary British Philosophy* (New York: Macmillan, 1925), 2d ser.
4. In *Proceedings of the British Academy,* XXV (1939).
5. Above, p. 201.
6. The conclusion of Malcolm's essay, "Moore and Ordinary Language," in Paul Schilpp (ed.), *The Philosophy of G. E. Moore* (Evanston, Ill.: Northwestern University Press, 1942), pp. 345-68.
7. Malcolm, p. 213 above. It is important to notice that Malcolm's strictures also apply to the simpler utterance, "That is a hand."

8. "If you take away from that sentence its connection with actions of investigation you turn it into an empty utterance (*ibid.*, p. 213).

9. Malcolm's three criteria of correct use of language are: (1) there is a doubt to be removed; (2) a reason can be given for the assertion; (3) there is an investigation which, if carried out, would settle the question at issue (*ibid.*, p. 203).

10. Observe that the utterance "I know that there's a hand before me" is not treated as a symptom. It is *understood* in the same way as it would be if it were an answer to a question.

11. The modified procedure suggested would have some advantages. The philosophical skeptic would *continue* to say, "I don't really know"; the defender of common sense would finally say, "*Now* I know." And this difference in their behavior makes prominent an important difference in their respective uses of the word "know."

Twelve

MOORE AND
PHILOSOPHICAL ANALYSIS

Morris Lazerowitz

OCCASIONALLY THERE HAS appeared in the history of philosophy a thinker who has become aware of the chaotic condition of philosophy and of the intellectual anarchy that exists in all of its branches and has attempted to remedy the situation. Descartes cast about for a guiding principle, a compass which would show him the way through the treacherous terrain of philosophy. As is well known he devised the method of systematic doubt, by means of which he hoped to discover an axiom on which he could securely erect a system of basic and reassuring beliefs. Leibniz had before his mind the notion of an ideal language which would by calculation solve problems with certainty. With this he thought we "should be able to reason in metaphysics and morals in much the same way as in geometry and analysis." Descartes' attempt was a failure; and nothing came of Leibniz's ideal, even with the development of modern symbolic logic. Russell's claim that "logic is the essence of philosophy" frightened many philosophers and gave new hope to others; but his claim was as empty as the proverbial political promise. With

Reprinted by permission of the author and the editor from *Philosophy*, XXXIII (1958), 193-220.

G. E. Moore we have a further attempt to introduce sobriety and certainty into philosophy and to make fruitful research possible in it. He has made prominent a method for obtaining results in philosophy; and he has also formulated a philosophical platform, i.e., set out a list of Common-sense propositions which he says are known to be true by everyone, philosopher as well as non-philosopher, and are not, therefore, open to debate. The method, which he used extensively and with great skill, is the method of analysing concepts. It held out great promise, and Moore's influence on the direction philosophy has taken is generally acknowledged to be enormous. In this paper it is my purpose to examine the technique of analysis in order, if possible, to see what it is and what it can accomplish.

What philosophical analysis is, its nature, is something of a mystery, and it has never been made clear and definite by those who practise it the thing or various things which are or might be achieved by it. One thing, apparently, which it is not designed to do is to enable us to apply our various concepts with greater accuracy;[1] or to put the matter in terms of the use of expressions, the object of philosophical analysis is not to improve in any way our ordinary use of terms, which, as everyone knows, remains unchanged by what is done in philosophy. The everyday speech of neither the layman nor the philosopher is affected in the slightest by the results of philosophical analysis. Moore recognized this long ago when in *Principia Ethica* he wrote that "verbal questions are properly left to the writers of dictionaries and other persons interested in literature; philosophy, as we shall see, has no concern with them."[2] The definitions yielded by philosophical analysis are not about customary usage, are not concerned with "mere questions of words."[3]

If we look at Moore's writings, in which he makes extensive use of the techniques of analysis, we see that analysis appears to have as its aim different types of results, additions to our knowledge of the world[4] as well as clarifications of concepts. Moore's paradigm of analysis is *to be a brother is to be a male sibling*, in which the analysans simply makes explicit what is implicit in the analysandum; conceptual clarification is here the sole result. It does not bring us to *new* properties which things answering to the concept *brother* must have; it only makes explicit properties in virtue of which a thing is a brother. It therefore is not, as it so often is represented as being, *the* model for *all* analysis done in philosophy. Of course, an important feature of this example is that the subject and predicate are connected by logical necessity; its denial gives rise to a logical impossibility. And this is a feature which all cases of the correct analysis of a concept must have, regardless of whether the analysis is only clarificatory[5] or is more than this.

We can discern at least two distinct uses of clarificatory analysis (more than two, in fact). One is to bring to light hidden contradictions in philosophical theories. Moore, of course, is practised in laying bare the self-contradictions in theories of other philosophers, contradictions which are internal to them and the exposure of which reduces them to logical absurdities. For example, by analysis he appears plainly to show a contradiction in the philosophical claim expressed by the words "Each man's happiness is the sole good"; and he does this by showing that the criteria for the use of "the sole good" are in conflict with the criteria for the use of "each man's happiness." Or to express the point non-linguistically, he shows that equating the concept *the good* with the concept *each man's happiness* leads to the consequence that something which is only one thing is also a plurality of things, or, "that several different things are *each* of them the *only* thing desirable."[6] Another instance is the contradiction he discovers in the metaphysical-ethical theory that the good is self-realization. The contradiction, which as his analysis claims to show is internal to the view, is that since the self and the Absolute are in the end identical, the self is in the logically impossible position of having to realize what is already and necessarily realized: "For it is plain that what exists eternally cannot be affected by our actions."[7]

It is interesting to note the surprising and not adequately explained fact that laying bare a contradiction in a philosophical view is no guarantee that philosophers will agree that it is a contradiction. This is one of the disconcerting and not unfamiliar things that happens in philosophy. Once it was established, as in Euclid, that to suppose that $x^2 = 2$ had a rational solution was to suppose something self-contradictory, there was no question whatever of mathematicians' disagreeing as to whether it was self-contradictory. But the situation is radically different in the case of philosophical contradictions, and one cannot help but wonder how this difference is to be explained.

A further use of clarificatory analysis is to bring philosophical theories into direct connection with matters of fact for the purpose of testing their truth-values. For this Moore used a technique which he called "translation into the concrete." A philosophical view which on translation into the concrete turned out to be inconsistent with a truism of Common Sense was condemned as an unquestionable falsehood. Instances of such translations are "Time is unreal" into "There are no temporal facts," and "There are no material things" into "There are no such things as hands, desks, and the like." No internal contradictions are discovered. A vague statement is, so to speak, de-mystified, made manageable and brought down to earth where it can be checked against fact. Some philosophers thought that Moore brought a breath of fresh air into philosophy when he wrote: "Of course, Time, with a big T, seems to be a highly abstract kind of entity, and to define *exactly* what can be meant by saying of an entity of that sort that it is unreal does seem to offer difficulties. But if you try to translate the proposition into the concrete, and to ask what it *implies*, there is, I think, very little doubt as to the sort of thing it implies. The moment you try to do this, and think what it really comes to, you at once begin thinking of a number of different *kinds* of propositions, all of which plainly must be untrue, if Time is unreal. If Time is unreal, then plainly nothing ever happens before or after anything else. . . ."[8] Other philosophers thought that Moore was dogmatic, that he assumed the very thing at issue, and, moreover, that he had not really grasped what it was that they were doing.

It should be noted that Moore's use of his technique of translation to refute theories rests on the unformulated assumption that philosophers who hold them make two *logically* different kinds of mistake, and not only one kind of mistake. The effect of a translation appears to be no more than to make an abstractly stated view more concrete and in this way to disperse the metaphysical fog that surrounds it so as to enable us to see that the theory collides with known fact. It would seem therefore that a translation into the concrete simply brings out in sharper relief a theory which is in conflict with fact in order to make us aware that it is an empirically false view. And it would seem thus that the technique of translation is designed to expose only one kind of error, an empirical error. But if we look at the technique more closely we can, I think, see that its use is designed to expose another and different kind of mistake. It is grossly unrealistic to think that a philosopher who holds that time is unreal *needs* a translation of his view into the proposition that there are no temporal facts in order to recognize the view for the empirical "howler" it is. It is entirely unlikely that a philosopher wishes with the words "Time is unreal" to deny the existence of temporal facts and somehow fails to realize that this is what he is doing.

It can be seen that a translation into the concrete calls attention to an *entailment*. For example, ·the statement that "Time is unreal" translates into "There are no events, such as eating breakfast" implies that

"Time is unreal" entails "There are no events, such as eating breakfast,"

and the statement that "Matter is unreal" translates into "There are no hands" implies that

"Matter is unreal" entails "There are no hands."

A philosopher who holds his view in disregard of Moore's translation would plainly seem to be making a logical mistake, and if he accepts Moore's translation it would seem that he accepts logical correction. Reformulated in terms of language, Moore's translations call attention to usage. A philosopher who resists this translation would seem to have a mistaken notion about usage and a philosopher who accepts the translation would seem to let himself be corrected. The above two translations amount to stating that "material thing" applies to whatever "hand" applies to, and that "temporal" applies to whatever "event" applies to, which in turn applies to what "eating breakfast" applies to. Moore's translations give every appearance of being designed to expose two logically different kinds of mistake, one empirical and the other linguistic. They are intended to correct misapprehensions of language and also mistakes about the existence of things and occurrences. Moore seems to suspect that his translations are meant to do more than expose empirically false views when he ventures a possible explanation of Bradley's claim that time both is and is unreal: "The kind of thing which I imagine may be happening to him when he insists so strongly that Time *does exist, is a fact,* and *is,* is that, properly speaking, he is not attaching to these phrases any meaning whatever—*not,* therefore, that which they properly bear."[9] The implication is that Bradley has misapprehended the use of the word "time" and that with his translation Moore is attempting to correct it and to show him what its use actually is. But what the connection is between the two kinds of mistake a philosopher who holds that time is unreal is charged with making, is left unclear. At present we can only think that the philosophical utterance "Time is unreal" is made to do double work; it is made to deny that the word "time" has a use and it is also made to deny matter of fact, the existence of familiar phenomena.

Doing philosophy has, of course, a positive as well as a negative side. In philosophy we wish not only to refute false positions, but also to establish the correctness of some views. Our concern is not only to expose falsehoods by using analysis, but also by analysis to discover important truths about the world. The latter is undoubtedly the most important task of analysis; for it would hardly be worth our while to upset false views if we had no hope of discovering true ones. The propositions of Common Sense are, of course, not discoveries, and a philosopher who accepts them and resists views which go or apparently go against them wishes also to discover new truths, truths not merely on a footing with Common-sense claims but which go deeper. Thus in a specific connection Moore has said that what needs "to be taken seriously, and what is really dubious, is not the question, whether this is a finger or whether I know that it is, but the question *what,* in certain respects, I am knowing, when I know that it is."[10] In other words, according to Moore, Common Sense knows that some among things are fingers, chairs, and ink-wells, yet still has something further to learn about the nature of these things, something which a correct philosophical view can provide. In his *Some Main Problems of Philosophy* Moore said: "It seems to me that the most important and interesting thing which philosophers have tried to do is no less than this; namely: To give a general description of the *whole* of the Universe. . . ."[11] It is, of course, a common notion that the primary concern of philosophy is to arrive at true views which give basic information about the world. There can be no doubt that consciously or semiconsciously every philosopher harbors the belief that in doing philosophy he is attempting to gain insight into the nature of various phenomena. And Moore seems to be no exception in this regard. For Moore, as for others, understanding Common-sense statements and knowing them to be true is not enough. A Common-sense philosopher is not one who remains at the level of Common Sense. His quest is for knowledge which penetrates further into the nature of things than unaided Common Sense is able to. And his procedure is not that of the natural sciences. Whatever the results, actual or only possible, achieved by philosophical investigation, looking and experiment play no role. Like the analytical part of his refutations Moore's demonstrations are *a priori*. They result from some sort of scrutiny of concepts, not from a more careful observation of things.

Wittgenstein has said that philosophers have the idea that the analysis of concepts is something like chemical analysis. And it is not to be denied that they do give the impression of thinking that just as in chemistry substances are decomposed into their constituent elements, with a consequent increase in our knowledge of the composition of the substances, so in philosophy concepts are resolved into their ultimate components with a consequent increase in our knowledge of the nature of phenomena falling under the concepts. By analytical penetration into a concept, by a process of intellectual dissection, we seem able to get an inside look into the nature and workings of things. Leibniz clearly seems to have had this idea when he developed his theory of the monadic composition of things. He appears to have arrived at his view that things are really collections of non-extended sentient entities by performing an analysis on the concept *matter* or *extended body*. Locke, who arrived at a different view, also seems to have come to it via analysis, the analysis of the concept *thing*, which involves the distinction between substance and attribute. What analysis shows according to him is that substance, which is that which has attributes, is not itself an attribute, is unknowable and, furthermore, is a "necessity of thought." Berkeley, as is well known, by using a technique of investigation not different from Locke's, arrived at the view that substance as the unknowable support of attributes is an impossibility of thought. There are, of course, still other views about the nature of things which are arrived at by analysis.

All these, Moore would allow, are analyses of the concept of *material thing*, such that if any one of them is true it gives information which is over and above and in addition to what Common Sense claims to know about them. Moore has distinguished between three classes of philosophical views in relation to Common Sense.[12] Some theories add to Common Sense, for example, the proposition that God exists, and, perhaps, the proposition that there are such entities as universals. Some theories contradict Common Sense, for example, those which "positively deny the existence of space and material objects."[13] Still other theories both contradict and go beyond Common Sense, theories such as that a thing is a colony or collection of monads or an unknowable substratum which presents various appearances. It would seem plain that theories of the first and third class inform us of the existence of new things, or of new properties "never thought [of] before"[14] in familiar things. The plain implication is that analysis can bring us to new knowledge, to something more than clarification of what is already known.

This is borne out by the fact that in one of his important studies[15]

Moore includes in a list of philosophical theories about the nature of
physical things the theory that physical things are "as Reid and some
scientists would say . . . Certain configurations of invisible material
particles."[16] The scientific theory that matter is molecular is, of course,
not arrived at by the analysis of concepts. Experiment and observation
alone could suggest and *confirm* such a theory; and by including it with
the philosophical theories he unavoidably implies that like it they go
beyond our everyday knowledge of the nature of things and, if true,
add to it. We may say that the model in Moore's mind of a view arrived at by analysis which is more than clarificatory is a scientific view
which gives us information in depth about phenomena, knowledge of
their inner constitution.

And this is borne out further by a curious mistake he makes in *Principia Ethica* where he discusses definitions "which describe the real
nature of the object or notion denoted by a word, and which do not
merely tell us what the word is used to mean. . . ."[17] He says that
"We may, when we define horse, mean . . . that a certain object, which
we all of us know, is composed in a certain manner: that it has four
legs, a head, a heart, a liver, etc. etc., all of them arranged in definite
relations to one another."[18] Quite obviously mention of liver and heart
is no part of any sort of definition of "horse," whether it is "arbitrary
verbal definition," "verbal definition proper,"[19] or analytic definition.
And the only plausible way of accounting for Moore's apparently making the curious mistake of thinking that mention of a heart enters into
the *definition* of the concept of a horse is that he was using it to tell
us what the work of an *important* piece of analysis should be like. His
mistake went unnoticed because its *point* was to tell us that an important piece of analysis is one which takes us beyond what we know about
things to new properties "of which we had never thought before," gives
us more information than could an ordinary definition of the concept
to which the things answer. Dissection of horses and not a definition
of the word which applies to them can tell us that they have hearts
and livers; and we can only think that a philosopher's words are mo-
tivated by a semi-hidden idea when he gives the impression of imagining that analysis can yield a definition which will give us the kind of
information which dissection alone can yield. The hidden, or partly
hidden, idea is that analysis is in some respects like dissection. Like
the anatomical dissection of horses, an analysis of the concept *horse*
which is more than clarificatory takes us beyond the definition that a

horse is a "solid-hoofed perissodactyl quadruped" and informs us of the existence and function of unobserved parts. It is enlightening, in conjunction with Moore's curious definition of "horse," to read what he has to say about *good* definition: "A good definition of the sorts of things you hold to be in the Universe, obviously adds to the clearness of your view. And it is not only a question of clearness either. When, for instance, you try to define what you mean by a material object, you find that there are several different properties which a material object might have, of which you had never thought before; and your effort to define may thus lead you to conclude that whole classes of things have certain properties, or have *not* certain others, of which you would never have thought, if you had merely contented yourself with asserting that there are material objects in the Universe, without inquiring what you meant by this assertion."[20] It is natural in this connection to think of the Kantian claim that there are synthetic *a priori* propositions, since analysis is an *a priori* procedure which apparently can lead to additional knowledge. But this connection is never made explicitly. Later, perhaps, we shall be able to see whether there is a connection between them. Analysis, it is to be supposed, consists of some sort of examination of concepts, a sort of mental penetration into them, which helps make more distinct their components, and in many cases does more than this.

This notion of the positive work of analysis underlies all forms of rationalistic philosophical doctrines: by thinking on concepts nature's secrets, its cosmic fabric and innermost workings, can be revealed. Indeed, it seems also to be at the basis of philosophical empiricism. Thus, for example, Hume gives the impression of arriving at his startling view about causation as the result of having made careful observation of cases ordinarily described as those in which a change is brought about by the action of one thing on another. "When we look about us towards external objects, and consider the operation of causes, we are never able, in a single instance, to discover any power or necessary connexion; any quality, which binds the effect to the cause, and renders the one an infallible consequence of the other."[21] Or again, "Let us therefore cast our eye on any two objects, which we call cause and effect, and turn them on all sides, in order to find that impression. . . ."[22] But Hume's words describe an illusion and not a fact. No observation of any sort has *actually* been resorted to; and this can easily be seen from the following consideration.

A basic claim of Hume's, which he repeats frequently, is that our ideas derive from impressions, such that if a supposed idea cannot be traced back to a source in some form of experience it is no more than a pseudo-idea. Phrased less misleadingly, Hume's claim is that a word does not denote an idea and is literally without sense if the criteria for the use of the word do not state features which individually or in combination are features of things met with in experience. Hume appears to claim that we have no idea of "necessary connexion," on the grounds that *inspection* of instances of causation shows no necessary connection between occurrences, that it shows no more than invariant conjunction. But obviously, if we have no idea of necessary connection between events, or, what is the same thing, if we do not know what it would be like for them to be necessarily connected, we cannot examine occurrences to see whether they are necessarily connected or not. Hume could no more, on his accounting, have been making an observation or series of observations than could the mistreated daughter of the wicked stepmother have searched for strawberries which were green all over and also red. In Hume's case, not finding necessary connection, unlike an ordinary case of looking for something and not finding it, shows that he could not have been looking for anything in the first place. For not finding it shows that he had no idea whatever of necessary connection, which in turn shows that he had no idea of what to look for. The point is that if he had an idea of necessary connection he did not have to look for instances since the existence of the idea would imply the existence of instances. And if he had no idea then he could not look for instances. Interestingly enough, Hume was aware of this, and the curious thing is that he was not disturbed by it nor was he led to correct his description of what he was doing: "We have no idea of this connexion, nor even any distinct notion of what it is we desire to know, when we endeavor a conception of it."[23] Nothing could be more plain than that Hume misdescribed what he was doing. His theory about the nature of causation springs from an analysis of the notion of causation and from nothing else. His argument is a piece of analysis.

Philosophy abounds with instances in which it is made to appear that an intellectual experiment or an observation is being made to establish a claim, when in fact it is a piece of analysis that is being given. And the interesting thing is that in every such case analysis apparently does something comparable to what observation or an experiment does. To cite one further example, Moore makes it appear as if he arrives at the position that ". . . it is better that the beautiful world should exist, than the one which is ugly . . ."[24] by making a Gedankenexperiment of some sort. Verbally he makes it appear that he is imagining himself examining two worlds, one which is exceedingly beautiful and the other exceedingly ugly, each of which is to exist without being experienced by anyone. But in this case, as in Hume's, a hidden analysis backs the conclusion. For, together with the not explicitly formulated version of the view that beauty is a non-natural *property of things* (is objective),[25] the considerations which distinguish between extrinsic and intrinsic value and which make beauty out to be a good in itself are an attempted analytic demonstration of the claim that it is better for beauty to exist than not to exist, regardless of whether it is enjoyed. And this in conjunction with the consideration that ugliness is intrinsically bad, so that its eradication counts as a good, is an analytic argument for the proposition that of two worlds, one beautiful and the other ugly, it is better that the beautiful world exist rather than the ugly one, even though no one is there to enjoy it: ". . . the existence of a more beautiful thing is better *in itself* than that of one more ugly, quite apart from its effects on any human feeling. . ."[26] Contemplating the two universes and coming to a decision, as if on the basis of an empirical examination, actually plays no role in the philosophical demonstration of the proposition. Again, analysis leads, or purports to lead, to the establishing of a philosophical claim which is misleadingly described as being established empirically. And again the interesting thing is that analysis does, or appears to do, for philosophy what observation and experiment do for science: lead to new results. The feeling is unavoidable that philosophers misdescribe their procedure because they think their *actual* procedure does the kind of thing that their described procedure normally does.

To summarize briefly the most important things apparently accomplished by analysis in philosophy. It lays bare, for one thing, hidden contradictions in theories. For another, it clarifies theories by a process of translating them into the concrete for the purpose of bringing them into confrontation with matters of fact. And finally, and undoubtedly the most important of the aims of analysis, it discloses new facts not referred to in the definition of the term analysed. The first and the second are to be expected, and hardly anyone would think of contesting them as being legitimate and possible objectives of analysis although actual claimed results might be challenged. The last-mentioned goal seems to some philosophers natural and possible as a goal of analysis and to others it seems unnatural and delusive. In fact some philosophers have maintained outright that analysis cannot lead to new information about phenomena and that it has as its sole possible end-result clarification, the making explicit of what is implicit in concepts.

The picture of themselves that philosophical analysts create is that of people who examine the meanings of terms, or the concepts denoted by them, more carefully and with greater skill and penetration than is done by others. And furthermore, they make it look as if they are examining *objects* of a special, perhaps rarified, kind. They make it look as if they are examining objects which *accompany* terms and are given with them by psychological contiguity, the terms being present to sight or hearing and the objects to the mind. The written word "elephant," for example, is present to sight; its meaning, the concept *elephant,* is present to the mind. And a philosopher who practises analysis with the last of the above objectives in mind gives every appearance of believing that by carefully scrutinizing the concept *elephant* he will learn zoological facts about actual elephants. We are presented with a mystifying, if engaging, picture of the philosophical analyst at his work. The medical radiologist examines X-ray pictures in order to learn medical facts about patients. And the philosopher examines subtle objects with the probing eye of his mind in order to learn whatever he can about phenomena in nature, e.g., that an elephant has "a heart, a liver, etc. etc., all of them arranged in definite relations to one another."

We are reminded of the view, expressed in the *Cratylus,* that "the name is a revelation of the thing," that ". . . names rightly given are the likenesses and images of the things which they name." Of course, if a name were a revelation of a thing, "a likeness and image" of it, then by examining the name more carefully, looking at it more closely, noticing relations between its parts, etc., we should expect to learn new things about the object named. But, of course, names are not images of things. To suppose that they are is sheer intellectual grotesquerie, which may have its source in the fact that language did once consists of pictographs. Apart from onomatopoetic words which imitate the sounds they denote, ordinary words do not picture what they denote. But despite the fact that the notion that they are pictures is patently false, many people seem to have it. Thus Russell seems to have had some such idea when he said, "For my part, I believe that, partly by means of the study of syntax, we can arrive at considerable knowledge concerning the structure of the world."[27] And Heinrich Hertz has said:

"One cannot escape the feeling that these mathematical formulas have an independent existence and an intelligence of their own, . . . that we get more out of them than was originally put into them."[28] Having this idea is, of course, by no means to act on it, and most people would certainly *act* on the view, expressed in the *Cratylus,* that ". . . the knowledge of things is not to be derived from names. They must be studied and investigated in themselves." However, some philosophical analysts, and perhaps all, appear to act on the idea that things need not be "investigated in themselves" and that an examination of conceptual surrogates will yield "knowledge of things."

The picture of the penetrating gazer into concepts changes if we replace the expression "meaning of a term," or "concept denoted by a term," by the expression "literal use of a term." It is clear that no linguistic distortion is introduced by making this substitution; and the importance of making it is that it removes an idea which blinds us to what actually is being done. It removes the false notion that the meanings of words contain hidden facts about things which analysis can bring to light. The words "concept" and "meaning," unlike the term "literal use," suggest objects, whereas the term "literal use" suggests no more than an activity. The phrase "the meaning of w" has the form of a phrase like "the father of Jones," where "the father of Jones" denotes an object which is related in a special way to Jones; and one is naturally tempted to imagine that "the meaning of w" denotes an object which is related in a special way to w. But, of course, whereas an object is denoted by the one it is not by the other, and to suppose that it is is to be made the dupe of a semantic illusion which we ourselves create[29] by unconsciously exaggerating a grammatical similarity. We may echo here a complaint about language which Moore makes in a different connection: "It seems to me very curious that language . . . should have grown up just as if it were expressly designed to mislead philosophers; and I do not know why it should have. Yet it seems to me there is no doubt that in ever so many instances it has."[30] It may, as Moore complains, be that language misleads philosophers, but it may be that language does no more than offer opportunities for philosophers to practice a special kind of artistry on it.

The expression "the meaning of a term" is not used to denote objects, and this is brought out by the fact that the expression "the literal use of a term" substitutes without serious distortion for it. This is not to say, of course, that the two expressions are *exact* synonyms; nevertheless the fact that one can in a vast number of cases be used in place of the other shows that "meaning of a word" is not used to name an entity. In the present case the importance of calling attention to this is that it dispels an intellectual illusion, the illusion that analysis consists of resolving a kind of object into its components or of gazing into its interior. The expression "use of a term," like the expression "use of a knife," denotes an activity actual or dispositional, and no mystery attaches to the idea of analysing an activity. Plainly, analysing the use of an expression E comes to nothing more than stating the rules for E's use, and nothing over and above this is suggested. It consists in stating explicitly the features in virtue of which E is applied to a situation. Thus, the analysis of the use of the word "brother" informs us that the word applies to x's that are male and that are siblings. Making explicit what is implicit in a *concept* can now be seen to come to nothing more than describing features the presence of which makes it correct to apply a term to an object. It consists of stating rules which, without our conscious awareness for the most part, determine our use of an expression. The feeling that analysis teaches us something new is in part justified; for analysis makes us conscious of criteria which normally we unconsciously use. When Moore distinguishes between the meaning of a word and the analysis of its meaning, and maintains, quite rightly, that we can know the first without knowing the second, what he is doing is remarking this fact, namely, that we can know perfectly well the use of a word without being consciously aware of criteria which determine its use. But the way he expresses himself carries the suggestion that knowing the analysis of the meaning of a word comes to something more than knowing explicitly the criteria for its use. His language suggests that something more than linguistic fact is thrown into clearer light, that hidden facts about things are revealed. With the dissipation of the picture of philosophers learning secrets of nature by a sort of mental X-raying of concepts, the notion that philosophical analysis can have as a possible aim the disclosure of matter of fact about phenomena is clearly seen to be a deception. When we see that analysing the meaning of an expression E is nothing more than analysing E's use, we see that analysis can be nothing else but clarificatory. How, we wish to ask, have philosophers been able to think themselves doing more by analysis than this? How is this to be explained?

The objection will undoubtedly be raised that analysing a concept is not the same as explicating the use of a word. It will be said that analysing a concept is a process which uses words to record its findings, but is not about the words, and that ideally analysis could go on without the help of words. You cannot analyse the use of an expression without bringing into the analysis an expression which has that use; but you can, it will be maintained by some philosophers, analyse the meaning of an expression without bringing the expression into the analysis. You could, conceivably, analyse a concept without using any word which names the concept. The correct result of an analysis is an *a priori* true proposition, and an *a priori* proposition is not verbal. Furthermore, an *a priori* proposition could exist in verbal nakedness, prior even to the existence of language.

It will be maintained, moreover, that some *a priori* propositions are synthetic, the predicates of which, unlike the predicates of analytic propositions, tell us something new and in addition to what the subject tells us about the kind of phenomenon referred to. It is thus possible for analysis to take us beyond a given concept ∅ to new concepts into which ∅ is not resolvable but with which ∅ is connected by logical necessity. For example, the proposition that a uniformly green surface is nowhere pink is *a priori*, and, according to some philosophers, would count as synthetic, on the grounds that being not pink is not a conjunctive constituent of *being uniformly green*. Thus, it will be urged, analysis of a given concept can lead us to new knowledge of the nature of things falling under the concept. These two counter-claims have to be met before we can go on: the claim that the analysis of concepts is not the same as the analysis of usage, and the claim that analysis can yield new knowledge, can be more than clarificatory, because there are synthetic *a priori* propositions.

Let us consider first the claim that analytic propositions are not verbal. It can be seen that it is this, primarily, on which is made to rest the contention that the analysis of concepts is not to be identified with analysis of usage. Now as the word "verbal" is actually used, it is true to say that analytic propositions are not verbal. But insight into the nature of analytic propositions will make us see that the analysis of concepts is nothing more than the explicit listing of rules for the use or application of terms, stated in the ontological or nonverbal idiom. The proposition, "A brother is a male sibling," is the result of a verbal analysis; it states the criteria for the use of the word "brother," but does this without mentioning words.

To see this, consider the *sentence* in English which expresses the analytic proposition that a brother is a male sibling. What we know and all that we know in understanding this sentence is usage, the use of "brother," of "male," of "sibling," and the fact that "brother but not a male sibling" has been assigned no application; but the sentence itself says nothing about usage. This has been argued elsewhere,[31] but a consideration which leads to this may be looked at briefly. In place of the sentence "A brother is a male sibling," let us consider the associated sentence "It is logically impossible for anyone to be a brother and not be a male sibling." And now let us note the difference between this latter sentence and "It is physically impossible for anyone's brother to jump to the moon." The difference between the impossibilities expressed by these two sentences is enormous. It is a difference in kind and not one of degree. The difference between them is not like the difference between the impossibility expressed by the second sentence and that expressed by "It is physically impossible for anyone's brother to jump twenty feet straight up." With regard to the two sentences which describe physical impossibilities, we know what it would be like to do what the sentences declare impossible. This is to say that the phrases "brother who jumps to the moon" and "brother who jumps twenty feet straight up" have a descriptive use. They describe what is declared by the sentences to be impossible, such that, in understanding sentences, we know what it would be like for there to be situations which would render false the propositions expressed by the sentences. Plainly, a sentence describes a situation which would, if it obtained, upset the proposition expressed by the sentence only if the proposition is empirical, only if it could, theoretically, have a truth-value other than the one it has.

With regard to the sentence "It is logically impossible for anyone to be a brother and not a male sibling," the position is altogether different. If in understanding it we imagined a situation the existence of which would upset a claimed impossibility, the impossibility would not be the *a priori* impossibility of logic. It would be only if the phrase "brother who is not a male sibling" did not denote a situation the conceiving of which is equivalent to conceiving the proposition to be false. And this means that what we know in understanding the sentence "It is logically impossible that anyone be a brother and not a male sibling" is that "brother and not a male sibling" is not used in our language to describe a creature, actual or mythical, although, to be sure, this linguistic fact is not part of what the sentence asserts. The sentence "It is logically impossible . . ." does not say the same as "It makes no literal sense to say . . . ," although what we know in understanding the first sentence is that what the second sentence says is true. And this is brought about by the fact that these sentences are in different idioms. It is plain that what we know in understanding the sentence "A brother is a male sibling" is not different from what we know in understanding the sentence "It is logically impossible . . ." Hence what we know and all that we know in understanding the first sentence are facts of linguistic usage.

An analytic proposition which is the end-result of an analysis of a concept is, to put the matter loosely, verbal in content but non-verbal in form. It presents an array of features the presence of which is required in anything which exemplifies the concept. This is a non-verbal form of presenting information about the use of terminology. Talk about analysis of concepts is equivalent to talk about analysis of usage, but is talk carried on in the "object language." And although the first mode of speech in no way affects the practice of analysis, it creates a misleading picture of what the philosopher does when he analyses various concepts.

To consider now the second point, namely, that some logically necessary propositions are synthetic, and that this makes it possible for analysis to take us, *via the bridge of a priori connection,* beyond the concept under analytic scrutiny to new concepts. A sentence which expresses a synthetic *a priori* proposition, e.g., "A uniformly green surface is nowhere pink," is a sentence which expresses a logically necessary one. It is this fact which such sentences share with sentences expressing analytic propositions. But quite in general, as has been seen, any sentence which expresses a logically necessary proposition is such that understanding it is equivalent to knowing facts about usage. And whether the proposition expressed by a sentence is analytic or synthetic *a priori* does not affect this point. So long as the proposition is *a priori* true the sentence will be non-verbal and such that all that we know in understanding it is a matter of verbal facts. Thus, the sentence "A uniformly green surface is nowhere pink" is non-verbal, but what we know in understanding it is that what is said by the sentence "As a matter of usage 'nowhere pink' applies to whatever 'uniformly green surface' applies to" is true. Hence, a synthetic *a priori* proposition does not give us new information about the nature of a phenomenon; its predicate does not tell us something about what is denoted by the subject term which we do not already know in knowing the meaning of the subject term. Analytic investigation of a concept, which terminates in a synthetic _a priori_ proposition, does not, as it might seem, lead us to knowledge of new properties of things. It is not, to take an expression from Dr. Margaret Macdonald, a kind of "interior looking" into a subtle object ø and thereby learning unobserved facts about things of which ø is the archetype. Plato's Ideal Theory comes to mind.

Again we come back to our question, How have philosophers been able to think that _a priori_ synthetic propositions give knowledge about the nature or existence of phenomena, and also, how could any philosophers have imagined that by purely _a priori_ procedures they could learn facts about the world? What has produced the remarkable illusion which many and perhaps all philosophers have embraced, the illusion, namely, that their utterances make deep factual claims to which they were led by the non-experimental procedure of analysing concepts, a procedure which actually comes to no more than making explicit rules governing usage?

To explain this we have to show how it is possible to create the appearance of arriving at and establishing theories by a procedure which does no more than list feaures which we automatically use in applying expressions to situations. A straightforward analysis of the use of a term can hardly be said to give us exciting information; and it would not normally be thought to issue in a proposition about reality. The tendency to think that "A brother is a male sibling" or that "A green surface can nowhere be pink" are about persons and things is not great, although there is some tendency to think this because of the idiom in which the statement is made, the idiom, that is, in which expressions are not mentioned and in which, most often, they are used to describe situations. And it is a relatively simple matter to dispel the idea that "A brother is a male sibling" is about persons by bringing that statement into connection with the statement " 'Brother' means male sibling": their underlying identity is too obvious to be denied. And the idea, of course, is completely dispelled if in addition to this we point out how different "A brother is a male sibling" is from "A brother eats more than his sister does": the latter has no verbal import.

A non-philosophical analysis, like that illustrated by the paradigm, even when it does appear to be about the world, never seems to be a _theory_ about the world. In philosophy, however, the case is otherwise. Analysis in philosophy invariably leads to a variety of "theories," all of which are in dispute. If we give the name "actual analysis" to cases of ordinary analysis which do no more than list the features which make the application of the definiendum correct, then we can see that there must be an important difference between it and a philosophical analysis. For unlike the former, the latter issues in a permanently controversial proposition which has the air of being a theory about phenomena. An actual piece of analysis, which in effect constitutes a report about established usage, would not be permanently debatable nor would it have the appearance of being a theory about things. A *philosophical* analysis cannot therefore be *merely* an actual analysis, and I shall give it the designation "conversion analysis." I use the term "conversion analysis" because, as I shall try to show, in philosophy an analysis is used to make a linguistic alteration, it is used to justify a manoeuvre with terminology. It is a linguistic conversion which in every instance creates the semantic illusion that a theory about phenomena is being stated. Thus, in marked contrast to the paradigm of analysis, Hume's famous analysis of causation issues in what looks to be a theory about how occurrences are related, a theory, moreover, which has been controversial for two hundred years. To show that Hume's view is a deceptive manoeuvre with terminology, that his analysis is a conversion analysis a full and detailed examination of his position is required, and this is too much for the present paper. A short account will have to suffice.

We can gather from Hume's comment about how "cold, and strain'd, and ridiculous" his speculations at times seemed that he did not intend his view about causation to be accepted as an everyday proposition, but intended it rather for acceptance in what Moore calls a "philosophic moment." Moore's expression is helpful because of what it suggests. It suggests that a philosophical theory, particularly one which is in flagrant violation of Common Sense, can, unlike a glaringly false scientific proposition, be believed in a special moment, in which, perhaps, we are under the domination of a special mood. We do not hear of scientific theories, the falsity of which is known, being believed in a special kind of scientific moment. What are we to make of the "theories" which are to be believed only in philosophic moments? The suggestion that irresistibly presents itself is that a philosophical theory is not the kind of thing it seems to be. And indeed, it is plain that it cannot be; for it cannot both be a theory and result from an analysis of usage. And it cannot be a description of usage, since if it were it would not be permanently controversial. Hume's position is no exception.

Hume maintains that all events are "loose and separate,"[32] and that "Objects have no discoverable connexion together."[33] The discerning reader of Hume will know that he held at least two different views with regard to causation: (1) that words like "cause," "force," "necessary connection" have no literal meaning, are "wrong apply'd," and (2) that "cause" means no more than constant conjunction. The second position, however, seems to be the one most often attributed to him, and if we suppose that this is the one that he himself would have wished to hold exclusively, we shall have to say that he distinguishes between "cause" and "necessary connection." The fact, of course, is that sometimes he uses them interchangeably and sometimes not. The theory which arises from keeping their use distinct is to the effect that a statement like "α causes β" is equivalent to a statement to the effect that α is followed by β, "and where all the objects similar to the first are followed by objects similar to the second."[34] This is an astonishing view and Hume himself recognized that it was a "violent" paradox and that only "by dint of solid proof and reasoning" could he ever hope to "overcome the inveterate prejudices of mankind." What are his reasons for holding that causation is nothing more than constant conjunction? Russell represents the dispute over whether it is or not as being empirical. He says: "The controversy is thus reduced to one of empirical fact. Do we, or do we not, sometimes perceive a relation which can be called causal [i.e., a necessary connection]? Hume says no, his adversaries say yes, and it is not easy to see how evidence can be produced by either side."[35] How seriously this misrepresents the controversy is evident (apart from what has already been noticed about Hume's pseudo-search for necessary connection) from the quite unacceptable consequence, namely, that either some philosophers perceive what others, strangely enough, fail to perceive, have a kind of visual blindness which can neither be explained nor described, or else that some philosophers "see" what is not there and, furthermore, cannot describe to others what they see. This is absurd, and has to be rejected, and with its rejection goes the description which represents the controversy as being empirical. Hume's reasons are analytical and not at all the kind that could be characterized as constituting testimony of the senses.

Hume maintains that ". . . there can be no demonstrative arguments to prove, *that those instances of which we have had no experience, resemble those, of which we have had experience.* We can at least conceive a change in the course of nature; which sufficiently proves that such a change is not absolutely impossible. To form a clear idea of anything, is an undeniable argument for its possibility, and is alone a refutation of any pretended demonstration against it."[36] And again, he writes: "If we reason *a priori,* anything may appear able to produce anything. The falling of a pebble may, for aught we know, extinguish the sun or the wish of a man control the planets in their orbits."[37] With these words Hume unmistakably calls attention to the difference between causal statements, such as that bodies in friction heat and "water refreshes," and entailment statements, such as that a pyramid has four faces. The one is *a priori* and the others are not. The negation of the entailment results in a proposition which is "absolutely" or logically impossible, whereas the negation of either causal statement does not result in a logical impossibility and gives us a "clear idea" of a state of affairs. No causal statement, nor the denial of any causal statement, can be ruled out as "absolutely impossible" if we "reason *a priori*" only. This fact indicates how linguistically different the "if . . . then——" of causation is from the "if . . . then——" of entailment. Hume's words constitute a piece of actual analysis. They correctly signalize the difference between two uses of "if . . . then——," the difference between the "if . . . then——" in "If two bodies are in friction then necessarily they heat" and the "if . . . then——" in "If anything is a pyramid then necessarily it has four faces." The necessity of one is the necessity of logic and the necessity of the other is not. And these are utterly different. The one, we may say, has its source in language, the other in nature.

Consider now the further thing that Hume has to say about causation: ". . . we are never able, in a single instance, to discover any power or necessary connexion; any quality, which binds the effect to the cause, and renders the one an infallible consequence of the other. We only find, that the one does actually, in fact, follow the other."[38] Consider also his further words: "It may be thought, that what we learn not from one object, we can never learn from a hundred, which are all of the same kind, and are perfectly resembling in every circumstance. . . . From the mere repetition of any past impression, even to infinity, there never will arise any new original idea, such as that of a necessary connexion; and the number of impressions has in this case no more effect that if we confin'd ourselves to one only."[39]

It can be seen, for one thing, that in a colourful but descriptively misleading way Hume is saying something about the use of "necessary" as it occurs in such causal statements as "Friction necessarily generates heat," namely, that it is a word which is not the name of anything. His remarking that we have no impression of necessary connection comes to pointing out the linguistic fact that it makes no literal sense to speak of *seeing* necessary connection between occurrences, as it does make sense to speak of seeing a link which unites two objects. His words call up the picture of someone in search of something, but the reality behind this false picture is linguistic in nature; to put it shortly, "we have no impression of necessary connection" = " 'necessary connection' denotes nothing which could with literal sense be said to be perceived." Hume goes on to argue that what we do not perceive in one instance we do not perceive in any number of like instances, "even to infinity," and consequently that causation is nothing more than constant conjunction. This part of his argument is used to demonstrate that it makes no sense to say that causation is anything more than constant conjunction. It would seem plain that his argument is a piece of analysis. Hume is to be taken as saying something like the following: the analysis of the use of "cause" makes explicit the linguistic fact that "cause" applies to occurrences to which "constantly conjoined" applies, and further, that the term "necessary connection" has no use. The statement, "Friction causes heat," can without change of meaning be replaced by "Friction is invariably accompanied by heat," and "Friction necessarily causes heat" contracts without loss of meaning into "Friction causes heat." Philosophers who have rejected this view have done so on the grounds that there is more to causation than *mere* repeated conjunction of occurrences, that causation entails invariable conjunction but is not entailed by it. And some present-day philosophers even go so far as to maintain that the term "necessarily" as it occurs in causal statements denotes logical necessity and that causation involves entailment.

It is plain that philosophers who reject Hume's view wish to point out the difference between causal conjunctions and *accidental* ones, a difference which Hume's view seems to obliterate. Their protest is that according to Hume's analysis "cause" means repeated *accidental* conjunction, and Hume seems to acknowledge this when he says such things as that events are "loose and separate," "Objects have no discoverable connexion together," and "We cannot penetrate into the reason of the conjunction." His view does seem to represent causation as recurring accident.

The *point* of remarking that we perceive no "necessary connection" in a single instance of a conjunction of occurrences and that any number of similar conjunctions does not reveal any more than the original conjunction is to urge that occurrences which we say are causally connected are all accidentally conjoined. There is no perceived necessary connection in the first conjunction, which is to say that for all we know it is accidental; and since no further conjunctions reveal (or could reveal) anything not revealed by the first they are all accidental, all "loose and separate." Causation is nothing more than a miraculous repetition of independent occurrences. Hume's further words heighten the impression that this is his view: "If we believe that fire warms or water refreshes, 'tis only because it costs us too much pain to think otherwise." What these words appear to come to is the view that although fire and warming are constantly associated, there is no connection between them in addition to their occurring together; and it is the same with drinking water and being refreshed. The straightforward implication with regard to such words as "warms," "refreshes," "supports," "shatters," that is, what we may call causal verbs, is not that they describe processes between occurrences which *in fact* do not exist but that they do not describe processes. In holding that *all* events are loose and separate, he tells us that we have no idea what it would be like for events to be other than loose and separate. In other words, his claim is *a priori*, not empirical. Thus, his view is, or certainly appears to be, that causal verbs are literally meaningless, describe neither an actual nor a conceivable process or action. "Warms" does not describe what fire *does*, nor does "heats" describe what friction does.

Many philosophers, and all non-philosophers who are first introduced to Hume's position, protest against his implied claim about causal verbs without making clear and explicit what it is they are protesting against. Russell appears to have divined the linguistic import of Hume's position when in commenting on the statement, "Generally speaking, the errors in religion are dangerous; those in philosophy only ridiculous," he says: "He has no right to say this. 'Dangerous' is a causal word, and a sceptic as to causation cannot know that anything is 'dangerous.' "[40] Thus Russell is led to charge Hume with insincerity: "In a sense, his scepticism is insincere, since he cannot maintain it in practice."[41] Hume's "insincerity" is that of a person who denies, or appears to deny, that all of a particular class of verbs have literal sense while acknowledging, by his use of them in sentences to convey information about matters of fact, that they are perfectly intelligible. When Russell protests that Hume has no "right" to say anything is "dangerous," he is objecting to the use of the word by a philosopher who denies that it has a use.

Is Hume's position, however, what it now looks to be, an analysis of causation which shows causally connected events to be no different from accidentally conjoined events, and which, furthermore, shows that an entire class of verbs in frequent everyday use are semantic hoaxes, are without sense? If it is, it is an incorrect analysis, the incorrectness of which could not for long have failed to strike him. "α causes β" does not mean that α-like occurrences are invariably but fortuitously conjoined with β-like occurrences; and that it does not mean this could not for long have escaped Hume and his later followers, if his view is what it appears to be. And it is just fantasy to think that he and others could have held, whether explicitly or by implication, that such causal verbs as "ignites," "quenches," "endangers," are meaningless because analysis shows them to be such. No one can take such an unreal attitude about the magical persuasive powers of analysis.

F. H. Bradley has said that "It is a very common and most ruinous superstition to suppose that analysis is not alteration. . . ."[42] And we may usefully apply his words to the present case. I think, indeed, that we can understand what Hume is doing and why his view gives the delusive impression of being a theory about the nature of causally connected events if we construe his analysis to be, not an actual analysis, but a conversion analysis, an analysis the object of which is *alteration*. We can understand what he is doing and how he produces his remarkable and dramatic effect if we interpret him as pointing out certain linguistic dissimilarities and similarities between causal statements and entailment statements, and between causal statements and accidental joint-occurrence statements. It is not necessary again to note the linguistic difference between causation statements and entailment statements and the difference between "necessary" in the causal sense and "necessary" in the logical sense. It is sufficiently plain that Hume calls attention to the unlikeness between the statements, glossed over by their identity of form (both being of the form "if . . . then——"), and that he wishes to heighten this unlikeness. His argument for the position that events are "loose and separate," namely, that there is no discernible connection in any single instance of causally conjoined events nor therefore in any number of such instances, however great, "even to infinity," calls attention to an important similarity between causal statements and coincidental-occurrence statements. It calls attention to the fact that however well established a causal correlation between α's and β's has become, *it always makes literal sense* to say "α's and β's are only accidentally connected" or to say that the next α will be unaccompanied by a β, even though it is false to say this. For example, it makes sense to say, even if only in jest, "The window happened to shatter just as the stone struck it." And this shows a linguistic likeness between causal statements and non-causal joint-occurrence statements. In order to make more conspicuous, linguistically more visible, this likeness, and at the same time make more pronounced the linguistic gulf between causal statements and entailment statements, Hume re-describes causal statements in such a way as to bring out the likeness at the cost of muting their difference, without completely obliterating it. Causal sequences are made to look more like accidental conjunctions by describing them as *conjunctions* or joint occurrences, while their difference is preserved in a shadowy way by characterizing causal conjunctions as "invariable" or "constant." But even this verbal shadow of causal "necessity" is made more indistinct by academically ruling out from use causal verbs. He does not hold that they are in ordinary language senseless; he only makes them senseless, deprives them of their use, by linguistic fiat. And he does this in order to exaggerate the likeness between causal statements and non-causal joint-occurrence statements in order to make their actual likeness more transparent.

To sum up, Hume's analysis of causation consists, for one thing, of pointing out the difference in the uses of the term "necessary" in *a priori* implication statements and in causal implication statements. For another thing, it points out the likeness between the descriptions of causal conjunctions of events and non-causal fortuitous conjunctions of events. And this likeness and unlikeness he uses to justify a linguistic conversion or alteration. He re-edits our causal terminology, and he does this in such a way as to make linguistically more pronounced than does ordinary terminology the unlikeness as well as the likeness which strike him with their importance; he academically banishes the term "necessary connection" and causal verbs.

The difference between "A brother is a male sibling" and "Causation is nothing more than invariable sequence" is that the first is an actual analysis, and reports, in the ontological idiom, accepted usage, and the second announces, also in the ontological idiom, a linguistic alteration. It is the combination of being in the non-verbal idiom and announcing in a concealed fashion a non-workaday reclassification of causal sentences with non-causal joint-occurrence sentences which creates the illusion that Hume's theory makes a factual claim about a well-known kind of phenomenon, shows us a new and surprising thing about how it operates. As has already been noted, the ontological idiom in which *a priori* propositions are expressed can give one the idea that objects and their properties are being discussed, when nothing of the sort is the case. To illustrate, one philosopher has maintained that "the Law of Contradiction is metaphysical or ontological."[43] This he maintains on the grounds that "*We cannot think* contradictory propositions, because we see that *a thing cannot have* at once and not have the same character; and the so-called necessity of thought is really the apprehension of a necessity in the being of things."[44] The "necessity in the being of things" is, as we might say, linguistically created: that the sentence "*A thing cannot have* at once and not have the same character" expresses a necessary proposition implies that the expression "thing which both has and does not have character ϕ" has no theoretical application, and knowing this verbal fact is what understanding the sentence comes to. An impression which is produced merely by a statement being formulated in the ontological idiom is plainly heightened when the statement does more than convey information about customary usage, when it introduces a hidden re-editing of terminology. What Hume actually does when he states and argues for his position is, so to say, to re-draw linguistic lines, but in doing this in the non-verbal form of speech, and, furthermore, in presenting his analysis in the guise of a demonstration, he falsely depicts himself as stating something about the nature of a phenomenon. What he does is made to look like the announcing of a theory which is supported by powerful evidence. The theory, which hides a language revision, looks either like a mistaken view about the nature of causation (and to some it even appears to deny the existence of causation) or like a true view which destroys a common superstition. Thus, e.g., Wittgenstein has said that "Belief in the causal nexus is a superstition."[45]

This account of the nature of Hume's view of causation explains the source of the idea that by analysing concepts it is possible to obtain new information about phenomena coming under the concept. It explains how we come to think that analysis can disclose new properties, properties into which the concept under analytic inspection does not resolve itself. The new "properties" are nothing more than disguised language alterations. Truly, Hume's view can be characterized as synthetic *a priori*. The words "Causation is nothing more than invariable conjunction" and the words "Causally connected events are loose and separate" express, in Hume's recomposed language, propositions which are both *a priori* and synthetic, or to use a term which brings out the point more clearly, they are *ersatz a priori*. These words, as they are ordinarily used, do not express *a priori* propositions, but Hume academically *makes* them express *a priori* propositions by Humpty Dumpty fiat. He achieves the effect of demonstrating a startling fact about a familiar type of phenomenon by making a non-workaday manoeuvre with language against the backdrop of unaltered everyday language. The effect is theatrical. Semantically, the existence of two terminologies makes it look as if there are two theories about the nature of causation,[46] one a piece of "primitive metaphysics" of the common man and the other a sophisticated theory held by the penetrating analyst. But philosophical analysts are not mental gazers into concepts from which they learn the secret workings of the world. They are subtle changers of language. We may say that on its constructive side philosophical analysis is creative rather than explicative.

There remains to be seen what Moore's translations into the concrete come to and why they so often fail to achieve their intended objective.[47] A translation into the concrete has two jobs to do, or perhaps it would be better to say it has a job with a special point. So to speak, it has an aim-directed task. The avowed work of a translation into the concrete is to effect a clarification in a concept by showing what in a concrete way it entails. Thus, the concept of time is so connected with the concept of event that the proposition that time is unreal entails the proposition that there are no events. To exhibit such an entailment is to effect a clarification. The *point* of a translation into the concrete is to bring a theory into confrontation with matter of fact in order to test it, and such testing seems to be empirical. The puzzling thing about such translations is that they fail to do their intended work, viz., to refute a philosophical theory which goes against Common Sense. As is known, philosophers have continued to hold their theories in disregard of Moore's refutations. And in doing so they appear either to have mistaken notions about usage or mistaken notions about non-linguistic matter of fact, neither of which, for some strange reason, will they give up on confrontation with the relevant facts. But what is even more puzzling is how the two kinds of mistake could be made *in the same utterance*. It is much as if a person said "Colour does not exist" and used these words to express two utterly different sorts of proposition, one that the word "colour" had no use and the other that there are in fact no coloured things, that rubies are not red, buttercups not yellow, etc. In making a linguistic mistake a philosopher is not mistakenly denying matter of fact, and in mistakenly denying matter of fact he is not making a linguistic mistake. What the *function* of a translation into the concrete could then be is a mystery. For in the hypothetical colour case, for example, it could not be to show that the word "colour" *has a use* by holding up rubies and buttercups, nor could it be to show that *there exist* red and yellow things by showing that the word "colour" has a use. In its application to philosophical theories, the technique of translation cannot be to correct a philosopher's language in order to expose his non-linguistic empirical mistake. Moore cannot be supposed to be correcting Bradley's notion about the use of the word "time" with the object of showing him that the statement "Time is unreal" is in fact false. There is only one explanation which in an intelligible way clears up these puzzles. After the discussion of Hume the explanation here can be given briefly.

A philosopher who holds a view like "Time is unreal" and resists its translation into "There are no temporal facts" is not failing to see an obvious implication. His resisting the translation means that his words do not have that translation. And they do not have that translation because he has, in the way usual in philosophy, changed language. In the light of this supposition, Moore's translation, which takes the philosopher's words in their everyday sense, is to be construed, not as correcting a mistaken idea about the use of the word "time," but as countering an academic decision to cast out "time" with a vote for the *status quo*. This explanation of what has happened must be conceded to have the merit of making intelligible to us a philosopher's being able to remain obdurate when faced with a translation into the concrete, and indeed it explains how he could even come to hold his view.

The ostensible point of a translation into the concrete, which is to bring a philosopical theory into juxtaposition with confuting fact, could not be the actual point. Moore's translations are not at all comparable to deductions in the form of complicated mathematical calculations used to establish that a scientific theory is not consistent with empirical fact. And if we preserve our sense of reality we cannot accept as a fact that philosophers are mistaken about the existence of time, space, material bodies, etc. Moore's empirical-seeming refutations are actually countermoves with language. His technique is wholly linguistic, although it does not appear to be because of the manner in which he phrases his refutations. The propositions which he lays down as truisms, his philosophical platform, are not statements of fact as to what exists and what things are, but examples of the kind of everyday utterance which are not to be tampered with by metaphysically inclined philosophers under the guise of making actual analyses. This is the linguistic prohibition implied both by Moore's distinction between the meaning of ordinary words and the analysis of their meaning, and by the paradigm he gives of analysis. The analysis of the meaning of a word like "time" cannot show that "time" has no meaning, and it will not show this so long as the analysis is an actual and not a conversion analysis. What Moore is telling us is that philosophy should be done within the confines of ordinary language, and should not be done with the subterranean purpose of changing it. Thus, Moore's translations into the concrete of theories which go against Common Sense are to be interpreted as showing that they go against the language of Common Sense, that they are attempts to change it which, according to his lights, should be resisted. A translation does not show, nor is it in fact designed to show, that a philosophical theory is in conflict with matter of fact. It is designed to oppose an idle innovation in a language which works well enough. A philosopher who holds a bizarre anti-Common-sense view has, like Hume, performed a conversion analysis and has not governed himself by Moore's prohibition against using analysis to justify radical alterations of ordinary speech. With Moore philosophy gains sobriety and the appearance of rigor but loses most of its dramatic appeal; and it is taste and nothing else which dictates which we choose in philosophy, the extravaganza of metaphysics or the sobriety of Common Sense with its semblance of science. We may say with Hume: "'Tis not solely in poetry and music we must follow our taste and sentiment but likewise in philosophy."[48]

Notes

1. Broad gives the impression of thinking otherwise. See *Scientific Thought* (New York: Harcourt Brace, 1923), Introduction.
2. G. E. Moore, *Principia Ethica* (Cambridge: Cambridge University Press, 1903), p. 2.

3. G. E. Moore, *Some Main Problems of Philosophy* (London: George Allen & Unwin, 1953), p. 24.

4. This will be justified later.

5. For this adjective I ask the purist's forbearance.

6. *Principia Ethica*, pp. 104-105.

7. *Ibid.*, p. 117.

8. G. E. Moore, *Philosophical Studies* (London: Routledge & Kegan Paul, 1922), pp. 209-10.

9. *Ibid.*, p. 218.

10. *Ibid.*, p. 228.

11. *Some Main Problems of Philosophy*, p. 1.

12. *Ibid.*, pp. 17-23.

13. *Ibid.*

14. *Ibid.*, p. 24.

15. *Philosophical Studies*, pp. 64-65.

16. *Ibid.*

17. *Principia Ethica*, p. 7.

18. *Ibid.*, p. 8.

19. *Ibid.*

20. *Some Main Problems of Philosophy*, p. 24.

21. Hume, *An Enquiry Concerning Human Understanding*, Sec. VII, Pt. i.

22. Hume, *A Treatise of Human Nature*, Book I, Pt. III, Sec. ii.

23. *An Enquiry Concerning Human Understanding*, Sec. VII, Pt. ii.

24. *Principia Ethica*, p. 84.

25. *Ibid.*, pp. 201-202.

26. *Ibid.*, p. 84. Italics added.

27. Bertrand Russell, *An Inquiry into Meaning and Truth* (London: George Allen & Unwin, 1940), p. 438.

28. Heinrich Hertz, quoted in *Men of Mathematics* by E. T. Bell (New York: Simon & Schuster, 1937), p. 16.

29. This is argued in my *The Structure of Metaphysics* (London: Routledge & Kegan Paul, 1955), Chap. III.

30. *Philosophical Studies*, p. 217.

31. *The Structure of Metaphysics*, Chap. XII.

32. *An Enquiry Concerning Human Understanding*, Sec. VII, Pt. ii.

33. *A Treatise of Human Nature*, Bk. I, Pt. III, Sec. viii.

34. *An Enquiry Concerning Human Understanding*, Sec. VII, Pt. ii.

35. Russell, *A History of Western Philosophy* (London: George Allen & Unwin, 1945), p. 669.

36. *A Treatise of Human Nature*, Bk. I, Pt. III, Sec. vii.

37. *An Enquiry Concerning Human Understanding*, Sec. XII, Pt. i.

38. *Ibid.*, Sec. VII, Pt. i.

39. *A Treatise of Human Nature*, Bk. I, Pt. III, Sec. vi.

40. Russell, *op. cit.*, p. 672.

41. *Ibid.*

42. F. H. Bradley, *Principles of Logic* (London: Oxford University Press, 1883), I, p. 95.

43. H. W. B. Joseph, *An Introduction to Logic* (London: Oxford University Press, 1916), p. 13.

44. *Ibid.*

45. Wittgenstein, *Tractatus Logico-Philosophicus*, 5.1361.

46. The following news report, taken together with Hume's theory, provides an interesting illustration: "An experiment that suggests that smoking thickens the blood of the smoker is reported in the Canadian Medical Association Journal. According to the article, the results may explain the reason for the higher statistical death rate from coronary artery disease among smokers. . . . Up to now the connection between heart disease and smoking has been statistical" (*New York Herald Tribune,* Oct. 8, 1956, p. 13). A Humeian would say that there never will be more than a statistical connection between heart disease and smoking, because there never will be more than a statistical connection between blood thickening and smoking. Causal correlations are *never* more than statistical.

47. I shall not in this paper attempt to deal with the contradictions in philosophical views brought to light by analysis.

48. *A Treatise of Human Nature,* Bk. I, Pt. III, Sec. viii.

Thirteen

THE PARADOX
OF ANALYSIS

M. S. Gram

THE PARADOX of analysis is deceptively easy to formulate. It runs like this:

1) Every analysis is a statement of identity holding between *analysans* and *analysandum.*
2) If every analysis is a statement of identity, then every analysis must be a tautology.
3) If a proposed analysis is not a statement of identity, then it is not an analysis.
4) Hence, either a sentence expressing an analysis is a tautology—in which case it is uninformative and not an analysis—or it is not a tautology—in which case it is not an analysis.

To generate (4) an uncontroversial auxiliary premise is required; namely, that every analysis deserving the name must be informative and therefore separable from an expression which is tautological. If the foregoing argument is sound, what it shows is that a sentence expresses an analysis if and only if it does not express an analysis. The conclusion of this argument cannot, of course, be true, for there are cases of anal-

258

yses which are *prima facie* successful. This shows that, even if such analyses are not successful, they are at least free from the general defect that the conclusion of the foregoing argument demands that we attribute to every analysis. But this is not enough to show the argument to be unsound. It is no answer to the argument to say that it must be unsound because we often succeed in giving nontrivial analyses: One does not show that an argument is unsound by showing that its conclusion contradicts other propositions which we accept as true. For all we learn, when we are told this much, is that one or the other of the propositions in question is false; we are not told which one is false. And this is the reason why the mere claim that we give successful analyses is not enough to show that the paradox of analysis yields a false conclusion.

The paradox of analysis is, nonetheless, unsound. What I shall argue here is that it is generated only by a faulty assumption of what philosophical analysis is and that the solution of the problem given us by the paradox has profound consequences both for the relation between common-sense and ontological descriptions of the world as well as our understanding of the verification of philosophical analyses in general. G. E. Moore first stimulated discussion of the paradox in its present form; hence I begin with his remarks on the paradox as a way of exposing the error on which it feeds.[1]

I. Moore's Suggestions

Moore nowhere claims to solve the paradox of analysis, but he does offer a variety of suggestions for doing so. My point in considering them here is to show that the paradox will remain even if a proposed solution does fulfill the conditions which Moore sets forth. Moore does, to be sure, offer his suggestions as members of a set of necessary and sufficient conditions for a correct solution. I shall treat them separately here. Should any solution of the paradox fulfill any one of the conditions which Moore sets down, it would be sufficient to show that the argument generating the paradox is unsound and would thus count as a solution of the paradox.

What I shall consider as one suggestion for a solution of the paradox is associated with the distinction Moore makes between two senses of knowing something. In *Some Main Problems of Philosophy* he contrasts our ability "to know quite well, in one sense, what a word means, while at the same time, in another sense, we may not know what it means. We may be quite familiar with the notion it conveys, and understand sentences in which it occurs, although at the same time we are quite unable to *define* it."[2] The distinction Moore makes here between knowing how to use sentences in certain contexts and knowing the analysis of those sentences might be used to solve the paradox. For it could be used to fulfill the primary condition of solving the paradox: We must explain which elements in the sentence expressing the analysis are different and which are identical. Given the distinction I have just mentioned, we have the following alternative explanation. We can say that the analysans and the analysandum are related by an identity of concepts or meanings, but that what distinguishes this relation from that which holds in tautologies is the epistemic relation in which we stand to that relation of identity. Thus I can know the meaning of the analysandum and still not be able to give an analysis of it. To know$_1$ the meaning of an analysandum is to be able correctly to apply it in various contexts and correctly to refuse to apply it in others. I am not here concerned to give adequate criteria for possessing this kind of knowledge. All I want to do is to point out that there is such knowledge and to ask whether the fact of such knowledge can be used to solve the paradox. It is an uncontroversial point that we possess this kind of knowledge when we have certain kinds of recognitional abilities. And we must distinguish this kind of knowledge from the kind of knowledge we have when we are able to state the analysis of sentences which we can correctly assert or refuse to assert under certain circumstances. (Let us call the ability to give an analysis of the sentence we can otherwise correctly or incorrectly assert 'knowledge$_2$.')

This distinction is a philosophical commonplace. What does not enjoy the same status is the power of this distinction to solve the paradox of analysis. Let us reconsider the formulation of the paradox given at the beginning of the paper and ask how this distinction can be made to exhibit the unsoundness of the argument generating the paradox. There are two ways in which we can seek to apply the distinction to solve the paradox: we can apply it to the analysandum considered in itself; or we can apply it to the whole sentence expressing the analysis. Thus we can say that the difference between the analysandum and the analysans lies in our epistemic relation to them. We know$_1$ the analysandum but we know$_2$ the analysans. And so, while the analysis itself expresses a conceptual identity, we do not, on this account, have to have the same epistemic relation to one part that we have to the other. In this sense, then, the analysis might be held to be informative and hence not tautological, while the relation holding between the concepts analyzed is that of identity. The argument generating the paradox would, on the present account, be unsound because of the falsity of premise (2). It would be replaced by the following allegedly true but very different sentence:

2') If every analysis is a statement of identity, then the relation of concepts in the sentence expressing the analysis must be that of identity but need not therefore yield a tautology because of the different epistemic relation in which we can stand to the concepts comprising the analysis.

But the application of the distinction between two types of knowledge to the paradox fails immediately. The substitution of (2') for (2) does not solve the paradox but merely conflicts with the requirement, stated in premise (1), that every analysis must express an identity of concepts. The result of this conflict is this: Either the sentence to whose parts we have different epistemic relations is not an identity—in which case the sentence in question does not state an analysis; or the sentence does express an identity—in which case we must have the same epistemic relation to one side of the analysis that we have to the other. And in either case what this shows is that the substitution of (2') for (2) merely reproduces the paradox without solving it. The paradox is not solved by showing that one of the premises conflicts with another. For all we learn in such a case is that one premise must be false without learning which one is false. And this is precisely the difficulty which sustains the paradox.

Can the distinction between two types of knowledge remove the paradox if we apply it, not to the two sides of the sentence expressing the analysis, but rather to the sentence expressing the analysis as a whole? I think not. Consider the strategy of such an application. We can say that we have one epistemic relation to the sentence expressing an analysis when we can apply the analysandum, while we have a different epistemic relation to that same sentence when we can state the analysans. What must be explained is how, on this account, the relation I have to the analysis when I know$_2$ it can be a relation to anything more than a tautology. The explanation cannot, however, be supplied.

For the paradox of analysis is not solved but merely reproduced by applying the epistemic distinction to the whole analysis. And so the epistemic distinction cannot explain how an analysis is informative. It does not give us such an explanation because the paradox which such a distinction might be introduced to solve can be formulated all over again with respect to one part of that distinction: either the reflective knowledge we have of an analysis is knowledge of a tautology; or such knowledge is not knowledge of an analysis. My conclusion, then, is that Moore's distinction between knowing how to apply a concept in certain contexts and knowing the analysis of that concept cannot be used to solve the paradox of analysis.

The same point can be made with regard to those philosophers who, unlike Moore, seek to connect the paradox of analysis with the more general problem of intensional contexts.[3] We are sometimes told that the beginning of a solution of the paradox is the realization that the left-hand side and the right-hand side of an analysis are not extensional and hence cannot be substituted interchangeably *salva veritate* in all contexts. The reason given for this is, accordingly, that I can know the meaning of one side of an analysis without knowing the meaning of the other side. But this way of approaching the solution of the paradox is hopeless. It has, in fact, nothing to do with that paradox. The point of a solution, it must be remembered, is to preserve the informativeness of an analysis without sacrificing the identity of the left- and right-hand sides of sentences expressing analyses. However, suppose that we try to prevent the reduction of analyses to tautologies by first pointing out that sentences expressing analyses are not truth-functional and then going on to restrict the application of the principle of substitutivity with regard to those sentences. *This will not solve the paradox because the problem which generates the paradox arises before any such substitution takes place.* Take any sentence which purports to express an analysis and is not tautological. Even if you say that one side cannot be substituted for the other side of the analysis, you still must explain how the original sentence purporting to express an identity can be informative. Thus to say that one side cannot be substituted for the other merely perpetuates the problem without solving it, for if we cannot substitute one side for the other, what we are given is a reason for believing that one side is not identical with the other. And this is a reason for believing that the sentence does not express an analysis. All of this shows that calling the left and right hand sides of an analysis nonextensional merely provides a symptom of a problem that has not been solved.

Let us return to the conditions which Moore lays down for a solution of the paradox. What he offers, as I have already said, is not a solution but the conditions which any solution must meet. I consider these suggestions in turn. Moore says that, if any analysis is to be correct, it "must, in some sense, be *the same concept*" but "the *expression* used for the *analysandum* must be a different *expression* from that used for the *analysans*."[4] If this condition can be fulfilled by any proposed solution, then it is easy to understand how the paradox would be removed. The paradox is generated by our apparent inability to explain how the analysandum is both identical with but different from the analysans. One way out of this difficulty would be to say, as Moore suggests, that the entity under analysis must be distinguished from the expression whose meaning it is supposed to be. We could then say that the *expressions* in a sentence expressing an analysis are different while the *meaning* of the expressions is the same. An analysis would thus be informative because we may not know that one expression conveys the same meaning as another. The strategy of this solution, then, is to remove premise (2) of the original argument and substitute the following:

2″) Every analysis is an identity statement; but an analysis is not a tautology because the expression for the analysandum is different from the expression for the analysans.

If (2″) is true, then the paradox disappears.

The claim formulated by (2″) is true; but it states a condition to be fulfilled by a proposed solution to the paradox and is not itself a solution. And I think that the condition in question cannot be fulfilled. My reason is that any attempt to fulfill it would render it impossible to state the analysis of anything. The difficulty I have with (2″) centers on the notion of an expression, and Moore does not help us here by giving a precise account of an expression. Let me, accordingly, introduce the following notational devices in order to understand what he might plausibly mean by an expression. Consider the English word 'cat.' It is a component of at least three elements. There are, first of all, the physical shapes or sign designs of the configuration flanked by single quotes. If we consider the word merely as a collection of sign designs, let us flank it by asterisks: Thus *cat* is a collection of sign designs.[5]

Collections of sign designs as such imply nothing about the status of those collections in a natural or artificial language. The asterisk-flanked entity, *cat,* is an entity because it has certain physical features. The single-quoted entity, 'cat,' is an entity because it obeys certain grammatical rules. Thus 'cat' is an entity while 'tca' is not since the latter has no linguistic status. While 'cat' is governed by a set of syntactical conventions, the only sense in which *cat* is governed by convention is that in which there are rules governing its correct reproduction.

There is a third kind of entity to be distinguished both from sign designs on the one hand and from linguistic entities on the other. We can distinguish a word as an entity governed by syntactical or formation rules of a language from a word as interpreted in a certain way. Thus 'cat' and 'Katze' are different words in that they obey different syntactical rules, but they have the same meaning. The meaning which different words have in common can be isolated in discourse by dot quotes. We can, accordingly, say that •cat• is a meaning, or concept. The reason for separating this third entity from the other two is basically common-sensical: Although words obey different sets of syntactical rules, we can still say that they have the same meaning. And whatever the correct philosophical account of this fact may be, it remains a fact and must, as such, be separated from the other two phenomena I have been distinguishing.

The semantical hierarchy I wish to articulate, then, is this. The entity, *cat,* is the vehicle of the word, 'cat.' But the word, 'cat,' is a vehicle or linguistic embodiment of a meaning expressed in English which is indicated by •cat.• One peculiarity about the device of dot quotes must be noted. Meanings cannot be isolated in their pristine purity by that quotation device. They must be indicated by means of a linguistic (i.e., syntactical) device which also occurs between the dot quotes. Thus •cat• refers to that meaning which is expressed in English by 'cat.' In the context of the dot quotes, however, 'cat' is used and not mentioned. What is mentioned is a meaning, concept, or intension which can be shared by many different entities enclosed by single quotes.

There are two remarks to be made about the distinctions which I have just drawn. First, they are all common-sensical and, as such, they commit me to no philosophical theory. This is why I introduce them by simply pointing them out and do not offer any argument for them. Second, I do not claim that they constitute an exhaustive classification of linguistic entities. The fact is that I do not know how to give such a proof for the classification. But this should not be confused with another, very similar, point from which it is nonetheless different. What I cannot prove is that the classification I have given is the only way of looking at the relation between meaning and language. But it is exhaustive for the problem at hand. What is required is an explanation of how the sentences expressing analyses can contain elements that are the same and elements that differ. That I have given an exhaustive classification for this purpose can be shown as follows. We are not required to give a specific interpretation of the entity which is enclosed by dot quotes. I have called it a meaning or a concept. But these words can be viewed as place markers for any third entity—whatever its description—that is distinguishable from collections of sign designs and words in a natural or artificial language. And if it can be shown that, whatever the description given of the entity which is distinguishable in this way from the other two entities, the paradox is insoluble, the classification I have offered will be exhaustive for the present purpose.

Let us use the classification to clarify the notion of expression which Moore deploys in the requirement he lays down for the solution of the paradox. He says that an analysis must contain different expressions but also a concept which is identical despite the difference of expressions. Consider the three candidates for an expression which I have distinguished.

1) An expression might be regarded as a collection of sign designs. An analysis would, on this account, relate two such collections. And this would make an analysis non-tautologous, for we need not allow two occurrences of the same collection of sign designs to count as an analysis. But this would still be compatible with the identity of the concept or meaning which is expressed by two different collections of sign designs.

However, this will not solve the paradox because the information we get from an analysis thus construed will not be the information we want. All we will be told by an analysis is that two different collections of shapes are vehicles of the same meaning. But what an analysis purports to tell us is the constituents of a concept or meaning, not that a concept or meaning is embodied by certain physical shapes or designs. We can, for example, know that °rational animal° is a vehicle of the same concept as that of which °man° is a vehicle and still not know the analysis of the concept of which these collections are vehicles. The difference of expression which, according to Moore, must hold between expressions in an analysis cannot be explained by saying that the two expressions are collections of different sign designs: The condition formulated by (2″) cannot, on this interpretation, be fulfilled.

2) Let us, then, take an expression to be a word in a natural or artificial language. The difference of expression which should assure informativeness would hold between different words as distinct from collections of sign designs. But this alteration of what is to count as an expression will not rescue the position from the same objections which were already pressed against expressions construed as sign designs. For now we can learn from an analysis only that a concept or meaning is expressed in a certain way in a certain language. To be told that 'rational animal' is the linguistic vehicle of the same concept as that for which 'man' is the linguistic vehicle is not to be told the analysis of the concept of which these words are the linguistic vehicles. And this only reproduces the problem raised with regard to collections of sign designs: The informativeness we are given is irrelevant to the informativeness demanded of an analysis.

3) There are, finally, the entities which I have called concepts or meanings. Can they serve as expressions? That they cannot can be seen at once. Concepts or meanings are entities which are enclosed by dot quotes. And anything thus enclosed contains two elements—a meaning, and a word which is used but not mentioned in order to express the meaning. To offer entities that are dot-quoted as candidates for expressions does no more than propound a dilemma: If the difference of expression in an analysis is attributable to the word which is used but not mentioned in the dot quotes, the same objections will apply that applied to words when they were enclosed by single quotes. And if the difference for which we are looking is attributable to the concepts or meanings which are enclosed by dot quotes, the result will conflict with the requirement that an analysis state an identity of concepts. In either case, concepts cannot serve as expressions. And it should be noted that the same conclusion will hold no matter what theory one has of a concept or meaning. As long as an analysis must express an identity of concepts, then the difference of expression required by this account of an expression cannot be a difference of concepts.

But there is another suggestion which I find in Moore that may help us keep the notion of expression while making it more serviceable for the solution of the paradox. Moore says:

> I think that, in order to explain the fact that, even if "To be a brother is the same thing as to be a male sibling" is true, yet nevertheless this statement is *not* the same as the statement "To be a brother is to be a brother" one *must* suppose that both statements are in *some* sense about the expressions as well as about the concept of being a brother.[6]

This passage suggests a new sense of 'expression.' It approximates the view according to which an expression is a concept in conjunction with a word or words. But it is, nonetheless, significantly different from that view. On the previous view, an expression consisted of a concept together with a word that is used but not mentioned. On the present view, an expression consists of a concept together with a word that is mentioned and a word that is used. Let us call a linguistic device of this latter kind a meta-expression. Each such expression would be distinguished from ordinary expressions in that it would contain a word which is mentioned and not used and which refers to another word.

The notion of a meta-expression will not solve the paradox. The success of any such solution depends upon the power of a meta-expression to explain what we learn when we are told something about the expression to which the meta-expression refers. And the entity about which we are told something in this way must either be a collection of sign designs, a word properly so called, or a concept. And difficulties have been previously raised about all of these entities. So the notion of a meta-expression does not mark any advance over the previous interpretations of an expression.

Moore makes one more suggestion which formulates a condition for the solution of the paradox of analysis. One of the requirements of a correct analysis is that the expressions for the analysans and analysandum must differ "in this way, namely, that the expression used for the *analysans* must *explicitly mention* concepts which are not explicitly mentioned by the expression for the *analysandum*."[7] Consider an instance of explicit mention: The word 'brother' does not mention either the word 'male' or the word 'sibling'; hence 'brother' does not explicitly mention the concepts whose linguistic vehicle it is. The difference between analysandum and analysans is that one implicitly mentions what the other explicitly states. The sentence relating them is thus not tautologous because it lacks the characteristic of a tautology in virtue of which the concept explicitly mentioned by the left-hand side is explicitly mentioned by the right-hand side. And so premise (2) of the original argument is transformed into:

2''') Every analysis is a statement of identity; but no such statement is tautological because the analysandum implicitly mentions what the analysans explicitly mentions.

The difficulty with this suggestion is that there is no reason to say that one side of the analysis does not explicitly mention a concept while the other does. Moore does not give us a criterion for explicit mention. There is, however, a criterion implicated by what Moore says: A concept is explicitly mentioned when a separate linguistic entity is used to mention it. A concept is, accordingly, implicitly mentioned when an expression stands for it but does not single it out by a separate linguistic entity. But this view is easily reducible to the view that the only entities accounting for the difference of each side of an analysis are the linguistic entities I have called words, as distinct from sign designs on the one hand and concepts on the other. Explicit mention can, to be sure, tell us how many concepts are expressed by the analysandum. But this tells us only that the linguistic entities which express the same conceptual complex can themselves be more or less complex. It does not succeed in telling us—and this is what we must be told by an analysis—whether what we grasp when we know an analysis is anything more than the fact that the same conceptual complex can be expressed by linguistic entities of differing complexity. The objection that was previously raised against the notion of an expression construed as a word or words in a language is not removed by saying, as this suggestion of Moore's would have us say, that the linguistic configuration on one side of an analysis is more complex than that on the other side.

This concludes my catalogue of Moore's suggestions. They are so many attempts to account for the sense in which an analysis can express the same thing while yet telling us something new. These suggestions are, indeed, different in that each tries to remove the paradox by making use of a different distinction. But all of them fail. The distinction between two types of knowledge fails because it duplicates the problem. The distinction between expressions fails because it cannot account for how the information we obtain from an analysis is anything more than linguistic and hence irrelevant to the entities under analysis. And, finally, the distinction between explicit and implicit mention of concept fails because it reduces to the distinction, already rejected, between expressions. If we are to accept Moore's suggestions, then, we must be prepared to accept the unacceptable—that no analysis that lays claim to giving us information can give us anything more than linguistic information.

II. The Assumptions Generating the Paradox of Analysis

The conditions which Moore lays down for a solution of the paradox have two things in common. They all assume, first, that only identity statements can express analyses, and, second, that statements of analyses can be assimilated to synonymies. These assumptions are not of equal weight, for only the former generates the paradox. I mention the latter because acceptance of it can mislead one into thinking that only identity statements can express analyses. Once you hold that analyses are expressions of synonymies, then it is an easy, though not a necessary, step to the conclusion that analysis expresses an identity of meaning and hence can be provided only by means of an identity statement. In the present section, then, I want to show that the paradox of analysis does rest on the two assumptions I have mentioned, that it is in principle insoluble on one of those assumptions, and that both the assumptions in question are false.

Consider the assumption, basic to the paradox, that only identity statements can express analyses. That it is basic to the paradox hardly needs arguing. This is the assumption which has to be reconciled with the informativeness of every analysis, and this is what makes the paradox insoluble. As long as you assume that the elements of the statement expressing an analysis must be related by identity, you will be forced to introduce another kind of entity, different from that which you are analyzing, which will account for the informativeness of the statement, for informativeness is accounted for by a difference of entities. And this is what makes the paradox insoluble: The only way of accounting for the informativeness of an analysis is to provide a kind of information that implies a difference between the two entities that are related. And this uncovers the real conflict in the argument generating the paradox. It arises because of the following assumption:

A) The constituents of the statement of the analysis must have the same relation to one another as their referents.

As long as (A) presides over the argument, the paradox can neither be avoided nor solved. This will be the case as long as we are forced to introduce an entity to account for the informativeness of an analysis which is different from the entities being analyzed. If one says that one is analyzing things or objects in the order of nature, one must introduce concepts or meanings to account for the informativeness of the statement expressing such analyses: The concepts are different while the objects which they are about are identical. But then the paradox can be formulated all over again in terms of concepts. And if one says that he is analyzing concepts or meanings as distinct from the things they are about, the informativeness of an analysis can be rescued only by talking about some such thing as an identity of concepts and a difference of verbal expressions—which merely clothes the paradox in new garb. No matter what the garb in which one chooses to dress an analysis, the result will be the same as long as one accepts the assumption in question. This does not, to be sure, prove that the assumption is false. It does prove, however, that the paradox cannot be solved as long as the assumption is accepted.

But is assumption (A) false? I think it is. It implies the proposition that the statement of an analysis must have the same property that it asserts its referent has. And this is false, for if it were true, it would imply the impossibility of synthetic identity statements. Here we can only conjecture why someone should have been misled into accepting such a patently false assumption. I can suggest one explanation that makes the acceptance of a disguised form of assumption (A) plausible. Someone might reason that no analysis could be expressed by a synthetic identity statement because the denial of such statements does not generate a contradiction. But if this is so, then it is logically possible to say that one of the concepts in such a statement is instantiated while the other is not. And if this is possible, it may be argued, no such statement could express an identity. When we analyze something, we want to be able to say—to put it very roughly—that certain kinds of entities are reducible to others. And if it is possible to have instances of one kind of entity without having instances of the other, then it would seem that no analysis has been offered and, further, that we are forced to accept assumption (A) after all.

However, this way of defending the inevitability of assumption (A) rests on a serious confusion. When we say that a synthetic identity statement permits us to have instances of the entity denoted by the expression on one side without having instances denoted by the expression on the other side, all that is being said is that we can *conceive* of one kind of entity without conceiving of the other. This does not prove that the objects referred to by means of these concepts can exist separately. All the defense proves, then, is that one *concept* in a synthetic identity statement can exist without the other. This is very different from saying that the referent of one concept must therefore be able to exist without the referent of the other. Hence the identity of the objects related by a synthetic identity statement is quite compatible with the syntheticity of such statements.

There is another assumption on which the paradox feeds—the assumption (call it assumption [B]), namely, that synonymies can count as analyses. This assumption is presupposed by premise (1) of the argument generating the paradox. That premise requires that the statement of an analysis express an identity of meaning. And since all such expressions are synonymies, it follows that every analysis must be a synonymy. It is, of course, true that all tautological synonymies are excluded from this requirement. But the restriction to non-tautologous synonymies will not affect anything I say here. Assumption (B) is not logically independent of assumption (A). My reason for singling it out for independent consideration is that it can tempt one in its own way to accept assumption (A).

That no synonymy can be an analysis can be shown by considering what a synonymy is. All we are told by a synonymy is that tokens of a certain type are interchangeable *salva veritate* in all extensional contexts. There is no claim here that one of the expressions is the analysis of the other with which it is synonymous, for all we are told when we discover that two expressions are synonyms is that one can be substituted for another in certain contexts. And even if we expect a synonymy to give us an analysis of something, our expectation is bound to fail for another reason. Since synonymous expressions have the same meaning, we cannot learn any more from one expression than we can from the other, and this prevents a synonymy from counting as an analysis.

When I say that no synonymy can be an analysis, I am not claiming that we learn nothing new from synonymies or that dictionary definitions, which are generally thought to formulate synonymies, tell us nothing new. All I am claiming is that what we are told in each case is not an analysis. When we learn that two expressions are synonymous, we discover that one expression is equivalent to another. And this is a case of genuine discovery. But we can discover this without knowing the analysis of either expression. Dictionary definitions also tell us things we do not know about the words we use, but these are reports of synonymies in use. This tells us a fact about equivalence of expressions in a certain language—all of which returns us to the difficulties mentioned earlier which prevent us from counting any synonymy as an analysis.

III. The Solution of the Paradox

I have already indicated what I believe to be the crucial step toward a solution of the paradox: We must deny that an analysis need be an identity statement.[8] But this solution brings a difficulty with it which must be settled before it can count as a plausible solution. Let us consider an example of philosophical analysis taken from ontology. An ontologist begins with a sentence like the following:

A) This is red.

He wants to discover the ontological constituents of (A). One ontological analysis of (A) is:

A') There exist a universal, redness, a bare particular, and a nexus of exemplification.

Some ontologists claim that (A') is the analysis of (A). There is an entity in the inventory of (A') which accounts for each feature of the world described by (A).

I hold that the sense of (A) is different from the sense of (A'). Thus to say that one sentence states the analysis of the other is to say something informative without plunging us into the paradox of analysis. But there is, as I have said, a difficulty standing in the way of this solution. It is this: Someone may argue that, on my account, (A') could never be the analysis of (A) just because one sentence could be true while the other is false. On my account, such a possibility is not self-contradictory. And if it is not self-contradictory to assert (A) and deny (A'), it would seem to follow that the state of affairs described by (A) can exist independently of the state of affairs described by (A'), and from this it follows that the fact stated by (A') cannot be identical with that stated by (A).

This objection is deceptively formidable. It shows that there is a possible world in which I can truly assert the conjunction of (A) and the negation of (A'). But this does not prove that there are two facts—that stated by (A) and that stated by (A')—which must be related to each other and which can exist independently of each other. It proves only that it is logically possible to assert one description of a fact and deny the other description given of that fact. If the two descriptions are truly applied to the fact, then what they describe is the same thing. If they are not truly applied to the same fact, then one must be wrong. All that this shows is that we can be mistaken about the generality of any analysis we give. It does not follow from our fallibility in giving analyses that a correct analytical description fails to refer to something which is identical with the ordinary description we give of it.

The root of the present objection to my solution of the paradox is the assumption that a correct analysis must be true in all possible worlds. Once we admit that a correct analysis need not be true in all possible worlds, an objector may think the conclusion inevitable that such an analysis is true in no possible world. But this would be a mistake. A correct analysis is a description of that in the fact under analysis which accounts for the features it has. But there can be equivalent ontological analyses. I do not say that there can be equivalent ontological analyses of the same world. All I contend is that there can be different ontological analyses of features that several worlds may have in common. Consider the following example. Some philosophers have argued that the particulars of the world are all bare. I do not wish to take any position about that issue here; I wish only to point out the possibility of another world with particulars but in which particulars are analyzed as spatial regions or moments. There are reasons why some ontologists do not accept these latter entities as particulars. But they could account for particulars in one world just as the entities called bare particulars account for this same phenomenon in our world. We can contrast both of these worlds with a world in which there is no space or time. It is logically possible to describe a world which would lack spatial or temporal features while still containing particulars.

The example I have just cited shows that entities called particulars can be common to a number of possible worlds, but the ontological analysis of particularity can differ from world to world. There may be some resistance to this conclusion on the ground that certain entities, like spatial and temporal moments, can be analyzed differently so that they become relations and hence can no longer individuate. This shows, not that spatial and temporal entities fail to individuate, but only that the spatio-temporal features of a world can be analyzed differently from world to world.

The foregoing example can be strengthened. We can conceive of a world in which there are particulars but in which entities totally different from those which philosophers have so far used to account for particulars serve to individuate. Let us call this entity a *phi*. I cannot, of course, describe the properties of *phi*'s save that they serve to individuate in the world under discussion. But unless it can be shown that there cannot be any such entities in any possible world, then it has not been shown that the analysis we give of particularity must be true in all possible worlds. I do not think that any such demonstration can be given, for the description of a world containing particulars that are accounted for by *phi*'s rather than bare particulars is not self-contradictory.

My conclusion is that an analysis does not have to be true in all possible worlds in order to count as an analysis. That an analysis is correct is a factual truth. It is, of course, a factual truth unlike other such truths; but this does not permit the inference that it must therefore be expressed by an analytic identity statement. And that an analysis which holds for this world can be false in another world does not disqualify it as an analysis. All that this shows is that there can be equivalent analyses.

This way of defending synthetic identity statements can be generalized to apply to any domain of entities which may be the subject of philosophical analysis. If we offer analyses, not of things, but of our concepts of those things, those analyses will still be expressed in synthetic identity statements. The concept being analyzed would be described in two ways, and it is possible to know about a concept that one description applies while not knowing that the other applies. But what we learn when we discover this analysis is not something linguistic but rather something about the objects being analyzed. The same point can, of course, be made *mutatis mutandis* for any object one chooses. And for this reason it is possible for every analysis to state an identity between analysandum and analysans without being a tautology. The relation of identity holds between the referents of the expressions comprising the analysis. But from this it does not follow that such a relation holds between the entities constituting the expression of the analysis.

And to say that the expression for the analysans can apply to something while the expression for the analysandum need not is only to say that there are possible worlds sharing features in common with ours which can be accounted for by different ontological entities.

Notes

1. Cf. C. H. Langford, "The Notion of Analysis in Moore's Philosophy," in Paul A. Schilpp (ed.), *The Philosophy of G. E. Moore* (2d ed.; New York: Tudor, 1952), p. 323. This is the formulation that started recent discussion. The origin of the paradox can be traced at least as far back as Hegel's criticism of the law of identity—that it must be the equation of one thing with another and thus violates the condition of a correct identity statement. Cf. Hegel, *Science of Logic*, ed. H. Glockner (Stuttgart: Fr. Frommans Verlag, 1958), I, 516.

2. G. E. Moore, *Some Main Problems of Philosophy* (London: Allen & Unwin, 1953), p. 205.

3. Cf. Feyerabend's article, "Die Analytische Philosophie und das Paradox der Analyse," in *Kant-Studien*, 1957-58, pp. 238-44; also Wilfrid Sellars, "The Paradox of Analysis: A Neo-Fregean Approach," in his *Philosophical Perspectives* (Springfield, Ill.: Charles C. Thomas, 1967), pp. 291-307.

4. G. E. Moore, in Schilpp, *op. cit.*, p. 666.

5. I assume here that what is enclosed by asterisks is a type and not merely a token of sign designs. I need not, for my present purpose, distinguish between token and type with regard to collections of sign designs.

6. Moore, *ibid.*

7. *Ibid.*

8. The position that I am arguing here differs radically from that argued by Wilfrid Sellars, *op. cit.* He rejects an entity theory of concepts and substitutes a view according to which a concept is the linguistic role played by words in a language. Very briefly, his strategy is to show that analyses are not identities but equivalences of linguistic functions; and he holds that the equivalence of linguistic function preserves the informativeness of an analysis. My problem with equivalence is that it is question-begging. To say that the analysandum and analysans have equivalent linguistic functions assumes the notion of sameness. But if that is what we learn in grasping an analysis, then what is on the left-hand side is still the same as that which is on the right-hand side. What has to be explained is what is meant by equivalence of linguistic function. Either there are some differences—in which case the right-hand side will not capture what is on the left-hand side; or there are none—in which case equivalence reduces to out-and-out identity. Sellars' solution does not make clear why linguistic function is not, after all, subject to the same objections as the previous solutions.

Fourteen

G. E. MOORE'S
PROOF OF AN
EXTERNAL WORLD

E. D. Klemke

THERE ARE doubtless many who might wonder why Moore or any other philosopher would want to try to prove the existence of an external world, or the existence of matter. John Wisdom relates that he once said to Moore, "Those philosophers who have said that matter does not exist did not mean to deny that you have two hands or a watch in your pocket." Moore's response was to reach for a copy of McTaggart's *Some Dogmas of Religion* and point to the words: "The result is that matter is in the same position as the Gorgons or the Harpies. Its existence is a bare possibility to which it would be foolish to attach the least importance, since there is nothing to make it at all preferable to any other hypothesis however wild."[1] Moore apparently took McTaggart (and others who said such things) seriously, and he was concerned that we recognize the falsehood of what they said. This, no doubt, is why he thought it important to insist that there really is an external world and to offer a proof of its existence.

Before asking such questions as whether Moore's proof is a good one or in what sense it is a proof, etc., we must state the proof, at least schematically, since there is much confusion in the literature as to just what *is* the proof. (Perhaps even Moore himself was not, at times, clear on this point.) Therefore I shall first outline the various steps of Moore's paper, "Proof of an External World."[2] There is little doubt, I think, that Moore thought that he was giving a genuine proof in this essay, but Professor Alice Ambrose has questioned this and maintained that Moore was actually doing something else. I shall, next, examine her views and raise some objections to them. Finally, I shall turn to the questions mentioned at the beginning of this paragraph. Let us, then, begin with an analysis of Moore's paper.

I

Moore begins with a quotation from Kant:

> It still remains a scandal to philosophy . . . that the existence of things outside of us . . . must be accepted merely on *faith*, and that, if anyone thinks good to doubt their existence, we are unable to counter his doubts by any satisfactory proof.[3]

Moore questions whether Kant's own attempted proof is satisfactory and sets out to give one which is conclusive. But we must first be clear as to what we are trying to prove. What are "things outside of us"? We could, of course, provide various synonymous definitions. We could hold that:

1) things outside of us

is definitionally synonymous with

2) external things

or with

3) things external to our minds.

But these expressions are not clear either. Hence we cannot merely define (1) as either (2) or (3), unless we know what the latter two expressions mean.

Kant himself noted the ambiguity of the expression 'outside of us.' He held that 'things outside of us' could have at least two very different meanings, namely:

4) transcendentally external objects

or

5) empirically external objects.

Following Kant, Moore uses expression (1) as in (5). Kant also refers to such objects as

6) things to be met with in space.

Moore says that (6) designates the sort of things whose existence he hopes to prove: the bodies of men and animals, stones, mountains, etc., that is, the sort of things which philosophers and others call physical objects. But (6) also refers to things which are not material objects, such as shadows.

Now Kant uses another expression as if it were equivalent to (6), namely:

7) things presented in space.

But according to Moore (6) and (7) are not equivalent. For there are some things which are presented in space yet are not to be met with in space, for example, negative after-images. 'To be met with' suggests that anyone could perceive some object under certain conditions, but no one can see my negative after-images. Likewise, there are things which are to be met with in space which are not presented in space, for example, certain trees or stones which no one had ever perceived. Such objects are not at any given time presented in space, yet they are to be met with in space, in that they might be perceived at some time. Thus the statement that an object falls under (6) does *not* entail that it falls under (7), and conversely.

By 'things outside of us' or 'things external to our minds' Moore has in mind the sort of things to which (6) refers. Thus after-images, double images, pains etc., are excluded from falling under (6), but the bodies of men and animals, stones, etc., are included. Moore emphasizes that he is so using (6) that, from the proposition that, say, two dogs exist, it (logically) follows that there are things to be met with in space. Thus from the proposition 'Dogs exist,' no further proof is required that there follows: 'There are things to be met with in space.'

But someone might object: How does all this prove that there are things external to our minds? As we saw earlier, 'things outside of us' may mean 'external things' or 'things external to our minds.' Although 'Two dogs exist' entails 'There are things to be met with in space,' it does not also entail 'There are things external to our minds,' unless we simply stipulate that 'external' is to be used as a synonym for 'to be met with in space.' But perhaps neither Kant nor anyone else held the former to be a mere synonym for the latter, or vice versa. Hence in order to give a proof of the existence of things outside of us or of an external world, we must get at the meaning of 'things external to our minds.' We may do so by contrasting 'external to our minds' with 'in our minds.' We generally refer to such things as a pain that I feel or an after-image which I see as being in my mind, and such things as my body or a star as being external to my mind. But how can we *account for* this difference of usage?

Consider the following classes of statements:

A) I heard a clap of thunder.
   I was thinking out a plan of action.
   Etc.
B) I was lying on my back.
   I was less than four feet high.
   Etc.

If we add a time to A-statements, the result is a proposition such that, if it is true, there logically follows a proposition that I was having an experience at the time in question. But if we add a time to B-statements, there does not follow a proposition that I was having an experience at the time. This provides us with a criterion for distinguishing those things which are in my mind from those which are external to my mind. For any object, X:

a) X is in my mind, if from a proposition that X exists at time t1, there logically follows a proposition that I was having an experience at t1.
b) X is external to my mind, if from a proposition that X exists at t1, there does not logically follow a proposition that I was having an experience at t1.

Furthermore, we may say that I was having an experience at a given time "if and only if either (1) I was conscious at the time or (2) I was dreaming at the time or (3) something else was true of me which resembled what is true of me when I am conscious and when I am dreaming, in a certain obvious respect in which what is true of me when I am dreaming resembles what is true of me when I am conscious, and in which what would be true of me, if at any time, for instance,

I had a vision, would resemble both."[4] From this it would follow that an after-image which I see is in my mind, whereas my body or a star is external to my mind. For not only does 'A star exists' entail 'There is a thing to be met with in space'; it also entails 'There is a thing external to our minds,' for the proposition 'A star exists at t1' does not logically imply that anyone was having an experience at t1.

Moore goes on to say that there are *many* things similar to stars, bodies, etc., such that if one can prove the existence of at least two of them, it will logically follow both that there are things (plural) to be met with in space and also things outside of us or external to our minds. Hence if by 'external world' we rightly mean 'things external to our minds,' then to prove the existence of any two of them is *ipso facto* to prove the existence of an external world. As is well known, Moore at this point says he can give a large number of such proofs. For example, "I can prove now that . . . two human hands exist. How? By holding up my two hands, and saying, as I make a gesture with the right hand, 'Here is one hand,' and adding, as I make a gesture with the left, 'and here is another.' "[5] By the premise 'Here is one hand, and here is another,' I have proved that two hands exist now. And by doing this I have *ipso facto* proved the existence of external things, or things external to our minds, or things outside of us.

Moore holds that the proof that 'Two human hands exist now' is a rigorous one and meets all the conditions for a good proof. (1) The premise differs from the conclusion. (2) He knew the premise to be true. And (3) the conclusion logically follows from the premise. Moore goes on to say that he could give a similar proof that external objects existed in the past. Here it is: "I held up two hands . . . not very long ago; therefore at least two external objects have existed at some time in the past. Q. E. D."[6]

Moore says he is aware that many philosophers will not be satisfied with either proof, because they want a proof of the premises used in the proofs or, rather, a general statement as to how any propositions of the sort which were used as premises can be proved. This, he says, he did not give, and he believes that it cannot be given. If *this* is what is meant by a proof of the existence of external things, then no proof can be given. Some will say: But if you cannot prove your premise then you cannot know it. Moore disagrees. He says: "I can know things which I cannot prove; and among things which I certainly did know, even if (as I think) I could not prove them, were the premises of my two proofs. I should say, therefore, that those, if any, who are dissatisfied with these proofs merely on the ground that I did not know their premises, have no good reason for their dissatisfaction."[7]

II

Before going any further, we must at this point ask just what constitutes the proof of an external world in Moore's paper? There is a great deal of confusion on this matter, both on the part of Moore himself and on the part of commentators on Moore's essay. One might say that the answer to this is easy: That Moore's first proof (that two hands exist now) is a proof of an external world, and so is the second (that two hands existed in the past). But this cannot be. Moore's first "proof" is ('P' designates premise and 'C' conclusion):

(I)   (P) Here is one hand and here is another.
       (C) ∴ Two hands exist now.

(I) cannot be the proof of an external world *as it stands,* for the conclusion is 'Two hands exist now' and *not* 'There exists an external world.' Moore's second proof comes closer to being a proof of an external world.

(II)   (P) I held up two hands not very long ago.
       (C1) ∴ two hands existed not very long ago.
       (C2) ∴ at least two external objects existed in the past.

But even (C2) is not the statement 'There exists an external world.'

Some may think this is mere quibbling, but I do not think so. It seems to me that much of the criticism of Moore's proof has been misdirected because of a failure to see just in what Moore's proof of an external world consists. It does not consist in either or both of what have been referred to as Moore's proofs, both by Moore and his commentators, namely, (I) and (II). I shall refer to (I) and (II) as Moore's *shorter* proofs. Ignoring (II), Moore's *proof* of an external world is a proof which runs throughout Moore's entire essay, and which includes the shorter proof (I) as a part of that larger proof. We must be clear about this. (I) by itself cannot possibly be a proof of an external world, for its conclusion is merely 'Two hands exist now' and not 'An external world exists.' The proof of the latter requires much more than the premise of (I). Let us adopt the following as abbreviations to be used in the full proof:

EW:	external world
OU:	outside of us
E:	external
EM:	external to our minds
EE:	empirically external
MS:	to be met with in space
H:	hand
HE,t:	has an experience, at time t

Then Moore's *proof of an external world* is:

1) $OUx \equiv Ex \equiv EEx \equiv MSx \equiv EMx$
2) $[(\exists x) \ (x = x, t1) \nrightarrow (\exists y) \ (HEy, t1)] \rightarrow EMx$
3) $(\exists x) \ (Hx, t1) \nrightarrow (\exists y) \ (HE, t1)$
4) $(\exists x) \ (Hx, t1) \rightarrow (\exists x) \ EMx$
5) $EWz \equiv (\exists x) \ (\exists y) \ [(EMx \cdot EMy) \cdot (y \neq x)]$
6) $(Ha \cdot Hb) \cdot (a \neq b)$
7) $\therefore \ (\exists x) \ (\exists y) \ [(Hx \cdot Hy) \cdot (y \neq x)]$
8) $\therefore \ (\exists x) \ (\exists y) \ [(EMx \cdot EMy) \cdot (y \neq x)]$
9) $(\exists z) \ EWz$

III

In "Moore's 'Proof of an External World,'" Alice Ambrose makes the common mistake of referring to one of the shorter proofs within the proof as Moore's proof of an external world. She writes: "The proof consists in proceeding from the assertedly known premise 'Here is a hand,' to the conclusion which logically follows from it, 'there exists a thing external to us.' "[8] She goes on to say that "It is clear that Prof. Moore considers the proposition, 'There are external objects,' to be an empirical one." Why? "Because it follows from a proposition which is established by empirical evidence, viz., the evidence of the senses. One has merely to show two hands and one has established that there are external objects."[9] Furthermore, she states that the skeptic would not be satisfied with Moore's proof because he "requires a proof of what

Moore has not tried to prove, namely, the *premise,* 'Here is a hand,' "
which (he holds) cannot be known.[10] Hence Moore's proof will not
refute the skeptic. Professor Ambrose goes on to say that it is her purpose "to investigate why neither Moore's 'refutation' nor any 'refutation'
will serve to convince the sceptic, and why no argument the sceptic
produces will seem conclusive to Moore."[11]

As she sees the matter, this is not a case of Moore's proof's failing
whereas some other proof might succeed, for no amount of further
evidence would change the skeptic's mind that no one can *know* that
external objects exist. In the case of a statement like 'No evidence is
sufficient for establishing the identity of the criminal,' we know what
it would be like for the statement to be false, and we could describe
what sort of additional evidence would be adequate for establishing the
guilt of a certain suspect. But when the skeptic says 'No one can know
that external objects exist,' he cannot describe what sort of evidence
would be needed in order to attain knowledge of the existence of
external objects. Therefore his statement, being unfalsifiable, is not an
empirical assertion. What the skeptic may seem to be arguing for is
"the *logical impossibility* of knowledge and not for any empirical fact."[12]
Yet this does not seem reasonable, for that would mean that any statement such as 'I do not know that hands exist' is necessarily true. But
"our present language is such that it is not necessary."[13] Thus what the
skeptic really is holding (says Professor Ambrose) is that the statement
'No one knows that hands exist' *should* be necessary. But then what
he is actually doing is "making a disguised proposal that it be accepted
as a necessary truth . . . he is proposing or recommending that certain
expressions in our language be deprived of their use."[14] However, according to Professor Ambrose, no argument that Moore can bring will
answer the skeptic. Since the latter is proposing a revision of language,
no facts about anything will lead him to change his conviction.

According to Professor Ambrose, in his proof Moore seems to be trying to establish the truth of the empirical proposition, 'There are external objects.' His argument is of the type one might use to convince an
ordinary man of the existence of something in question, for example,
the existence of a dime in a box. But by pointing out the dime we could
settle the argument about the existence of the coin. However, asks
Professor Ambrose, "can one 'point out an external object' and thereby
settle any questions about whether there is a thing of that kind?"[15] And
her answer is No, for one cannot point out to anyone anything which

is not an external object. 'External object' is not a name for a kind of thing. According to Professor Ambrose, this shows that Moore's proof is not at all like an ordinary empirical argument to establish the existence of something. What Moore is doing in asserting that 'There is a hand' entails 'There is an external object' is: calling attention to criteria for applying "external object words," words such as 'hand,' 'dime,' and showing that it makes sense to say, e.g., 'I know there is a dime in the box.' And hence Moore's argument does not establish the truth of any empirical proposition about the existence of some kind of thing, external objects. But it does have as a consequence that it is logically possible to know there are coins in a box, etc.

To sum up: The skeptic has recommended that it be incorrect to say that one knows that hands exist, etc. And what, then, has Moore done? "Moore's argument constitutes an insistence on retaining present usage—on retaining 'know' as well as 'believe' to preface statements about physical objects. . . . It is the great merit of Moore's position that it makes one see, by calling attention to ordinary usage, that the sceptic's linguistic recommendation is objectionable."[16] Professor Ambrose concludes:

> Moore *in doing philosophy* constantly holds ordinary language before one, so that one is made to feel, not only upon returning to one's views but while philosophizing, that they are 'strain'd and ridiculous.' Once one feels this one has taken the first step toward seeing why—toward seeing that a 'rectified' language only says in another way what ordinary language does. Our language is such that when we philosophize, certain considerations constantly tempt us to revision, while considerations which would make us see our language needs no revision and is adequate to express all we want to say, are discounted and forgotten. We are tempted to think that the sceptic weaves a verbal material which is much finer than the coarse fabric of ordinary discourse. But in forcefully reminding us of current usage, Moore sets us on our way to seeing that like the imposters of the tale of The Emperor's New Clothes, the sceptic is wearing nothing at all, and that in fact the Emperor is naked.[17]

IV

In his "A Reply to My Critics,"[18] Moore denies almost every one of Professor Ambrose's main assertions. He denies: (1) that there is such a great difference between 'external object' and 'coin' that the proof that a dime exists proves that at least one coin exists, whereas it cannot prove that at least one external object exists; (2) that his statement 'There are external objects' is nonempirical; (3) that in his "Proof" he was merely making a recommendation as to how words ought to be used or ought not to be used. And he maintains (4) that he cannot see that Professor Ambrose has given any good reason for saying that he was *mistaken* in thinking that what he gave as a proof that there are external objects really was a proof of the existence of such objects.

I think that Moore was wrong in claiming that the statement 'There are external objects' is empirical. But with regard to the other three points, Moore was surely right.

Professor Ambrose holds that, although one can prove that a coin exists by producing a dime, one cannot prove that an external object exists. Why not? Because of the vast difference between these terms. For example, one can teach someone by an experiential method what 'dime' means, but one cannot teach him what 'external object' means, because one cannot point out anything that is *not* an external object. As Moore said, if pointing does not mean literally pointing a finger, then this is false. And I think that Moore is clearly right in maintaining (*a*) that even if there are differences between terms such as 'coin' and 'external object,' this in no way provides an argument against proving the existence of external objects; and (*b*) that Professor Ambrose has given no good argument against such a proof.

I also believe that Moore is correct in maintaining that the skeptic who says 'There are no external objects' or 'No one knows that there are any' is not making a linguistic proposal as to how words ought to be used and that, therefore, Moore, in holding, 'There are external objects,' was *not* merely making a countering linguistic proposal. I fail to see how anyone who reads Moore's "Proof" could interpret his essay in this manner, unless he comes to it with some preconceived dogma and then reads it into Moore's paper, thereby grossly distorting Moore's aims and achievements.

On these grounds, I think Moore was correct in insisting that Professor Ambrose has given no good reason for saying that Moore was mistaken in thinking that what he put forth as a proof of external objects really was a proof of the existence of such objects. (I am not saying that no such reason can be given. I am only saying that I agree that Professor Ambrose has not given any.)

This leaves us with the last of the above assertions (the one numbered [2], above), Moore's denial that 'There are external objects' is nonempirical; i.e., his claim that it is an empirical statement. This seems to me to be clearly wrong. Surely the statement is a philosophical proposition. And that is why it cannot be proved in two or three sentences in one of the shorter proofs, and why the proof of it requires Moore's entire essay. Since it is a philosophical proposition it must be analyzed. In one sense we all understand the statement and, apart from skeptics, etc., as understood in this sense, we common-sensically know it to be true. What Moore's proof consists in is an analysis of 'There is an external world,' an analysis which shows us precisely *what* we know to be true when we common-sensically claim to know this statement to be true.

To be sure, both the premise and conclusion of (I) are empirical statements, as are the premise and first conclusion of (II). But the proposition 'There exists an external world' is not the conclusion of either (I) or (II), and furthermore it does not follow from the premise of either (I) or (II); and finally it does not follow from the conclusion of either (I) or (II), unless other premises are added. In effect, it was Moore's task in the major part of the paper (up to the point at which [I] was stated) to provide such premises. But not all of these premises are empirical propositions—a number of them are statements of philosophical explication. They explicate or analyze what it means to assert the existence of an external world. Now the analysis itself involves and is based on the existence of such things as hands, tables, stars, etc. And thus one may argue that Moore's shorter proofs are, in a way, irrelevant. For, since the philosophical statement 'There is an external world' is explicated via ordinary true statements about the existence of hands, tables, dogs, etc., then *its* truth is already guaranteed—otherwise the explication would not have been the proper one. Hence it would seem that the shorter proofs (I) and (II) are superfluous. They would be essential if, throughout the lengthy analysis, Moore had held the existence of dogs, stars, etc., to be hypothetical. Then (I) could serve to move from the hypothetical level to that of the actual: 'Now here, *in fact*, is one existent hand, and here, in fact is another.' But it is clear that, throughout the analysis, Moore did not hold the existence of dogs and stars and soap bubbles to be hypothetical. His whole analysis of such expressions as 'outside of my mind' vs. 'in my mind,' etc. is based on the assertion of the existence of members of both classes. Hence (I) and (II) are not, strictly, Moore's proofs, nor are they the most important components of Moore's proof.

All of this does not mean that Moore's proof is in no way a proof but merely a linguistic proposal, etc. Of course, it is not a proof in the sense of a mathematical demonstration. Nor is it a proof in the sense in which one might be said to prove experimentally, say, the laws of falling bodies or the laws of gases. It is a form of philosophical proof in which a philosophical thesis is analyzed and justified, partly in terms of ordinary concepts and statements of fact about ordinary objects. No one—apart from Ambrosian skeptics—doubts the existence of such objects in *some* sense. Part of the task of the analysis is to show *what* sense this is and then to show that all this provides a *correct analysis* and therefore a *justification* of the philosophical thesis. In *this* sense of 'proof,' I think that we must recognize that Moore *did* provide a proof of the external world and one which is worthy of our consideration.

Notes

1. John Wisdom, *Paradox and Discovery* (Oxford: Basil Blackwell, 1965), p. 83.
2. In *Philosophical Papers* (London: Allen & Unwin, 1959), pp. 127-50 (Paperback ed. [New York: Collier Books, 1962], pp. 126-48).
3. *Critique of Pure Reason,* B xxxix.
4. Moore, *op. cit.*, p. 141.
5. *Ibid.*, p. 144.
6. *Ibid.*, p. 146.
7. *Ibid.*, p. 148.
8. In Paul A. Schilpp (ed.), *The Philosophy of G. E. Moore* (2d ed.; New York: Tudor, 1952), p. 397. I ignore the fact that this statement inaccurately characterizes the shorter proof.
9. *Ibid.*, p. 398.
10. *Ibid.*
11. *Ibid.* p. 399.
12. *Ibid.*, p. 402.
13. *Ibid.*
14. *Ibid.*, p. 404.
15. *Ibid.*, p. 406.
16. *Ibid.*, p. 411.
17. *Ibid.*, pp. 416-17.
18. In Schilpp, *op. cit.*, pp. 670-74.

CONCLUSION

Fifteen
MEMORIES OF
G. E. MOORE
Morton White

G. E. MOORE was at once the most distinguished and the most admirable philosopher I have ever known personally, and I am sure that my feelings are shared by many philosophers all over the world. I also feel sure that he would have wished me to confine myself to analyzing or criticizing his philosophical views on this occasion, but I am moved to talk also— even primarily—about Moore as a teacher, about Moore as a guide and inspiration to young philosophers, and about Moore as a man. I should like, in some of my remarks, to make those of you who knew him feel his presence once again and to give others some impression of his character and of his impact on several generations of philosophers in England and America. And I hope I can do this without indulging in the kind of sentimentality which he avoided so successfully all of his life

A slightly revised version of a talk delivered at Columbia University on January 15, 1959, at a meeting in memory of G. E. Moore. The same talk, in abbreviated form, was delivered on the Third Programme of the British Broadcasting Corporation and printed in *The Listener* for April 30, 1959.

Reprinted by permission of the author and the editor from *The Journal of Philosophy*, LVII (1960), 805-10.

even though he was a man of deep and delicate feeling, as any one could tell by listening to him sing Brahms and Schubert *lieder.*

While he was lecturing at Columbia in the early forties he and Mrs. Moore lived in a tiny flat off Amsterdam Avenue, and some of you will remember how, at a certain point in the evening if you coaxed him just a little bit, he would go into his bedroom, where the piano was because the living room was so small, and accompany himself while you listened in the living room. And in 1945, when he was seventy-two, he wrote me from Cambridge: "Now that our youngest son is living with us, I have the pleasure of constantly playing duets with him. I think you get to know music better if you play it yourself, however inadequately, than if you merely hear it."

Moore would have said the same thing about philosophy, I am sure. You get to know *it* better if you play it yourself, than if you spend your life merely listening to others, recording them, and playing them back to yourself and your students. It was this passion for doing philosophy independently that made Moore such an exciting and encouraging teacher.

Young philosophers at Columbia were not altogether unprepared for Moore when he came here in 1942. Some of our teachers had made us aware of the value of clarity in philosophy, but the accepted view was that philosophy required great learning in the sciences and history, or technical expertise in logic, or a professional fondness for wisdom. And Moore was deficient in all of these respects. We had been taught that the theory of perception was a waste of time, that anti-naturalism in ethics was a dreadful heresy, and that Cartesian dualism was even worse. But Moore believed in them all. We had also been assured by political experts in the thirties that the situation in philosophy had become even more poverty-stricken than it was when Marx had described it so scathingly—that bourgeois philosophers were now not only not changing the world, they were not even interpreting it; instead they confined themselves to interpreting *words,* under the counterrevolutionary influence of Moore and his allies.

You can imagine, therefore, how militant young New York philosophers, raised on the teachings of Morris Cohen, Carnap, Dewey, or Marx, might have been struck by a fresh dose of Moore. He deviated from almost every New York doctrine—pragmatic, positivistic, or naturalistic. He spent one term trying to analyze the concept of *seeing* and introduced us to the despised sense-datum. He spent another worrying about the *ordinary* use of the words "if-then," after the logicians had assured us that nothing but the "horse-shoe" was worth talking about. He repeated (though with diminished confidence) his published statement that goodness was a non-natural quality. He insisted that he was quite distinct from his body, and one day said that his hand was closer to him than his foot was. He showed no inclination whatever toward encyclopedism. He announced to scandalized empiricists that he believed in the synthetic *a priori*. He seemed utterly unconcerned with changing the ways in which we speak about the world, to say nothing of the world itself.

In short, Moore challenged most of our philosophical beliefs, attitudes, and prejudices. And yet knowing him and talking with him when he was about seventy and when I had just received my Ph.D. provided one of the most refreshing episodes in my philosophical education. Why? He did not persuade me, I am bound to say, of the validity of a single one of his main philosophical doctrines. But he was living proof of the importance of honesty, clarity, integrity, and careful thinking in philosophy. Moore never asserted anything that he did not believe was true; he never said that a statement followed from another unless he was absolutely convinced that it did; he never said that he understood when he didn't. And how many philosophers are there of whom one can say this? These qualities of Moore meant more to me when I began to stand on my own philosophical legs than all of the machinery of *Principia Mathematica,* than all of the learning of the learned, than all of the wisdom of the ancients. When later I read John Maynard Keynes' reminiscences of Moore as he was at the turn of the century, I could see how deeply ingrained Moore's qualities were. I could also see why they had been so affecting in Cambridge, England, for I felt the same excitement and intellectual pleasure in Moore's presence when he was seventy as Keynes and his friends had felt when he was thirty. The same purity, the same incredible simplicity, the same lack of bluff—they were all still there at the end of his life as they had been at the beginning.

"Do your philosophy for yourself," I have suggested, was one of Moore's great messages to the young. And he helped you do it yourself. He gave you the feeling that there was something like a method in philosophy. And this made you feel the comparative unimportance of arriving at the same doctrines as he did. I believe that Moore, more than any of his distinguished contemporaries, communicated to his students the feeling that they could share his method even when they did not accept his philosophical beliefs. Characteristically, however, Moore shied away from talking of his method, as the following excerpt from a letter shows. It was written by William Frankena after a conversation with Moore in 1949: "One bit of conversation was about Keynes' *Two Memoirs.* I asked Moore if he knew at the time that he was having such an influence on Keynes, etc. He said, approximately, 'No, I didn't. I used to hear them speak of "The Method" sometimes, and understood that it was regarded as mine, but I never did know what it was.' "

Moore may never have known what the method of his philosophy was, but Moore was unusually agnostic on such matters. It fitted in with his dislike of philosophical pomposity. A student of his, however, could not fail to observe a few characteristic moves and a few characteristic gestures and grimaces. You watched him begin by disentangling the different senses of the expression in which he was interested, and then, after he specified the sense with which he was concerned, he would consider the various proposals for analyzing it. Almost all of them, it seems in retrospect, he found defective. "*Surely,* the word so-and-so doesn't *ordinarily* mean such-and-such," he said, as he wrinkled his nose. Or then there was that characteristic conversation-stopper as he wagged his head violently: "I shouldn't have thought anyone could possibly say that *that's* what we ordinarily mean by that expression!" Because he was so cautious about saying that one expression meant the same as another, Moore seemed to be left with a set of *un*analyzable concepts in one hand, and in the other a set of concepts about whose analysis he was never certain. The result was that one of the greatest philosophical analysts of our age found it hard to point, in all honesty, to a single successful analysis of an important philosophical idea.

Part of the reason for Moore's failure as a constructive analyst, is to be located in the difficulty surrounding the notions of *meaning, synonymy,* and *analytic* which are so central to Moore's conception of analysis. He may have been shy about characterizing his method, but in *The Philosophy of G. E. Moore* he was prompted to say something revealing about the nature of analysis as he conceived it—among other things, that you must be sure, before you can say that you have given an analysis of a concept, that the expression which expresses the *analysandum* must be *synonymous* with any expression which expresses the *analysans.* Moreover, Moore says in the same place that a fuller discussion of the topic of analysis would require a discussion of the distinction between an analytic necessary connection and a synthetic necessary connection, because, he says, the necessary connection between the *analysandum* "x is a brother" and the *analysans* "x is a male sibling" is analytic, while other necessary connections are synthetic. At this point he says: "It seems to me . . . that the line between 'analytic' and 'synthetic' might be drawn in many different ways. *As it is, I do not think that the two terms have any clear meaning.*"[1] I venture to call this support from Sir Hubert to those who have been campaigning against complacency about the idea of analyticity. But one is tempted to add that if the word 'analytic' doesn't have any clear meaning, then Moore's phrase 'giving an analysis' doesn't either. And this is one reason why Moore had justifiable doubts about so many of the "analyses" he considered.

Now I wish to insist that in spite of such fundamental difficulties in Moore's method Moore was a pedagogical genius, because he allowed you to see that even if his own conception of analysis was too stringent or too obscure for effective use, something like analysis was of fundamental importance in philosophy. For then you might weaken the requirements for a successful analysis, as Russell and his followers do when they ask for no more than extensional identity between *analysandum* and *analysans*. Or you might say with Wittgenstein that the meaning of the term under consideration is its use; or that philosophers should look for its use rather than its meaning. But in either case you would be building on Moore's conviction that clarification is a central task of philosophy.

So pertinacious and candid was Moore in his search for clarity that he had to admit, as we have seen, that the notion of analysis which was so central in his thinking was itself unclear. It was this same candor and this same pertinacity which made him so admirable. A few typical stories may show why. In telling them I feel fortified by Moore's own statement that "stories, whether purporting to be true or avowedly mere fiction, [had] a tremendous fascination for [him]." The stories that follow purport to be true and *are* true, approximately.

At Columbia in the early forties Moore held an informal seminar to which students and members of the faculty came. One day, after Moore had made a particularly slashing attack on some doctrine in epistemology, a graduate student asked: "But Professor Moore, why do you spend so much time refuting *that* doctrine; *surely* [this emphatic use of "surely" he had learned from Moore] no one holds it." To which Moore replied, in a rising crescendo of rhetorical questions: "*No* one holds it? *No one* holds it? *No one holds it*? But Montague holds it—don't you Montague?" Professor Montague rolled his eyes and shook his head affirmatively.

There was never a consideration, you see, which was to get in the way of *finding* the truth, never any sense that a distinguished colleague's pain should get in the way of *saying* what was true. And this was of immense educational value. For Moore was not nasty in these belligerent moods. He was not sarcastic. He was a simple, direct Englishman who did not speak or write with his eye on the gallery. He made the young feel that by using their wits they might say things of value in philosophy.

One day a Columbia colleague of Moore's was looking for a book by Whewell—the famous Dr. Whewell who played such a great part in the history of Moore's own college, Trinity. He met Moore as he was looking for the book in the offices of the *Journal of Philosophy*. As his colleague took the book down from the shelves he showed it to Moore, thinking that Moore would certainly know it, and asked him what he thought of Whewell. To which Moore replied without the slightest sign of embarrassment and even with a sly twinkle: "You know, I've *never* read Whewell. Should I?" I don't remember what the colleague said in reply.

Just two more typical stories. When I was staying with the Moores in the Spring of 1951, Mrs. Moore came into the room after dinner to announce that Bertrand Russell was about to speak on the B.B.C. Long silence. "Moore," she asked (she called him "Moore" when she didn't call him "Bill"), "Moore, don't you think we ought to listen to Russell? I feel an obligation to listen to him. Don't you?" And then there was another awfully long pause as Moore puffed on his pipe. One felt that Moore was tuning in on him*self,* to see whether *he* felt that obligation. After the pause he reported with utter seriousness: "Dear, *I* don't feel any obligation to listen to Russell tonight."

Lest this give a misleading impression of Moore's attitude toward Russell—as expressed in my presence, at any rate—I should supplement it with a story which reverses the picture somewhat. One night in New York Mrs. Moore was commenting on Russell's law suit against Albert Barnes to recover his salary after their dramatic falling out in the forties at the Barnes Institute. Mrs. Moore said that while Russell was probably right, he shouldn't have stooped to the point of suing Barnes. "Moore wouldn't have done that. Would you have, Bill?" Once again there was the long puff on the pipe, but this time Moore said, "Oh yes I should have, dear."

You will now see why I say that I have never known a philosopher with more integrity. Some in this audience may not agree with my high estimate of Moore as a philosopher. But I hope that no one—either in this room or out of it—will deny that he possessed in the highest degree those moral and intellectual qualities that every great philosopher should have. Once I heard a man say after a sharp exchange with Moore: "I hate Moore's mind." I can only say that I had many a tough bout with Moore that I lost, but I never came out of one with any doubts about how I felt about Moore *or* his mind. I loved them both.

Notes

1. Paul A. Schilpp, (ed.), *The Philosophy of G. E. Moore* (Evanston: Northwestern University Press, 1942), p. 667. Italics added.

BIBLIOGRAPHY

*Compiled with the
assistance of G. Moor*

ABBREVIATIONS:

PS: *Philosophical Studies*
PP: *Philosophical Papers*
SMPP: *Some Main Problems of Philosophy*
PAS: *Proceedings of the Aristotelian Society*
PASS: *Proceedings of the Aristotelian Society, Supplement*
PGEM: *The Philosophy of G. E. Moore*

I. WORKS BY G. E. MOORE

"In What Sense, If Any, Do Past and Future Time Exist?" *Mind*, VI (1897), 235-40.
"Freedom," *Mind*, VII (1898), 179-204.
"The Nature of Judgment," *Mind*, VIII (1899), 176-93.
"Necessity," *Mind*, IX (1900), 289-304.
"Identity," *PAS*, VI (1900-01), 103-27.
"The Value of Religion," *International Journal of Ethics*, XII (1901), 81-98.
"Mr. McTaggart's 'Studies in Hegelian Cosmology,'" *PAS*, II (1901-02), 177-214.
Articles in Baldwin's *Dictionary of Philosophy* (1902).
   Vol. I: "Cause and Effect," "Change"; Vol. II: "Nativism," "Quality," "Real," "Reason," "Relation," "Relativity of Knowledge," "Substance," "Spirit," "Teleology," "Truth."

"Experience and Empiricism," *PAS*, III (1902-03), 80-95.

Principia Ethica. Cambridge: Cambridge University Press, 1903.

"Mr. McTaggart's Ethics," *International Journal of Ethics*, XIII (1903), 341-70.

"The Refutation of Idealism," *Mind*, XII (1903), 433-53. (Reprinted in *PS*.)

"Kant's Idealism," *PAS*, IV (1903-04), 127-40.

"Jahresbericht über 'Philosophy in the United Kingdom for 1902,'" *Archiv für Systematische Philosophie*, X (1904), 242-64.

"The Nature and Reality of Objects of Perception," *PAS*, VI (1905-06), 68-127. (Reprinted in *PS*.)

"Mr. Joachim's 'The Nature of Truth,'" *Mind*, XVI (1907), 229-35.

"Professor James' 'Pragmatism,'" *PAS*, VIII (1907-08), 33-77. (Reprinted in *PS*.)

"Hume's Philosophy," *The New Quarterly*, November, 1909. (Reprinted in *PS*.)

"The Subject Matter of Psychology," *PAS*, X (1909-10), 36-62.

Ethics. London: Williams & Norgate, 1912. (Reset edition, London: Oxford, 1947.)

"The Status of Sense-Data," *PAS*, XIV (1913-14), 355-80. (Reprinted in *PS*.)

"The Implications of Recognition," *PAS*, XVI (1915-16), 201-23.

"Are the Materials of Sense Affections of the Mind?" *PAS*, XVII (1916-17), 418-29.

"The Conception of Reality," *PAS*, XVIII (1917-18), 101-20. (Reprinted in *PS*.)

"Some Judgments of Perception," *PAS*, XIX (1918-19), 1-29. (Reprinted in *PS*.)

"Is There Knowledge by Acquaintance?" *PASS*, II (1919), 179-93.

"External and Internal Relations," *PAS*, XX (1919-20), 40-62. (Reprinted in *PS*.)

"Is the 'Concrete Universal' the True Type of Universality?" *PAS*, XX (1919-20), 132-40.

"The Character of Cognitive Acts," *PAS*, XXI (1920-21), 132-40.

Philosophical Studies. London: K. Paul, Trench, Trubner & Co., and New York: Harcourt Brace & Co., 1922. Includes two unpublished papers: "The Conception of Intrinsic Value" and "The Nature of Moral Philosophy."

"Are the Characteristics of Particular Things Universal or Particular?" *PASS*, III (1923), 95-113. (Reprinted in *PP*.)

"A Defence of Common Sense," *Contemporary British Philosophy: Second Series*, ed. J. H. Muirhead (New York: Macmillan, 1925), pp. 193-223. (Reprinted in *PP*.)

"The Nature of Sensible Appearances," *PASS*, VI (1926), 179-89.

"Facts and Propositions," *PASS*, VII (1927), 171-206. (Reprinted in *PP*.)

"Indirect Knowledge," *PASS*, IX (1929), 19-50.

"Is Goodness a Quality?" *PASS*, XI (1932), 116-31. (Reprinted in *PP*.)

"Imaginary Objects," *PASS*, XII (1933), 55-70. (Reprinted in *PP*.)

"The Justification of Analysis," *Analysis*, I (1933-34), 28-30. (Lecture notes trans. M. McDonald)

"Is Existence a Predicate?" *PASS*, XV (1936), 175-88. (Reprinted in *PP*.)

"Proof of an External World," *Proceedings of the British Academy*, XXV (1939), 273-300. (Reprinted in *PP*.)

"An Autobiography," *PGEM*, pp. 3-39.

"A Reply to My Critics," *PGEM*, pp. 535-677.

"Russell's 'Theory of Descriptions,'" *The Philosophy of Bertrand Russell*, ed. P. A. Schilpp (Evanston and Chicago: Northwestern University Press, 1944), pp. 175-225. (Reprinted in *PP*.)

"Addendum to My 'Reply,' " *PGEM*, 1952 ed., 677-687.
Some Main Problems of Philosophy. London: George Allen & Unwin, 1953. (Lectures given in 1910-11).
"Wittgenstein's Lectures in 1930-3," *Mind*, LXIII and LXIV (1954-55), LXIII, 1-15, 289-316; LXIV, 1-27. (Reprinted in *PP*.)
"Visual Sense-Data," *British Philosophy in the Mid-Century*, ed. C. A. Mace. (Cambridge: Cambridge University Press, 1957), pp. 205-11.
Philosophical Papers. London: George Allen & Unwin, 1959. Includes two unpublished papers: "Four Forms of Scepticism" and "Certainty."
Commonplace Book, 1919-1935 (ed. C. Lewy). London: George Allen & Unwin, 1963.
Lectures on Philosophy (ed. C. Lewy). London: George Allen & Unwin, 1967.

II. WORKS ON G. E. MOORE

Ambrose, A. "Moore's 'Proof of an External World,' " *PGEM*, pp. 397-417. Reprinted in *Essays in Analysis* (London: George Allen & Unwin, 1966), pp. 214-32.
―――. "Three Aspects of Moore's Philosophy," *The Journal of Philosophy*, LVII (1960), 816-24. Reprinted in *Essays in Analysis* (London: George Allen & Unwin, 1966), pp. 205-13.
Ayer, A. J. "The Terminology of Sense-Data," *Mind*, LIV (1945), 289-312. Reprinted in *Philosophical Essays* (New York: St. Martin's Press, 1964).
Bar-Hillel, Y. "Analysis of Correct Language," *Mind*, LV (1946), 328-40.
Barnes, W. H. F. *The Philosophical Predicament* (London: A. C. Black, 1950), Chapters 2-5.
Bentley, A. F. "Logicians' Underlying Postulations," *Philosophy of Science*, XIII (1946), 3-19.
Bergmann, Gustav. "Inclusion, Exemplification, and Inherence in G. E. Moore," *Inquiry*, V (1962), 116-42. Reprinted in *Logic and Reality* (Madison: University of Wisconsin Press, 1964), pp. 158-70.
Black, Max. "The 'Paradox of Analysis,' " *Mind*, LIII (1944), 263-67.
―――. "The 'Paradox of Analysis' Again: A Reply," *Mind*, LIV (1945), 272-73.
―――. "On Speaking with the Vulgar," *The Philosophical Review*, LVIII (1949), 616-21.
Blanshard, Brand. *Reason and Goodness*. (London: George Allen & Unwin, 1961), pp. 266-74.
―――. *Reason and Analysis*. (London: George Allen & Unwin, 1962), pp. 310-16.
Bouwsma, O. K. "Moore's Theory of Sense-Data," *PGEM*, pp. 203-21.
Broad, C. D. "Certain Features in Moore's Ethical Doctrines," *PGEM*, pp. 43-67.
Chappell, V. C. "Malcolm on Moore," *Mind*, LXX (1961), 417-25.
Ducasse, C. J. "Moore's 'The Refutation of Idealism,' " *PGEM*, pp. 225-51.
Dummett, Michael. "A Defense of McTaggart's Proof of the Unreality of Time," *The Philosophical Review*, LXIX (1960), 497-504.
Duncan-Jones, Austin. "Intrinsic Value: Some Comments on the Work of G. E. Moore," *Philosophy*, XXXIII (1958), 240-73.
Edel, Abraham. "The Logical Structure of G. E. Moore's Ethical Theory," *PGEM*, pp. 137-76.
Ewing, A. C. "Knowledge of Physical Objects," *Mind*, LII (1943), 97-121.

Field, G. C. "The Place of Definition in Ethics," in *Studies in Philosophy* (University of Bristol Studies #3, 1935). Reprinted in Sellars & Hospers, *Readings in Ethical Theory* (New York: Appleton-Century-Crofts, 1952), pp. 92-102.

Frankena, William K. "The Naturalistic Fallacy," *Mind*, XLVIII (1939). Reprinted in Sellars & Hospers, *Readings in Ethical Theory* (New York: Appleton-Century-Crofts, 1952), pp. 103-14.

————. "Obligation and Value in the Ethics of G. E. Moore," *PGEM*, pp. 93-110.

Garnett, A. Campbell. "Moore's Theory of Moral Freedom and Responsibility," *PGEM*, pp. 179-99.

Haezrahi, P. "Some Arguments Against G. E. Moore's View of the Function of 'Good' in Ethics," *Mind*, LVII (1948), 322-40.

Hall, E. W. "Proof of Utility in Bentham and Mill: Critique of G. E. Moore's Analysis," *Ethics*, LX (1949), 1-18.

————. "Review of Schilpp's *The Philosophy of G. E. Moore*," *The Philosophical Review*, LIII (1944), 62-68.

Hancock, R. "The Refutation of Naturalism in Moore and Hare," *The Journal of Philosophy*, LVII (1960), 326-34.

Hicks, G. Dawes. "Mr. G. E. Moore on 'The Subject Matter of Psychology,'" *PAS*, X (1909-10), 232-88.

Hochberg, Herbert. "Moore's Ontology and Non-Natural Properties," *The Review of Metaphysics*, XV (1962), 365-95. Reprinted in Allaire *et al.*, *Essays in Ontology* (Iowa City: University of Iowa Press, 1963), pp. 121-47.

Holmes, A. F. "Moore's Appeal to Common Sense," *The Journal of Philosophy*, LVIII (1961), 197-207.

Jones, E. E. C. "Mr. Moore on Hedonism," *International Journal of Ethics*, XVI (1906), 429-64.

Jones, J. R. "Dr. Moore's Revised Directions for Picking Out Visual Sense-Data," *The Philosophical Quarterly*, I (1951), 433-38.

Klemke, E. D. "Mr. Warnock on Moore's Conception of Philosophy," *Philosophical Studies*, XIII (1962), 81-84.

————. *The Epistemology of G. E. Moore*. Evanston: Northwestern University Press, 1969.

Laird, J. "Review of *Philosophical Studies*," *Mind*, XXXII (1923), 86-92.

Langford, C. H. "The Notion of Analysis in Moore's Philosophy," *PGEM*, pp. 321-42.

Lazerowitz, M. "Moore's Paradox," *PGEM*, pp. 371-93.

————. "Moore and Philosophical Analysis," *Philosophy*, XXXIII (1958), 193-220.

Lewis, D. "Moore's Realism," in Addis and Lewis, *Moore and Ryle: Two Ontologists* (Iowa City: University of Iowa Press, 1965).

Lewy, C. "Terminology and Sense-Data; Reply to A. J. Ayer," *Mind*, LV (1946), 166-69.

————. "G. E. Moore on the Naturalistic Fallacy," *Proceedings of the British Academy*, L (1964), 251-62.

Mace, C. A. "On How We Know That Material Things Exist," *PGEM*, pp. 283-98.

Malcolm, Norman. "Moore and Ordinary Language," *PGEM*, pp. 345-68.

————. "Certainty and Empirical Statements," *Mind*, LI (1942), 18-46.

————. "Defending Common Sense," *The Philosophical Review*, LVIII (1949), 201-20.

————. "Philosophy for Philosophers," *The Philosophical Review*, LX (1951), 329-40.

————. "Moore's Use of 'Know,'" *Mind*, LXII (1953), 241-47.

————. "George Edward Moore," in *Knowledge and Certainty* (Englewood Cliffs, N.J.: Prentice-Hall, 1963), pp. 163-83.

Marhenke, Paul. "Moore's Analysis of Sense-Perception," *PGEM*, pp. 255-80.

McGill, V. J. "Some Queries Concerning Moore's Method," *PGEM*, pp. 483-514.

McKeon, Richard. "Propositions and Perceptions in the World of G. E. Moore," *PGEM*, pp. 453-80.

Mettrick, E. F. "G. E. Moore and Intrinsic Goodness," *International Journal of Ethics*, XXXVIII (1928), 389-400.

Metz, R. *A Hundred Years of British Philosophy* (London: George Allen & Unwin, 1938).

Murphy, A. E. "Moore's 'Defence of Common Sense,'" *PGEM*, pp. 301-17.

Nagel, E. "Impressions and Appraisals of Analytic Philosophy in Europe," *The Journal of Philosophy*, XXXIII (1936), 10-16.

————. "The Debt We Owe to G. E. Moore," *The Journal of Philosophy*, LVII (1960), 810-16.

————. "Review of Schilpp's *The Philosophy of G. E. Moore*," *Mind*, LIII (1944), 60-75.

Nakhnikian, George. "On the Naturalistic Fallacy," in *Morality and the Language of Conduct*, H. N. Castañeda and G. Nakhnikian, eds. (Detroit: Wayne State University Press, 1963), pp. 145-58.

Nelson, John O. "Mr. Hochberg on Moore: Some Corrections," *The Review of Metaphysics*, XVI (1962), 119-32.

————. "Moore, George Edward," *Encyclopedia of Philosophy*, P. Edwards, ed. (New York: Macmillan, 1967), pp. 372-81.

Passmore, John. "Moore and Russell," *A Hundred Years of Philosophy* (London: Duckworth, 1957), Chapter 9, pp. 203-41.

Paton, H. J. "The Alleged Independence of Goodness," *PGEM*, pp. 113-34.

Paul, G. A. "G. E. Moore: Analysis, Common Usage, and Common Sense," in Ayer, *et al.*, *The Revolution in Philosophy* (London: St. Martin's, 1957), pp. 56-69.

Pratt, J. B. "Mr. Moore's Realism," *The Journal of Philosophy*, XX (1923), 378-84.

Presson, V. "G. E. Moore's Theory of Sense-Data," *The Journal of Philosophy*, XLVIII (1951), 34-42.

Prior, A. N. *Logic and the Basis of Ethics* (Oxford: Oxford University Press, 1949), Chapter I, pp. 1-12.

Riddell, J. G. "New Intuitionism of Dr. Rashdall and Dr. Moore," *The Philosophical Review*, XXX (1921), 545-65.

Roberts, H. W. "Some Queries Suggested by G. E. Moore's Beautiful and Ugly Worlds," *The Journal of Philosophy*, XXXVIII (1941), 623-27.

Rogers, A. K. "Mr. Moore's Refutation of Idealism," *The Philosophical Review*, XXVIII (1919), 77-84.

Ryle, G. "G. E. Moore's Commonplace Book," *New Statesman*, LXV (1963), 85.

Schilpp, P. A. (Ed.). *The Philosophy of G. E. Moore*, 2d ed. (New York: Tudor, 1952).

Stace, W. T. "The Refutation of Realism," *Mind*, XLIII (1934), 145-55.

Stebbing, L. S. "Moore's Influence," *PGEM*, pp. 517-32.

Stevenson, Charles L. "Moore's Arguments Against Certain Forms of Ethical Naturalism," *PGEM*, pp. 71-90.

Strong, C. A. "Has Mr. Moore Refuted Idealism?" *Mind*, XIV (1905), 174-89.

Swabey, M. C. "Mr. G. E. Moore's Discussion of Sense-Data," *The Monist*, XXXIV (1924), 466-73.

Tredwell, R. F. "On Moore's Analysis of Goodness," *The Journal of Philosophy*, LIX (1962), 793-802.

Veatch, Henry B. *Rational Man* (Bloomington: Indiana University Press, 1964), pp. 188-203.

Warnock, G. J. "G. E. Moore," in *English Philosophy since 1900* (London: Oxford University Press, 1958), Chapter II, pp. 12-29.

Warnock, M. *Ethics since 1900* (London: Oxford University Press), Chapter II, pp. 11-55.

White, A. R. "Moore's Appeal to Common Sense," *Philosophy*, XXXIII (1958), 221-39.

―――. *G. E. Moore: A Critical Exposition* (Oxford: Blackwell, 1958).

White, M. G. "A Note on 'The Paradox of Analysis,'" *Mind*, LIV (1945), 71-72.

―――. "Analysis and Identity; A Rejoinder," *Mind*, LIV (1945), 357-61.

―――. "Memories of G. E. Moore," *The Journal of Philosophy*, LVII (1960), 805-10.

Wisdom, John. "Philosophy, Anxiety and Novelty," *Mind*, LIII (1944), 170-76.

―――. "Moore's Technique," *PGEM*, pp. 421-50.

―――. "G. E. Moore," in *Paradox and Discovery* (Oxford: Blackwell, 1965), pp. 82-86.

―――. "Mace, Moore, and Wittgenstein," in *Paradox and Discovery*, 148-66.

Wright, H. W. "The Objectivity of Moral Values," *The Philosophical Review*, XXXII (1923), 385-400.

INDEX

QUADRANGLE PAPERBACKS

American History

Frederick Lewis Allen. *The Lords of Creation.* (QP35)
Lewis Atherton. *Main Street on the Middle Border.* (QP36)
Thomas A. Bailey. *Woodrow Wilson and the Lost Peace.* (QP1)
Thomas A. Bailey. *Woodrow Wilson and the Great Betrayal.* (QP2)
Charles A. Beard. *The Idea of National Interest.* (QP27)
Carl L. Becker. *Everyman His Own Historian.* (QP33)
Ray A. Billington. *The Protestant Crusade.* (QP12)
Allan G. Bogue. *From Prairie to Corn Belt.* (QP50)
Kenneth E. Boulding. *The Organizational Revolution.* (QP43)
Gerald M. Capers. *John C. Calhoun, Opportunist.* (QP70)
David M. Chalmers. *Hooded Americanism.* (QP51)
John Chamberlain. *Farewell to Reform.* (QP19)
Alice Hamilton Cromie. *A Tour Guide to the Civil War.*
Robert D. Cross. *The Emergence of Liberal Catholicism in America.* (QP44)
Richard M. Dalfiume. *American Politics Since 1945.* (NYTimes Book, QP57)
Chester McArthur Destler. *American Radicalism, 1865-1901.* (QP30)
Robert A. Divine. *American Foreign Policy Since 1945.* (NYTimes Book, QP58)
Robert A. Divine. *Causes and Consequences of World War II.* (QP63)
Robert A. Divine. *The Illusion of Neutrality.* (QP45)
Elisha P. Douglass. *Rebels and Democrats.* (QP26)
Felix Frankfurter. *The Commerce Clause.* (QP16)
Lloyd C. Gardner. *A Different Frontier.* (QP32)
Edwin Scott Gaustad. *The Great Awakening in New England.* (QP46)
Ray Ginger. *Altgeld's America.* (QP21)
Ray Ginger. *Modern American Cities.* (NYTimes Book, QP67)
Ray Ginger. *Six Days or Forever?* (QP68)
Gerald N. Grob. *Workers and Utopia.* (QP61)
Louis Hartz. *Economic Policy and Democratic Thought.* (QP52)
William B. Hesseltine. *Lincoln's Plan of Reconstruction.* (QP41)
Granville Hicks. *The Great Tradition.* (QP62)
Dwight W. Hoover. *Understanding Negro History.* (QP49)
Stanley P. Hirshson. *Farewell to the Bloody Shirt.* (QP53)
Frederic C. Howe. *The Confessions of a Reformer.* (QP39)
Harold L. Ickes. *The Autobiography of a Curmudgeon.* (QP69)
Louis Joughin and Edmund M. Morgan. *The Legacy of Sacco and Vanzetti.* (QP7)
William Loren Katz. *Teachers' Guide to American Negro History.* (QP210)
Burton Ira Kaufman. *Washington's Farewell Address.* (QP64)
Edward Chase Kirkland. *Dream and Thought in the Business Community, 1860-1900.* (QP11)
Edward Chase Kirkland. *Industry Comes of Age.* (QP42)
Adrienne Koch. *The Philosophy of Thomas Jefferson.* (QP17)
Gabriel Kolko. *The Triumph of Conservatism.* (QP40)
Walter LaFeber. *John Quincy Adams and American Continental Empire.* (QP23)
Lawrence H. Leder. *The Meaning of the American Revolution.* (NYTimes Book, QP66)
David E. Lilienthal. *TVA: Democracy on the March.* (QP28)
Arthur S. Link. *Wilson the Diplomatist.* (QP18)
Huey P. Long. *Every Man a King.* (QP8)
Gene M. Lyons. *America: Purpose and Power.* (QP24)
Jackson Turner Main. *The Antifederalists.* (QP14)
Ernest R. May. *The World War and American Isolation, 1914-1917.* (QP29)
Henry F. May. *The End of American Innocence.* (QP9)
George E. Mowry. *The California Progressives.* (QP6)
William L. O'Neill. *American Society Since 1945.* (NYTimes Book, QP59)
Frank L. Owsley. *Plain Folk of the Old South.* (QP22)
David Graham Phillips. *The Treason of the Senate.* (QP20)
Julius W. Pratt. *Expansionists of 1898.* (QP15)
C. Herman Pritchett. *The Roosevelt Court.* (QP71)
Moses Rischin. *The American Gospel of Success.* (QP54)
John P. Roche. *The Quest for the Dream.* (QP47)
David A. Shannon. *The Socialist Party of America.* (QP38)
Andrew Sinclair. *The Available Man.* (QP60)
John Spargo. *The Bitter Cry of the Children.* (QP55)
Bernard Sternsher. *The Negro in Depression and War.* (QP65)
Richard W. Van Alstyne. *The Rising American Empire.* (QP25)
Willard M. Wallace. *Appeal to Arms.* (QP10)
Norman Ware. *The Industrial Worker, 1840-1860.* (QP13)
Albert K. Weinberg. *Manifest Destiny.* (QP3)
Bernard A. Weisberger. *They Gathered at the River.* (QP37)
Robert H. Wiebe. *Businessmen and Reform.* (QP56)
William Appleman Williams. *The Contours of American History.* (QP34)
William Appleman Williams. *The Great Evasion.* (QP48)
Esmond Wright. *Causes and Consequences of the American Revolution.* (QP31)